**John Mercer** is Professor in Gender and Sexuality at the Birmingham School of Media, Birmingham City University.

'Mercer's book is dense and erudite, bedazzling in its connoisseurship, rich in the detail of case studies that ring a clear bell or make you wonder how you missed *that* one, as witty as it is weighty. Discerning contemporary gay porn – or any porn for that matter – through the "vortex" of "saturated masculinity" turns out to be immensely productive. It's all here, all of the inhabitants of the pornosphere from the 1970s celluloid twink to the 21st-century postporn amateur "care bear" virtual daddy, situated carefully in the astutely defined dynamics of fantasy and sociality that keep them all alive. Mercer's central place in the still-proliferating field of porn studies across the board is guaranteed.'
—Thomas Waugh, Professor of Film Studies, Mel Hoppenheim School of Cinema, Concordia University

'Hugely impressive, the most interesting thing I've read on these areas for years; it will be enormously helpful for scholars of pornography and a real gift to students.'
—Feona Attwood, Professor of Cultural Studies, Communication and Media, Middlesex University

# Library of Gender and Popular Culture

From *Mad Men* to gaming culture, performance art to steam-punk fashion, the presentation and representation of gender continues to saturate popular media. This new series seeks to explore the intersection of gender and popular culture, engaging with a variety of texts – drawn primarily from Art, Fashion, TV, Cinema, Cultural Studies and Media Studies – as a way of considering various models for understanding the complementary relationship between 'gender identities' and 'popular culture'. By considering race, ethnicity, class, and sexual identities across a range of cultural forms, each book in the series will adopt a critical stance towards issues surrounding the development of gender identities and popular and mass cultural 'products'.

## For further information or enquiries, please contact the library series editors:

Claire Nally: claire.nally@northumbria.ac.uk
Angela Smith: angela.smith@sunderland.ac.uk

## Advisory Board:

**Dr Kate Ames**, Central Queensland University, Australia

**Prof Leslie Heywood**, Binghampton University, USA

**Dr Michael Higgins**, Strathclyde University, UK

**Prof Åsa Kroon**, Örebro University, Sweden

**Dr Niall Richardson**, Sussex University, UK

**Dr Jacki Willson**, Central St Martins, University of Arts London, UK

**Library of Gender
& Popular Culture**

# Published and forthcoming titles:

# GAY PORNOGRAPHY

Representations of Sexuality
and Masculinity

JOHN MERCER

I.B. TAURIS

LONDON · NEW YORK

Published in 2017 by
I.B.Tauris & Co. Ltd
London • New York
www.ibtauris.com

References to websites were correct at the time of writing.

Library of Gender and Popular Culture 16

ISBN: 978 1 78076 517 4 (HB)
ISBN: 978 1 78076 518 1 (PB)
eISBN: 978 1 78672 091 7
ePDF: 978 1 78673 091 6

A full CIP record for this book is available from the British Library
A full CIP record is available from the Library of Congress

Library of Congress Catalog Card Number: available

Typeset by Out of House
Printed and bound in Great Britain by T.J. International, Padstow, Cornwall

MIX
Paper from
responsible sources
FSC
www.fsc.org    FSC® C013056

# Contents

# Contents

# Contents

# Acknowledgements

It's taken a long time to reach the stage where writing this book could become a practical reality and there is a very long list of people who have helped me along the way, from my initial postgraduate research in this area, to developing a career as an academic, writing, in part at least, about masculinity and gay porn. This includes many colleagues (and now friends) who have offered help and expressed enthusiasm for the work I was trying to do, back in those days when writing about gay porn still seemed like an odd career choice.

This project would not have been possible at all without the support of the Faculty of Arts, Media and Design at Birmingham City University, an institution which has provided the resources and time that have enabled the research and writing of this book. I owe a particular debt of gratitude to Professor Tim Wall, Associate Dean for Research, who has been a regular source of motivation and an invaluable supporter of my work over the years. I owe Tim a great deal.

I also want to thank my colleagues at the Birmingham Centre for Media and Cultural Research. A supportive, collegiate and enabling working environment really enables scholars to flourish and I've been lucky to have those kinds of working conditions. Thanks in particular to the centre directors Nick Webber, for working so hard to cultivate those conditions, and Paul Long, for leading the centre and for reading through drafts of this book, and to my research cluster colleagues, especially Inger Lise Bore and my dear friend Oliver Carter.

A special mention must also go to friends and editorial board colleagues at *Porn Studies* and this must inevitably include first and foremost the inspirational Feona Attwood and Clarissa Smith. You both already know how much I value your friendship but now you have evidence in print. Thanks also go to my fellow editors at *Journal of Gender Studies* and editorial board members of *Sexualities*. The Gorizia Spring School has become an especially important event in the calendar for porn studies scholars as it presents an almost unique opportunity for exchanging ideas, drawing together researchers from across disciplines. So I'd like to thank the Spring School organisers, Giovanna Maina, Federico Zecca and Enrico Biasin, for all of their hard work over the years and for this incredibly important annual event that we have all benefitted from.

Thanks to Mireille Miller Young and her grad student Beatrix McBride for confirming my suspicions, to Kevin Heffernan for making me laugh about Kink.com, to Evangelos Tziallas for locating some hard-to-find references, to Eric Anderson for being so enthusiastic about this project and of course to Richard Dyer and to Thomas Waugh for providing the inspiration to do this work in the first place.

Finally, and as always, my biggest debt of gratitude and the most love goes to Trevor.

# Series Editors' Foreword

Since the decriminalisation of homosexuality in Western societies in the 1960s, there has been a gradual mainstreaming of gay culture. As this book highlights, this was interrupted in the 1980s with the AIDS pandemic and associated moral panic that linked it with homosexuality, referring to it as the 'gay plague'. Mercer's book charts the shifts in social attitudes towards homosexuality and associated pornography, linking these with the development of new technologies that have aided access to such material, from VHS, to DVD, to the internet. Other books in this series explore pornography in other contexts (including its earliest manifestations on film), and here Mercer adds to these debates in his discussion of models of masculinity that are extremely diverse and constantly evolving and developing. By defining 'gay porn' as a particular genre that has an assumed primary audience of gay men, Mercer explores the notion of 'fantasy' in film, and thus links it with the wider issues surrounding the film industry that other authors in this series explore. Mercer's conclusion that gay porn has moved into the realms of popular culture is one that makes this book a thought-provoking addition to the Library of Gender in Popular Culture.

Angela Smith and Claire Nally

# Introduction: Coming to Terms (Again)

*Pornography is both a legitimate form of culture and a fictional, fantastical, even allegorical realm; it neither reflects the real world, nor is it some hypnotizing call to action. The world of pornography is mythological and hyperbolic, peopled by fictional characters. It doesn't and will never exist.*

Laura Kipnis, *Bound and Gagged* (1996:163)

In 1994, the American gay artist Bruce Cegur completed a painting entitled *Shop by Male 1-Make Me a Man*[1] that was eventually exhibited at the Kinsey Institute's Juried Erotic Art Show in 2006. Cegur's painting, bearing the influence of the photo-realist style of the Pop Art movement, acts as an ironic comment on the nature of desire in contemporary American gay culture. Imitating the layout of a mail order catalogue, the image presents a selection of idealised male body parts to an imagined consumer; each one is for sale at a 'new low price' with captions extolling their virtues. The artist, an avid gardener, found inspiration for this satirical work in seed catalogues where carrots are categorised by their length and pumpkins by their roundness and plumpness. Buttocks are wittily categorised and given titles – 'Sugar Baby' and 'Champion' – penises as 'Goliath' and 'Jersey Giant', and torsos as 'Olympian' and 'Californian Wonder'. The painting playfully (and perhaps prophetically) suggests a mechanism for organising

1

and categorising physical characteristics and types that has become one of the staple features of the ways in which porn is presented for consumption online. This is vividly illustrated by the tactics of porn aggregators and the architecture of tube sites. Pornhub, for example, organises gay content into categories that suggest practices but also preferred types, including Asian, bear, black, college, daddy, hunks and twink. Xhamster allows the consumer to browse in a similar fashion, with the addition of more specific categorisation, including types such as emo boys and transsexuals. Gaytube allows for even more detailed search parameters, including genre, number of performers, ethnicity, type, cock, cum, softcore or hardcore, clothing and location. Cegur's painting also suggests the possibility of constructing the ideally desirable man, an objective that is similarly attempted at points in the idealised physical types that populate the world of online gay pornography. It is these idealised masculine types that constitute the iconography of contemporary online gay pornography, their construction and the range of discourses that surround them, that is the concern of this book.

This book is the culmination, at the time of writing, of almost 20 years' research into gay pornography that started when I was a doctoral candidate in the 1990s and that has continued since then. When I first started writing about gay porn it was within a social, cultural and political climate that was in many respects profoundly different to the context in which this book now emerges. I started researching gay porn in the aftermath of the first wave of the AIDS pandemic, and the associated moral panic about the so-called 'gay plague'. The work that I chose to do at that point felt explicitly political and it was motivated by the desire to interrogate and to validate expressions of gay sexuality as they were represented in the material that, I wanted to argue, was at the very heart of anything that might be described collectively as 'gay culture'. The wider social acceptance of gay people, in many Western nations at least, that has grown exponentially in the intervening period means that, on the one hand, representations of gay men are no longer regarded as taboo and also that aspects of gay culture (and gay representation) have become assimilated by the mainstream culture. Indeed just as I will argue that the narrow binarisms of gay and straight sexual identities have become much more porous, so it's evidently the case that the seemingly straightforward distinctions between the mainstream and the marginal are now more vexed than they were when I first started writing about gay porn. Furthermore I should also note that attitudes towards porn research have changed a great deal over time. During the mid 1990s, researching gay porn at doctoral level was a choice that was regarded as outré to say the least and at worst was met with a mixture of incomprehension and suspicion, and I often found myself spending time trying to justify my research to any number of individuals. Why would anyone want to research material like this? What's your investment in gay porn? What is the point of this 'research' and what is there to say about this material? These were questions frequently asked. Times have, gladly, changed considerably since the mid-1990s. I now regularly meet research students in the UK and elsewhere who are producing PhDs, writing journal articles and delivering conference presentations on a subject that seemed, if not unimaginable, then rather distasteful some 20 years earlier.

Probably most profoundly, technological developments during this period have radically altered the context in which the material that is the subject of this book is located, accessed and understood. I started writing about gay porn before access to the internet was commonplace and my focus was primarily on material available on VHS, and latterly DVD, that was sold commercially in the US and Europe, but had a much less certain legal status in the UK. Now widespread access to porn online and the resulting concomitant set of debates around the so-called sexualisation and/or pornification of culture more widely (and popular culture specifically) mean that the iconography of gay porn can no longer be regarded as a marginal and minority concern. Instead this is material that, I argue, forms the fabric of the ways in which masculinity itself is understood. This then is a study that takes the iconography of gay porn as its primary object of study, but it is as much a book about contemporary constructions of masculinity as it is a work that is a contribution to the ongoing pornography debate. Gay porn, understood as a genre, a style, a mode of address or as a set of industrial practices, is in the business of producing models of masculinity for erotic consumption. My argument in this book is that these models of masculinity are extremely diverse and dynamic, they are iterative and more particularly they are generative; constantly evolving and developing. I am contending that this proliferation of types and modes of masculinity that are vividly illustrated in the world of gay porn cumulatively provide evidence of a phenomenon (discussed in the next chapter) that I describe as 'saturated masculinity'. This is a contemporary condition in which masculinity, historically tied to binarisms, has become overburdened with a range of meanings, associations and connotation to such an extent that it becomes a category that is increasingly indeterminate and threatens to collapse under the weight of its own hyperbole. Gay porn marshals and deploys a range of discourses that structure and position these iterative and generative models of masculinity, and it is these discourses of generation, orientation, ethnicity and self-hood that inform the organisation of the chapter structure of this book.

The first part of this book provides a set of contexts for the analysis of the paradigm of masculinities and their associated discourses that are discussed in the second part. So in this introduction I will consider the critical context in which gay porn scholarship has emerged and provide a rationale for the research presented in the subsequent chapters. This introduction is followed by Chapter 1, 'Saturated Masculinity', which outlines the conceptual framework for this book and the wider social and cultural context in which masculinities have become problematised and any contemporary analysis of masculinity in gay porn must be situated. In Chapter 2, 'History, Industry and Technological Change', which forms the final section of the first part of the book, I focus on the specific technological and industrial factors that have provided the conditions in which the iconography of gay porn has emerged and the generic conventions that have resulted from this.

In Part 2, 'Models, Patterns and Themes', the chapter structure has largely been derived from an articulation of the most common industrial categories used to describe gay porn for consumers/users. So in order to explore the discourses of masculinity that gay porn summons up, I have self-consciously chosen to draw upon the categories and language that commercial producers as well as the aggregators, mentioned at the start of this chapter, tend to use the most relentlessly. I also, in part, have been inspired by the lucidity of the organisation of chapters in Alan Sinfield's excellent *On Sexuality and Power* and to a lesser degree by Leo Bersani's classic *Homos*. Whilst I disagree with so much of what Bersani has to say, and his recourse to the psychoanalytic paradigm is not a strategy that

I adopt in this book, I admire his daring and uncompromising polemic, and his objective to assert the importance of sex (and especially the subversive power of sex) is a goal that also motivates the research that is presented here.

Chapter 3, 'Generation: The Boy-Next-Door, the Twink and the Daddy', explores the ways in which age is positioned as the locus of erotic investment and the masculinities that are represented as a consequence. Inevitably, given the preoccupations of wider society and the premium placed on youth and its connections to virility across popular culture, the primary focus of this chapter is the ways in which youthful masculinities are represented. However, in the concluding section of this chapter I discuss the figure of the 'daddy' and the eroticisation of intergenerational sex as a way into exploring the ways in which 'mature' masculinities are deployed in the subsequent chapter. In Chapter 4, 'Straight Acting? Heterosexuality, Hypermasculinity and the Gay Outlaw', I discuss the place of heterosexuality in gay porn and the category of the 'straight acting' gay male and provide examples to problematise both of these categories. I also here explore what I describe as gay hypermasculinity and the specific settings in which this version of masculinity is situated, through a discussion of the figure of the Bear, the Leatherman and fetish performance and finally through a discussion of the most controversial development in recent years; so-called bareback porn. In Chapter 5, 'A World of Men: Race, Ethnicity and National Identity', I look at the ways in which ethnic and racialised difference is presented as an erotic spectacle in gay porn, noting that whiteness is, to use Barthes' terminology, 'exnominated' in commercial, mainstream output. I look at the spaces and places in which non-Caucasian and specifically black masculinities are represented in gay porn, the eroticisation of national identity and the emergence of a homogenous 'international style' of sexualised masculinity. In the final chapter, 'The Celebrity, the Amateur and the Self', I focus on the emergence of the 'amateur' and the various manifestations of what is generically described as 'amateur porn' to illustrate that this category is far from straightforward. I discuss the porous nature of the divisions between the professional and the amateur in the digital age by discussing the changing status of the gay porn star and conclude by a focus on the ways in which gay porn may inform representations of the masculine self.

# Representing Gay Erotic Fantasy

This book, out of necessity, engages with some contested and vexed terminology: the mainstream, the amateur, heteronormativity, hypermasculinity. Indeed it has become something of a cliché that work in the field of porn studies has to grapple with unpacking (and unpicking) a lexicon that is often either under-theorised or used in uncritical ways, before any engagement with the manifest content of the genre itself can take place. Porn studies has become an increasingly confident field, however, and whilst it is not my intention, nor will I have the space, to indulge in protracted discussions of the implications of each and every term deployed here, there will, at points, be a necessity to define my terms of reference and point to the associated debates. Inevitably, though, a book that, in part at least, deals with the classification and organisation of masculine types needs from the outset to be clear about the types of material that will be interrogated. Consequently it's necessary to clarify what the term 'gay porn' means in the context of this study. Whilst this might seem to some readers as blindingly self-evident, this is far from an inconsequential matter and although the political ramifications that Richard Dyer noted in the essay written 30 years previously, and that inspired the title of this chapter, have become more complicated, the conjunction of the terms 'gay' and 'porn' mean that the material that is discussed here still has textual qualities, modes of address and networks of distribution and consumption as well as a social/cultural/political significance, that mark them as qualitatively different to other eroticised/sexualised representations of the male body that circulate within popular culture.[2] In order to draw my object of study into view, like Dyer I am using the term gay porn to describe a particular genre (or, more accurately still, a collection of subgenres) that address an assumed primary audience of gay men.[3] For the purpose of this study this will include material produced by commercial, gay-owned, web-based, adult entertainment media outlets as well as gay-oriented subsidiaries of corporate adult entertainment conglomerates such as Kink.com, Private and the online broadcaster AEBN. It will also include case studies drawn from specialist porn outlets catering to niche markets, and latterly some examples of artisanal and amateur material.

Fantasy is another term that will loom large over this study and the framing and contextualisation of the analysis that will take place here. In the first issue of *Porn Studies*, Martin Barker's essay 'The "Problem" of Sexual Fantasies' (2014) provides an incisive overview and critique of the ways in which the term fantasy is used in a range of settings, the problems associated with the ways in which interested parties make sense of fantasy, including some of the problems with the way in which sexual fantasy has been conceptualised in the field of porn studies. Barker observes that in popular discourse and scholarship fantasy carries with it a set of largely pejorative connotations. As he notes, 'sexual fantasies are seen as essentially unproductive; at best of limited value; at worst, adolescent, deficient, and dangerous' (2014:148). Barker sets out to challenge here the assertion that any potential harm that porn causes revolves around:

> (the common-sense) idea of 'losing the distinction between fantasy and reality'. This is an illusory notion, made possible simply by a linguistic oddity. One might as well worry if people might lose the distinction between cooking and reality.
>
> (p. 155)

As a corrective to these commonplace arguments and based on the responses of over 5,000 respondents to an online questionnaire and research project organised with Clarissa Smith and Feona Attwood, Barker offers five 'orientations' (ibid.) in order to shift debate away from an uncritical reproduction of the common sense and to provide a framework in order to make sense of sexual fantasy:

1. 'Fantasy' as magnifying glass: a conscious accentuation of a desire.
2. 'Fantasy' as mirror to self: a means to look at our responses to things.
3. 'Fantasy' as emporium: a world of possibilities to be explored and thought about.
4. 'Fantasy' as journey: a visitation to a distant realm of desires and activities.
5. 'Fantasy' as other self: what I might or might not be.

He notes that these orientations are provisional and that they require both more thought and empirical investigation but they nonetheless offer a

7

useful structure for conceptualising fantasy. The research presented in this book draws on these orientations as inspiration for exploring the meanings and significances of the representations and scenarios at play across a disparate range of texts and as a framework for thinking about how the discourses of masculinity that I identify in my research make meaning in the fantasy context of gay porn.

In concluding, Barker notes that:

> We are creatures who not only desire sex, but can enjoy the idea of desiring. [...] In between those responses, our feeling and understanding of them, and the world that delivers possibilities and constraints, is the field of sexuality. This is the zone of knowing and imagining how sex works, rewards and punishes. 'Fantasy' belongs here, in the zone of the relations between bodies, selfhood, and social and cultural permissions and forbiddings. [...] This is how and why the utterly explicit in pornography, the 'leaving nothing to the imagination', is at that exact same point the most fantastical. In this sense we might usefully see pornography as being like a huge library, a bookshop, or a film archive. Even to know that it is there, that it has something like a catalogue, is to begin to measure one's sexual self against all that it might offer.
>
> (p. 157)

Even whilst Barker's interests and methods are very different to my own, there is much to take away and make productive use of even in the case of the textually and contextually grounded research that is the basis of this study. In the first instance, he problematises a term that is central to an understanding of what it is that porn (and in this case gay porn) is doing. Secondly, the models of masculinity that gay porn offers and the discourses that surround them must be primarily understood through the framing lens of fantasy, and in this regard Barker's orientations are especially useful as a way into conceptualising the work that such representations are doing in specific contexts. My argument is that the articulations of masculinity that gay porn produces should be regarded as more than merely static and stereotypical (which of course would be to misunderstand the ways in which stereotypes operate in the first place).[4] Neither are they archetypical, unchanging and eternal, even whilst some of the models that I will present for analysis here (the athlete, the youth, the daddy, for example) seem to be exactly that. They are instead, as I have argued elsewhere, prototypes,[5] and therefore constantly changing, evolving and subject to revision. The iconography of gay porn presents heightened fantasies that articulate the erotic potentials, fluidity and ambiguity of contemporary masculinities. As Linda Williams succinctly notes,

> Pornography on film, video, or the internet is always two contradictory things at once: documents of sexual acts, and fantasies spun around knowing the pleasure or pain of those acts. Pornography studies needs to remember that it must always exist at the problematic site of this limit. (2014:37)

## The State of the Field

In an essay published in 2014 in two versions – firstly in the inaugural volume of the journal *Porn Studies* and subsequently in the *Porn Archives* anthology edited by Tim Dean, Steven Ruszczycky and David Squires – Linda Williams provides her diagnosis of the condition of porn studies as a field that, by her own reckoning, she played a fundamental role in establishing.[6] Williams' assessment of the state of porn scholarship is in many respects a rather surprising one, veering, sometimes rather uncomfortably, between an endorsement of a relatively small group of familiar names whose work she considers to be foundational, contrasted with a critique of a newer generation of scholars and what she regards as the lack of a strategic development of the discipline. The essay presents a challenge in two regards: a challenge to Williams' readers, who may well be discouraged by her assessment of current scholarship, and secondly a challenge that she sets for *Porn Studies* as a journal, which she sees as a necessary development for the field in order to raise the standard of scholarship. Williams also strikes a note of caution with regards to the use of language in this essay and especially to the term 'porn studies', revealing that whilst her own earlier edited collection had been marketed with this title, this was in fact as a result of publisher pressure rather than her own preference for the more formal term 'pornography', which she believes 'signals the higher ground of a more scholarly, distanced and critical approach' (2014:34). Unlike Williams, I see no pressing reason to avoid using the term 'porn', nor do I see any benefit to grandiloquence, and have consequently adopted the compressed and comprehensible 'porn' throughout this book. Putting to one side a debate around what Williams actually considers to be sufficiently scholarly, or indeed the necessity for 'distance', her broad argument is that the development of porn studies has been fairly asymmetrical, with some aspects of the field 'thriving' while 'others remain untended (p. 37). For instance she argues that 'mainstream, heterosexual hard core has been comparatively ignored by all but anti-pornography scholars' (p. 29) and that whilst a 'thriving subfield' of work on gay male porn is evident, even here 'there has been no equivalent to the ground-breaking articles on gay male pornography by Richard Dyer or of Thomas Waugh's' (p. 26). Whilst, as I have already noted, both of these remarks present a challenge and are intended to do so, these are important observations made by a figure whose work has shaped the agenda for the academic study of porn and necessarily informs the contribution that this book is intended to make. Additionally, and in particular, Williams points to a relative absence of monographs on the subject of porn in favour of what she sees as a preponderance of edited collections. She regards this as yet another significant problem for the development of the subject area, demonstrating a scholarly preference for 'dabbling rather than digging into a fertile field' (p. 32). This is not an insignificant point to make inasmuch as it relates to this book, as although Williams notes that gay male pornography has been one of the subfields that has been a particular beneficiary of the growth of porn studies more generally, this has not, in fact, translated into a critical mass of single-authored (and therefore sustained) investigations. Indeed, even if we include both John Burger's *One Handed Histories* (mentioned subsequently, which at 144 pages is scarcely a detailed study) and Tim Dean's *Unlimited Intimacy* (which contrary to Williams' view is not, first and foremost, a book about gay porn), this is only the fifth book that has been published on the subject. Notwithstanding Williams' remarks about a dearth of monographs, there is nonetheless a growing body of scholarship around gay porn to which this book should be regarded as a contribution.

I would argue that the overwhelming majority of research can be seen as taking place within two broad phases. These 'phases' (which are not entirely temporarily bounded in that there is some overlap) can, in short, be described as the pre-web, pre-digital phase of gay porn research, which is then followed by a post-web corpus. The first period is the one that Williams describes as producing the 'ground-breaking' work of Waugh and Dyer. This can perhaps be more productively understood as the first wave of gay porn scholarship and begins in the late 1970s, developing in the mid-1980s during the very early years of the AIDS crisis.[7] This period coincides with, and emerges from, the establishment of a conjunction of fields of study within the arts and humanities, in particular masculinity studies, gay and lesbian studies and the early signs of the nascent queer theory. This first phase generates work produced by scholars who share a similar set of interests and preoccupations that results in a particular sort of knowledge. Firstly an ideological interest in (and critique of) the cultural and political conditions under which gay pornography emerges. Secondly a concern with recovering lost and obscure cultural objects and therefore a privileging of the historical over the contemporary and a (mostly) unintentional canonisation of the object of study (so the work of 'important' directors or 'significant' films taking precedence.) Thirdly (and inevitably) a focus, set of concerns and method of analysis located in a pre-web, pre-digital landscape.

## Phase 1: Pre-Web, Pre-Digital

As Williams' essay implies, any discussion of the literature on gay porn must acknowledge the transformative early contributions of both Tom Waugh and Richard Dyer. However, neither of them were the first to write about the social and political implications of porn for gay men. For example, as early as 1978, Michael Bronski writes about gay porn magazines in 'What Does Soft Core Porn Really Mean to the Gay Male?' in Boston's *Gay Community News* and Greg Blachford produced a detailed Marxist critique of gay porn with 'Looking at Pornography', published in *Gay Left* and subsequently in *Screen Education* in 1979. This early work surveys out the terrain and sets an ideological agenda that would inform at least some of the work that subsequent researchers, and Waugh and Dyer in particular, were to undertake. So, in 1985 in 'Men's Pornography: Gay vs. Straight', an essay originally published in *Jump Cut*, Tom Waugh constructed what he described as a 'structural analysis' of gay pornographic video, comparing it – in formal, stylistic and content terms – to heterosexual porn. In his foreword

11

to the essay, reprinted in 1993, Waugh acknowledged the limitations of his scope and the changes that had taken place in the intervening period:

> The cultural and political context has muddied considerably since those days of clarity in the early eighties when I was writing this piece. For one thing the pandemic and the universal presence of home video have radically altered the sexual landscape; though each gets a mention or two in the text, it is obvious how this alteration requires that we look at 'Men's Pornography: Gay vs. Straight' as much as a historical document as an entry in our ongoing debates. (1993:307)

Notwithstanding the limitations that Waugh describes, which are as much to do with the political moment in which it was written, the essay is, in my view, a singularly important piece of writing on pornography for more than one reason. In the first instance Waugh acknowledges the mutable and ephemeral nature of porn and that these qualities mean that, all too often, the observations of scholars are necessarily provisional and contingent, and secondly the essay is important because it represents perhaps the first attempt to conduct the kind of formal analysis of the conventions of gay pornography as a genre that is in large part the intention of this study.[8] In his analysis Waugh identifies the conditions of production, consumption and modes of representation in both gay and straight pornographic texts as a way of identifying the similarities and differences between the two modes. Though Waugh's analysis is systematic, his attempts to identify what he describes as 'common narrative formulae' (1993:320) are inevitably too limited to be of use in the analysis of the huge proliferation of commercial gay video porn and online content that was to follow. What Waugh offers here is the beginnings of a method for analysis and the persuasive description of the necessity for work on porn (gay and straight) that is grounded in a consideration of both text and context.

Waugh was to continue his research into gay porn, moving away from an engagement with the contemporary in the exhaustive, rigorously researched and beautifully written historical study *Hard to Imagine: Gay Male Eroticism in Photography and Film from Their Beginnings to Stonewall* (1998). Beginning with the earliest examples of nude photography and ending with pornographic film and gay cinema of the late 1960s, Waugh's study stands as the most comprehensive historical overview of the development of homoerotic representation. Part social history and part critical analysis of the legal, cultural and political frameworks in which these representations have been produced, circulated and consumed, *Hard to Imagine* is undoubtedly the most significant and substantive contribution to the scholarly analysis of gay porn that has been undertaken to date and remains so. This historically grounded approach was to be adopted by several scholars, including Jack Stevenson in 'From the Bedroom to the Bijou: A Secret History of American Gay Sex Cinema' (*Film Quarterly*, 1997) and John Burger in *One Handed Histories: The Eroto-Politics of Gay Male Video Pornography* (1995). Burger's slim study, to some extent attempts to follow on from the point at which Waugh's book ends, and focuses on the emergence of gay home-video porn. Drawing on some work undertaken at the Birmingham Centre for Contemporary Cultural Studies into popular memory, Burger argues that gay male video porn can be considered as a form of social history, charting changing attitudes in the gay community regarding, for example, sexual conduct, practices and cultural trends. Bringing things relatively up to date, his study concludes with an analysis of the All Worlds Video, *More of a Man* (dir. Jerry Douglas, 1990), arguing that the incorporation of gay activism as a narrative theme in the video is evidence of a resurgent, progressive, political dimension to mainstream gay porn, an argument that was to be echoed by Mandy Merck in 'More of a Man: Gay Porn Cruises Gay Politics' (1993), Mark Simpson in 'A World of Penises: Gay Video Porn' (1994) and Rich Cante and Angelo Restivo in 'The Voice of Pornography' (2001). Though it was published in 2009, I would also include Jeffrey Escoffier's book *Bigger Than Life* as belonging to the lineage of Waugh's historical work. As a gay rights activist since the early 1970s, Escoffier has played an important part in, as well as having lived through, many of the scenes and changes on which he comments. His study, which is full of contextual detail and rich with fascinating anecdote, is ostensibly written for a popular readership and presumably was written with a much broader intended reach than Waugh's work. Nonetheless, as Williams remarks, the book is a 'model of the genre of popular writing about pornography' (2014:26).

Richard Dyer has also made significant contributions to the study of gay porn through a succession of articles, including 'Male Gay Porn:

Coming to Terms' published in *Jump Cut* at the same time as Waugh's foundational essay, and consequently over the years the two have become the scholars most often associated with the study of gay film and video porn. Dyer, like Waugh, has also produced work that is broadly historical, and in addition he discusses material positioned at the more experimental end of the spectrum of gay pornographic film as important in his own cultural history of gay and lesbian cinema, *Now You See It: Studies on Lesbian and Gay Film* (1990). In 'A Conversation About Pornography', collected in Simon Shepherd and Mick Wallis' *Coming on Strong: Gay Politics and Culture* (1989), Dyer offers personal reflections on gay porn in light of Andrea Dworkin's criticisms of porn, both gay and straight. Dyer notes, in a discussion that indicates the tenor of debate at the point at which the article was published, that issues of gender and gender difference are central to a discussion of gay porn, and as a result, consideration of the genre is tied into a complex network of debates:

> Because of the stigmatised position of both homosexuality and pornography, discussion of what's going on in gay porn can't be that straightforward. There are in fact very few images of women in gay porn. But we can't escape the fact that sexuality is informed by how gender is constructed in society at large [...] Now I think that, when I say I want to feel or be the man I desire, my reaction is informed by the notion that 'that image or object is different from women'. So a sense of gender difference is present, even when there's no specific reference to women.
>
> (1989:202/3)

Dyer's academic interest in the signifying practices of the film star are also drawn upon in his analysis of the gay porn star Ryan Idol in 'Idol Thoughts: Orgasm and Self Reflexivity in Gay Pornography' (1994). The essay discusses both Ryan Idol's performative qualities in the video *Ryan Idol: A Very Special View* (dir. Matt Sterling, 1990) and goes on to explore the formal and narrative qualities of gay pornographic video more generally. Similarly in 'Male Gay Porn: Coming to Terms' (1985), Dyer's focus is on narrative, which, he argues (counter to commonplace assumptions), is a fundamental feature of video porn, even in its most minimal form, indicating, for example, the progression of a sexual encounter from

**14**

initiation to climax. Likewise, Earl Jackson Jr., drawing on both the work of Metz and Lacan, in a chapter entitled 'Graphic Specularity' in *Strategies of Deviance: Studies in Gay Male Representation* (1995) discusses both the narrative construction of a selection of videos (notably *Le Beau Mec*, dir. Wallace Potts, 1976) and the implied viewing and subject/object relations that the gay pornographic text constructs.

By the early 1990s, debates surrounding the often problematic representation of racial difference in gay porn motivated the interventions of a group of scholars such as Richard Fung, in the essay 'Looking For My Penis: The Eroticised Asian in Gay Video Porn' and to a lesser degree Kobena Mercer in the frequently cited 'Skinhead Sex Thing: Racial Difference and the Homoerotic Imaginary' both collected in Bad Object Choices (eds.), *How Do I Look? Queer Film and Video* (1991). In this collection of essays, issues concerning the pedagogical function of gay porn, resulting as a consequence of the AIDS crisis and a call for safer sex education, are addressed by Cindy Patton in 'Safe Sex and the Pornographic Vernacular' as well as in 'Visualizing Safer Sex: When Porn and Pedagogy Collide' (1991), Richard Fung's 'Shortcomings: Questions About Pornography as Pedagogy' (1993) and Wieland Speck's 'Porno?' (1993), collected in M. Gever, J. Greyson & P. Parmar (eds), *Queer Looks* (1993).

In J. Elias et al. (eds), *Porn 101: Eroticism, Pornography and the First Amendment* (1999), Fung's essay on the representation of the Asian male in gay video porn is reprised by Daniel Tsang in 'Beyond "Looking for my Penis": Reflections on Asian Gay Male Video Porn', and in 'Notes on the New Camp: Gay Video Pornography', collected in the same volume, Joe Thomas argues that porn has superseded camp as a new form of politically motivated subversion of hegemonic masculinity for the gay community.

## Phase 2: Post-Web

What I would regard as the second wave of gay porn research emerges in the early 2000s, inspired by and responding to the interventions of Tom Waugh and Richard Dyer who had become the key reference points for subsequent work on gay porn by this stage. Just as importantly, though, this burgeoning body of literature was inspired by the publication of Linda Williams' agenda-setting *Hard Core: Power, Pleasure, and the 'Frenzy of the Visible'* (1989) and the analytical model that she developed, and latterly by Laura Kipnis' *Bound and Gagged Pornography and the Politics of Fantasy in America* (1998). From this period onwards, a diversity of research emerges that is equally various in its objects of study and methodological approaches. The emergence of queer theory and its role in shaping the ways in which porn might be conceptualised, as well as the inevitable and profound impact of the web, resulting in exponential growth of the volume, diversity and ease of access to gay porn during this period, meant that there was much more to talk about and perhaps an enhanced vocabulary with which to have that conversation.

This work is also increasingly multidisciplinary and transdisciplinary resulting in research not only in film, media and cultural studies, but also the social sciences, health and sports studies. So for example a special edition of *The Journal of Homosexuality* edited by Todd Morrison in 2004, which was simultaneously published as *Eclectic Views on Gay Male Pornography: Pornocopia*, has a title that speaks for itself and includes content that is illustrative of writing from a diversity of disciplines united by an interest in gay porn. The collection includes contributions concerning body image and eating disorders, sex and awareness education, the relevance of Radical Feminism for gay men, audience research and the perspectives of porn performers, as well as essays on the representation of ethnicity and my own contribution on prison scenarios. Retrospectively, perhaps one of the most interesting sections of the collection is to be found in Shannon Ellis and Bruce Whitehead's 'Porn Again: Some Final Considerations', a collation of responses to a set of questions posed to all of the contributors to the collection. These included questions related to the benefits and perceived harm that gay porn presents, the role of gay porn within gay culture, the perennial concerns around definitions (in this case the porn vs erotica debate), the relationship of gay porn to hegemonic masculinity, the extent to which porn can be seen as a tool of liberation and finally a question relating to the connections between gay porn and body image. These questions provide an insight into the issues of debate that motivated the collection in the first place and connected to wider concerns about porn more generally that have only gathered pace in the intervening years.

The same year as Morrison's collection, Linda Williams (who had previously remarked that she wished that she had written about gay porn in

*Hard Core*) included a section devoted to 'Gay, Lesbian and Homosocial Pornographies' in *Porn Studies*. Of the four essays in this section, only Rich Cante and Angelo Restivo take on gay porn (albeit primarily through an analysis of Jack Deveau's 1977 film *A Night at the Adonis*, which was by this stage a rather antique choice) in their excellent essay 'The Cultural-Aesthetic Specificities of All-Male Moving-Image Pornography'. In a highly sophisticated reading, the essay discusses the centrality of 'utopian' space in gay porn, comparing and contrasting the public sex represented in Deveau's film with the more contemporary example of listings of cruising areas on the website cruisingforsex.com. In a similar vein José B. Capino's historically located work focuses on conditions of consumption in 'Homologies of Space: Text and Spectatorship in All-Male Adult Theaters' in *Cinema Journal* (2005). In a section devoted to questions of race and class, Nguyen Tan Hoang's essay 'The Resurrection of Brandon Lee: The Making of a Gay Asian American Porn Star' provides detailed textual readings of several films featuring the eponymous star, and was to become the first chapter on his book on Asian masculinity and sexual representation, *A View From the Bottom* (2014).

More recently the bareback phenomenon has generated a wealth of debate that has translated into published research. Key in this arena is the work of Tim Dean and in particular his ethnographic study of the bareback subculture, *Unlimited Intimacy* (2009), which includes a lengthy discussion of bareback porn, specifically the work of the, now notorious, Paul Morris and his production company Treasure Island Media.[9] Likewise an increasing number of researchers have chosen web porn as their specific object of study and this is reflected in the edited collection *Porn.com* (2010), which includes Jennifer Moorman's survey of the field 'Gay for Pay, Gay For(e) play: The Politics of Taxonomy and Authenticity in LGBTQ Porn' and several submissions in the *C'Lick Me Reader* (2007).

Contrary to anything that might be implied by John Champagne's infamous injunction in 'Stop Reading Films!: Film Studies, Close Analysis, and Gay Pornography' (1997), which might suggest a proliferation of close textual readings of gay porn, the specific iconography of gay pornography remains, almost 20 years after the publication of his essay, a relatively unexplored avenue of critical enquiry and has certainly not been subjected to the kind of sustained and detailed textual analysis that Champagne opposed in his essay.[10] This is not to say that such examples do not exist. For example, the work of Nguyen Tan Hoang mentioned earlier is marked by its detailed and sensitive textual analysis, just as the work of Rick Cante and Angelo Restivo is perceptive and contextualised in a way that challenges Champagne's mistaken assertion that textual analysis is too often presented as 'value neutral and free from ideological underpinning' (1997:76). Similarly Brian Pronger's *The Arena of Masculinity: Sports, Homosexuality and the Meaning of Sex* (1990) includes a chapter on sporting iconography in gay video pornography, and in '"Ten men[...]hung and well built[...] some smooth, some hairy[...]but all insatiable" or Consuming the Buff Simulacrum' (2002) in Miller and Ward (eds), *Crime and Ornament: The Arts and Popular Culture in the Shadow of Adolf Loos*, drawing on the work of Deleuze, Pronger discusses the implications of the iconography of the muscular, gym-toned bodies of gay porn. However, I would suggest that whilst such examples exist, they are rarities and, to date, no major published study exists that addresses the iconography of contemporary gay porn in any sustained fashion, which constitutes something of a blind spot for the field. Instead iconography is overlooked altogether, or too often quick assumptions are made and the scenarios and models of masculinity in gay porn are written off as stereotypical, uniform and monolithic. It is this concern that has motivated my own interventions in the field and provides the impetus for this book. Since my first published article on gay porn in 2003, I have concerned myself with theorising the generic characteristics of the genre as it has developed, looking at the various masculinities that it produces and the settings in which they operate. Aspects of this work will be revisited and developed in this book.

## Methods and Scope

The object of study and field of view of this book is necessarily broad, as my concern is to look at the ways in which masculinities are produced across contemporary gay porn. This means that the book has a breadth of reach and frame of reference, given the size and variety of the industry, and in order to manage this I have had to be extremely selective in terms of the texts that I have chosen for analysis. Furthermore, given the volume of material that I had to draw on, my focus is as much on cross-textual as close-textual readings. The combination of close- and cross-textual analysis that I present here is fragmentary, and deliberately so, in order, as much as possible, to duplicate the contemporary conditions of consumption online, in which texts tend to be browsed and sampled rather than consumed in total. As Lister et al. note, 'consumption is browsing, surfing, using, "viewsing", we do not consume so much as we are "immersed"' (2009:248).[11] Notwithstanding the reservations that Lister et al. are suggesting here, my aim has been that this book should be critically engaged but also immersive in its engagement with texts, paratexts and associated debates around the nature of sexualised masculinity.

I have chosen to focus largely on what I am describing as contemporary 'mainstream' gay porn (a category that I will problematise) and within that on the dominant themes, models and discourses of masculinity that the mainstream deploys. Whilst I don't claim to have adopted a representative sampling method and this work is intentionally and unambiguously promiscuous in its scope and strategies, I have nonetheless decided to narrow my field of view largely to material since 2010 (though I freely deviate from the fairly arbitrary timeframe that I am setting myself here in order to manage the potentially vast range of material that is at my disposal for analysis when it's necessary). I have chosen texts for analysis on the basis that they have attracted sustained media or fan-based commentary and attention and through an analysis of nominees and award winners at the various trade and industry award ceremonies, in particular the Grabbies, the now defunct GayVN and the Cybersocket awards.

The method of analysis that I adopt is a triangulated one that pays attention to the gay porn text (and in particular the specifics of iconography, performance and setting), paratext and context.[12] The networks through which meanings are made and circulate are perhaps more proliferous (or to use Zygmunt Bauman's expression, more 'liquid') than ever before. Consequently, any analysis of any form of popular culture (and this relates as much to porn as any other form) must countenance and make account for the way in which the meaning of any text is produced and negotiated across a plethora of websites, social media, press releases and discussion fora. It's therefore important to acknowledge and make reference to the array of paratextual materials that will inform the analysis that is presented here. This material extends far beyond the websites through which the texts are accessed and accompanying promotional materials and discussion threads, Twitter feeds and so on, to the increasingly vigorous (and informed) growth of what might best be described as non-institutionalised research activity or para-scholarship.[13] In this respect, then, it might be argued that the reading of gay porn that is undertaken in this book can be thought of as a mode of textual analysis that Alan McKee has usefully defined as 'exegetical' (2014:56).

The project is ostensibly cartographic in that I am plotting and charting the shape of contemporary masculinities as they manifest and are represented in gay porn. This mapping has a wider purpose though over and above an exploration of the iconography and associated discourses of masculinity at play in gay porn. In *The Epistomology of the Closet*, Eve Kosofsky Sedgwick writes about the problems of classifying difference (1990):

> It is astonishing how few respectable conceptual tools we have for dealing with this self-evident fact. A tiny number of inconceivably coarse axes of categorization have been painstakingly inscribed in current critical and political thought: gender, race, class, nationality, sexual orientation are pretty much the available distinctions.
>
> (1990:22)

She says that her goal has been to 'repeatedly to ask how certain categorizations work, what enactments they are performing and what relations they are creating, rather than what they essentially mean, has been my principal strategy' (p. 27). Likewise my ambition in this book is to look at the ways that categories work in gay porn to reveal their complexity and their ambiguity. Inevitably the focus on the various discourses and iterations of masculinity that gay porn produces means that this work owes a debt to Foucault. As Leo Bersani notes in *Homos*:

> No one was more alert than Foucault to the connections between how we organize our pleasures with one other person and the larger forms of social organization. It is the original thesis of his *History* that power in our societies functions primarily not by repressing spontaneous sexual drives but by producing multiple sexualities, and that through the classification, distribution, and moral rating of those sexualities the individuals practicing

them can be approved, treated, marginalized, sequestered, disciplined, or normalized.

(1995:81)

Similarly I owe a debt to Judith Butler's work on gender performativity, to Linda Williams' work on porn but also to Laura Kipnis' important interventions, and similarly, to Thomas Waugh but also to Richard Dyer, to Raewyn Connell for her defining work *Masculinities* (2005), but also to Ken Plummer and Jeffrey Weeks.

Finally I should stress that this book is not meant (nor would it possible) to be a definitive study of masculinities in gay porn. Indeed my central argument is that contemporary masculinities have become so saturated with meaning that new categories and new articulations of masculinity emerge constantly. My intention instead is to illustrate that even within the context of the most generic and commercial examples of gay porn and through interrogating recurrent themes and patterns that seem so apparently transparent in meaning and intent, we can uncover the ways in which contemporary iterations of masculinity are nuanced and various. The reach and scope of this book is necessarily interdisciplinary as the intention of this study is to challenge a monolithic interpretation of gay porn and an equally monolithic comprehension of contemporary masculinities, as I will discuss in the next chapter.

# PART I
# Contexts and Frameworks

# 1

# Saturated Masculinity

*We cannot study masculinity in the singular, as if the stuff of man were a homogenous and unchanging thing. Rather we wish to emphasize the plurality and diversity of men's experiences, attitudes, beliefs, situations, practices and institutions along lines of race, class, sexual orientation, religion, ethnicity, age, region, physical appearance, able-bodiedness, mental ability and various other categories with which we describe our lives and experiences.*

Harry Brod and Michael Kaufman, *Theorizing Masculinities*
(1994:4–5)

This book, then, is concerned with the ways in which masculinities are constructed in and through gay porn, which is a mode of representation that cannot be understood in isolation. Whilst it has always been one of the fundamental tenets of cultural studies that any artefact or practice must be placed in its social, cultural and historical context in order to make sense of it, I have often thought that the narrow specificity that can sometimes frame the analysis of aspects of what has been described through custom and practice as 'gay culture' presents challenges for the researcher (and this is as true of my own work as of anyone else's). At its most extreme, a limited analytical and contextual field of view can easily ossify the chosen object of study. In this regard, I agree with John Champagne's critique, discussed in the introduction, of some of the issues presented by the close

25

textual analysis of porn films. At the very least, considering gay culture in isolation can lead to a stifling parochialism that sidesteps the wider political significances that can be attached to representations of gay identities and gay desires. That scholars have striven to carve out a demarcated space for the discussion of gay representation is, of course, of vital importance and that this space has become a quite narrow one, at points, is also hardly surprising given that before the late years of the last century, gay culture tended to be regarded as a marginal (or marginalised) interest within academe. In the previous chapter, I have described my own early experiences as a researcher, in order to acknowledge this. My view is that gay culture, however that term might be understood, must be situated within the context of a wider popular culture, not least because so much of what constitutes this 'gay culture' is based on interaction with, recycling and reappropriation of aspects of the wider culture.

This matters here because this study addresses a genre and a mode of representation that might at first glance be regarded as paradigmatically an exclusively gay interest and therefore of concern to gay men and a putative 'gay community' alone. I believe this to no longer be the case at all. There are a set of circumstances and shifts in cultural attitudes that had already begun by the late years of the 20th century, and which have gained a momentum of their own during the 21st century, that mean that the nature of the ways masculinity is figured and constructed within popular culture and the status of pornographic representation (and gay pornographic representation in particular) has fundamentally changed. These changes, discussed in this chapter, have arisen as a result of a set of cultural and social determinations and have been mobilised by widespread access to global culture as a result of the web and a set of concomitant shifts in attitudes towards sex, sexuality and masculinities that have gathered pace since the start of the 21st century.

One of the significant results of this set of factors is that porn, whilst still a politically charged form of cultural production and consumption in some circles, is no longer either marginal or taboo in any meaningful sense. Furthermore, on the basis of accessibility alone (though this is not the exclusive determinant), gay porn is not an obscure or a narrowly specific and marginal cultural practice, and consequently, in my view, it becomes an especially productive site through which we might explore modern masculinities.

One of the key premises of this book is that, in the developed West at least, masculinity as it is represented and inscribed into culture has undergone a radical transformation during the late 20th and early 21st century. As I will note in this chapter, drawing on the important work that theorists of masculinities have undertaken since the mid-1980s, it has become clear that a singular model of masculinity as it is prescribed and bounded by tradition and normative standards is no longer tenable and that in recent years the evidential basis for this claim has become increasingly compelling. Furthermore, my argument, based on an adaptation of Kenneth Gergen's terminology, used to describe contemporary identity, is that masculinity is now *saturated* with meaning. In short, masculinities are a multitude and are represented, likewise, in a multitude of ways, and this is vividly evidenced in the types that populate the fantasy worlds of gay porn.

## Masculinity and Popular Culture

Since the advent of the foundational scholarship of the 1970s, and the work of a range of researchers across disciplines during the 1980s and early 1990s – including but not limited to Komorovsky (1976, 2004), Pleck (1980, 1983), Cockburn (1983, 1985), Weeks (1985, 1986, 1991), Brod (1987, 1994), Kaufman (1994), Kimmell (1987, 1995, 2004, 2013), Messner (1995, 1997, 2010) and Hearn (1987), as well as the work of Messerschmidt (1993, 1997, 2000), Buchbinder (1992, 1994, 1998, 2012), Seidler (1989, 1997, 2006), Anderson (2009, 2010, 2012, 2014) and others)[1] – it has become an orthodoxy to argue, as do I in this book, that masculinity cannot be meaningfully understood as a monolithic entity and instead that it is more productive, indeed necessary, to conceptualise multiple *masculinities*. Looming large over these debates, though, and sometimes in a divisive fashion, is the figure of Raewyn Connell and her book *Masculinities* (1995, 2005) in which she describes the concept of hegemonic masculinity. Connell's contemporaries had concerned themselves with developing a field of knowledge that challenged a singular model by way of the production of knowledge that uncovered the diversity of experiences of masculinities across generations, class divides and cultures. Whilst not denying the variousness of the experience of men, Connell's work argued that what mattered was that power relations were at play in the ways in which masculinity is constructed, gender inequality is maintained and thereby patriarchy is perpetuated, by drawing on the Gramscian model of hegemony. Even whilst she notes that hegemony is a 'historically mobile' (2005:77) phenomenon and that its 'ebb and flow is a key element of the picture of masculinity' (pp. 77, 78), Connell's conceptual model presumes a dominant masculinity that is shored up by masculinities that she sees as variously subordinate and complicit. As Robert Hanke notes, this hegemonic masculinity is a 'model of masculinity that, operating on the terrain of "common sense" and conventional morality defines "what it means to be a man"' (1990:232).[2] Connell's work has had a wide-reaching influence in the field of masculinity studies and beyond and has framed the debate around masculinity for 20 years but it has also attracted some degree of controversy and criticism. This is something that Connell was to address herself when, ten years after the initial publication of *Masculinities*, she wrote the essay (with James Messerschmidt) 'Hegemonic Masculinity: Rethinking the Concept' (2005). Connell's response is an especially thorough reappraisal of the value and challenges her conceptualisation of hegemonic masculinity presented for the field and she is particularly generous in her thoughtful engagement with many of the scholars who were to take issue with her position. Connell and Messerschmidt conclude the essay with the admission that hegemonic masculinity is a concept that needs to be reformulated by attention to four areas, 'the nature of gender hierarchy, the geography of masculine configurations, the process of social embodiment, and the dynamics of masculinities' (2005:847), providing a set of research questions that should frame this work. This is a project that subsequent scholars have taken up, more or less, by either working within the constraints of the model (as in the case of Kimmel) or by proposing alternatives (see Anderson for example). Whilst the directions that Connell points towards are indeed useful, she makes it clear that she is wedded to the core tenets of her model, i.e. a 'dominant' hegemonic masculinity alongside what she describes as 'subordinated and marginalised groups' (ibid.) and the essay challenges many of the arguments presented elsewhere. For example she focuses some considerable attention on one of the most thoroughgoing critiques of her work, offered by Demetrakis Demetriou in his essay 'Connell's Concept of Hegemonic Masculinity: A Critique' (2001). Demetriou is critical of the ways in which Connell appropriates Gramsci, noting (correctly in my view) that her model of hegemony is ultimately static (though I would argue that this is largely a consequence of the ways in which her ideas have been put to use, and sometimes misuse, by subsequent scholars) and therefore almost by definition *not* hegemonic at all. He proposes an adaptation of Connell's model aligned more closely to Gramsci and also to the work of Brian Donovan (another critic of Connell) to propose what he describes as the 'hegemonic bloc' that he sees as 'hybridized':

> Donovan's studies reinforce the argument developed out of Gramsci's conceptualization of the process of internal hegemony: that the masculinity that occupies the hegemonic position at a given historical moment is a hybrid bloc that incorporates diverse and apparently oppositional elements.
>
> (2001:34)

This concept of hybridity becomes especially important for Demetriou, who then goes on to use the example of gay masculinity as an example of a masculinity where elements of hegemonic masculinity have become hybridised and assimilated through 'negotiation, appropriation, and translation into what he still prefers to describe as 'modern hegemonic masculinity' (ibid.). Connell, however, remains unconvinced that this hybridisation that Demetriou describes, is indicative of a challenge to hegemony (or indeed to her model):

> Clearly, specific masculine practices may be appropriated into other masculinities, creating a hybrid (such as the hip-hop style and language adopted by some working-class white teenage boys and the unique composite style of gay 'clones'). Yet we are not convinced that the hybridization Demetriou (2001) describes is hegemonic, at least beyond a local sense. Although gay masculinity and sexuality are increasingly visible in Western Societies – witness the fascination with the gay male characters in the television programs *Six Feet Under*, *Will and Grace*, and *Queer Eye for the Straight Guy* – there is little reason to think that hybridization has become hegemonic at the regional or global level.
>
> (2005:845)

Notwithstanding the clear irony that a field committed to challenging a monolithic conception of masculinity should become so dominated by a paradigmatically monolithic theoretical framework, the vigorous and productive debate that Connell's work has provoked has resulted in conceptual tools that are especially useful for my analysis of masculinities as they manifest in gay porn and the position of gay porn, vis à vis contemporary masculinity and popular culture. Sofia Aboim, for example, summarising the range of terms that have been adopted in recent years to describe the scope and range of masculinities, uses the term 'plurality' in more than an adjectival sense:

> Plurality is, in my view, an intrinsic feature of any masculinity. It is its formative and generative principle. Therefore any masculinity is always internally hybrid and is always formed by tension and conflict. Any masculinity, as any man, any individual, is plural both in relation to the material positions that locate him in the social world and the cultural references that constitute his universe of meaning and significance.
>
> (2010:3)

These dual notions of plurality and hybridity are helpful in my analysis of the expressions of sexualised masculinity that gay porn offers that are, to use Aboim's words, generative and hybridised. This is most evident in the web-based materials that are the subject of this study. A particular curiosity that I would observe here though is that whilst several scholars, including Connell and Kimmel (2005:415) and Acker (2004:29), have paid attention to the global conditions of gender and posited a 'global' hegemonic masculinity,[3] little, if any, mention is made in this research of the potential, as well as the challenges, posed for regional models of masculinity, normative standards and attendant conditions of power by the pervasiveness and global reach of the internet. Indeed, the web too often feels like a blind spot for the major thinkers and theorists in the field of masculinity studies, which inevitably the research in this book aims, in part, to address.

Within the realm of popular culture, it is increasingly common to see proliferating models of masculinity and instances where seemingly conventional 'dominant' masculinities (which we are often encouraged to read as variously old-fashioned, redundant or moribund) are supplanted by a panoply of new articulations and iterations of manhood. This of course is not new in and of itself. A historical view of the cultural construction of modern masculinities indicates that far from being static, masculinity is often in flux. Furthermore I would argue that the mass media have frequently played a pivotal role in the articulation and promotion of new modes of masculinity since at least the middle to late 19th century. So Dandyism, and more latterly the figures of the flaneur and the aesthete, were in part, at least, drawn into existence and popularised through newspaper reportage.[4] During the 20th century, we can observe a further blooming of models of masculinity through not just the press but also cinema, television and popular music, and this trend seems to have escalated in the 21st century.[5] In recent years we can see examples of 'new' masculinities that have been brought into view initially through the practices of the media and that have subsequently garnered scholarly attention. The most notable examples are the 'new man', the subject of Sean Nixon's *Hard Looks: Masculinities, Spectatorship and Contemporary Consumption* (1996), the 'new lad' (Benwell, 2002) and more recently still the 'metrosexual', who Matthew Hall interrogates in *Metrosexual Masculinities* (2015).[6] These models have already been joined by (and perhaps supplanted by) further media-generated soubriquets that have yet to attract the attention of scholars (but no doubt will), such as the 'lumbersexual',[7] a figure whose iconography draws on traditional hyper-macho signifiers including beards, tattoos and plaid shirts (ironically and largely unintentionally referencing the gay macho look of the mid-1970s), and the rather more heightened and aggressively sexual version of the metrosexual, the so-called 'spornosexual' (the term here is a conjunction of sport and porn), whose developed muscular body and highly groomed appearance speak unambiguously of an overt and assertive sexual desirability.[8] These proliferating contemporary masculinities might perhaps simply indicate an increasingly rapid pace of cultural and social change, or the rapacious demands of the modern media for constant novelty, but they certainly indicate a ramping up of the stakes regarding what can easily (and legibly) be ascribed as the constituent features of modern masculinities, not least because the term 'sexual' is so insistently a component of these portmanteau words and the attendant sexualised ways in which these masculinities are written about and received.

# Gay and 'Postgay'

Additionally there is evidence to suggest that the supposed fixity of specific masculine identities has become increasingly destabilised in recent times. Eric Anderson in *Inclusive Masculinity* (2009), for instance, makes a very useful distinction between what he describes as 'orthodox masculinity' that can be aligned with the model of masculinity that Connell's theorisation suggests as hegemonic, and a newer, liberal version that he describes as 'inclusive masculinity'. Those men who embody this inclusive model 'can act in ways once associated with homosexuality, with less threat to their public identity as heterosexual. I show that this has socio-positive effects for straight men, gay men, and women as well' (2009:7). For Anderson, this extends far beyond 'acting' out some of the traditional Western indicators of homosexuality: it has resulted in a new masculinity in which the dichotomous relationship between homo- and hetero-sexual (if not social or cultural) identities is increasingly less tenable or indeed meaningful. Anderson's work in the sociology of sport, as evidenced in *Twenty-first Century Jocks* (2014), results in a wealth of testimony about the ways in which young, straight men in contemporary settings demonstrate a masculinity that includes emotional connections, physical intimacy and even sexual contact with other men without overt concern that their masculinity or their sexuality is compromised. In a similar vein, sexologist Volkmar Sigusch suggests:

> The diversification of socially accepted lifestyles and forms of sexuality necessarily (has) led the way to differentiation within the old categories of hetero- and homosexuality, the previously monolithic character of which was shown in practical terms to be theoretical, in the sense that it was a product of culture. Modes of sexual and gender-based response once categorized as typically heterosexual, homosexual or perverse for lack of a more differentiated matrix have since drifted away from these prescribed orbits, defining and diversifying themselves as lifestyles.
>
> (2004:14)

This has intriguing consequences, as not only heterosexual but also gay masculinity has become problematised by the developments that Anderson observes and this seems to provide some evidence for the emergence of a phenomenon that had been the subject of discussion amongst gay theorists some years earlier. For instance, during the late 1990s, Alan Sinfield, in *Gay and After*, argued for the so-called 'Postgay'[9] era, suggesting that 'gay as we have produced it and lived it and perhaps lesbian also are historical phenomena and now they may be hindering us more than helping us' (1998:5). His view of a recent future was one in which a monolithic gay identity (like a monolithic masculinity) would be supplanted by multiple homosexualites and less limited and fixed sexualities. Sinfield's call now seems prophetic, based on the indications in the work of sociologists like Eric Anderson and a range of social and cultural theorists.[10]

For some, however, Sinfield's utopian vision is problematic and represents a loss rather than a gain for gay men, and consequently the term 'Postgay' has caused both a degree of controversy and a range of critical responses. Stephen Maddison, in his essay 'Is the Rectum *Still* a Grave?' (2012) in *Transgression 2.0*, for example opines that 'in a "Post gay" moment we are witnessing both the disappearance and assimilation of gay identities' and furthermore that 'male narcissism, fashion and grooming are no longer signs of queerness but of successful heterosexuality; gay men have thus not only disappeared culturally and politically but aesthetically and stylistically as well' (2012:97). Whilst Anderson observes the positive outcomes of what he regards as decreasing homophobia in Western society, Maddison notes that 'sexual tastes and sexual ideologies that police gender are increasingly driven by the needs of capital' (ibid.). Some of what Maddison has to say has echoes of an earlier and more fervent critic of the 'Postgay' phenomenon, Michael Warner. In the polemical *The Trouble With Normal* (1999), he takes a wrecking ball to what he sees as the 'utopian notion that somewhere one might not be defined by one's sexuality, that stigma might simply vanish' (1999:46) (that in his view has a strong under-current of self-loathing) expressed by the Mattachine Society in the 1950s, and that finds some parallel in Sinfield's writing in *Gay and After*. Warner's book was in part a response to the provocations of the conservative journalist and commentator Andrew Sullivan, who was the editor of the *New Republic* during the 1990s and the author of *Virtually Normal* in 1993, a book that suggests that the majority of gay people aspired for normalcy and integration into wider society. Warner considers that the separation of sex from identity and rescinding the radical power of gay cultural subversion is a dangerous move for the gay community, a term once again used to express a broad coalition.[11] Whilst it is clear to see the ways in which some of Warner's concerns about the assimilation of gay identities have come to fruition (gay identity has, perhaps, become increasingly depoliticised), he did not (and probably could not) anticipate that far from a diminution of manifestations of non-normative sexualities and identities, in fact in the years since he wrote *The Trouble With Normal* we have seen an exponential increase in expressions of sexuality in and across culture, and the emergence, some would argue, of a so-called 'sexualized' even 'pornified' culture.

## Sexuality, Sexualisation and the Web

The German sexologist Volkmar Sigusch, often regarded as one of the key figures of the sexual revolution of the 1960s, is an author whose work is rarely translated into English. This is a significant loss to Anglophone scholarship, given the wealth of material that he has published since the late 1960s and especially in recent years. Rather than the ebullient proponent of free love and liberal attitudes that one might expect, Sigusch instead has many pithy and critical observations to make about contemporary sexuality. In the essay 'On Cultural Transformations of Sexuality and Gender in Recent Decades' (2004), one of the rare translations of his work, he argues that 'sexuality is no longer an issue of prominence' and furthermore that it is 'largely banalized. Like egotism and mobility, it is simply taken for granted by many people today (3/14). He regards this condition, which he has described elsewhere as the 'Neosexual revolution' (1998:331–59), as a necessary consequence of a post-Fordist, late capitalist, neoliberal logic wherein the demands of the flexible market have permeated all areas of social life including, but not limited to, sexuality. There are obvious similarities in what Sigusch has to say and the argument that Stephen Maddison proposes in 'Is the Rectum *Still* a Grave?' Most notably, the proposition that the status of sexuality has changed as a result of the primacy of the market is at the heart of Sigusch's description of modern sexuality:

It is during intervals between significant and unmistakable transformations of sexuality as a cultural form that most people most firmly believe that sexuality is something unified and unalterable. In truth, however, it is a composite, an associated phenomenon that is subject to continuous change and recoding [...] The supposedly whole and complete sexual form is fragmented again and again in order to ascribe new desires and meanings to it, to implant new urges and new fields of experience, to market new practices and services. In some cases, change takes place rapidly over a period of just a few decades.

(2/14)

And more explicitly still:

Rationalization, dispersion, deregulation, commercialization and the compulsion to diversify have combined to create a new form of sexuality. The outcome of the neosexual revolution that conforms most closely to the social objectives could (with reference to the post-Fordian strategies of lean management and lean production) be called lean sexuality.

(11/14)

So, for Sigusch, the symbolic power of sexuality has been replaced in the contemporary moment with a diversity of sexual practices, the 'dissociation of the sexual sphere from the sphere of gender relations' (2014:141) and the commercialisation of sexuality.[12]

In an essay that provides a very useful summary of Sigusch's argument, Volker Woltersdorff takes issue both with the negative diagnosis that he offers and the static nature of his argument. In 'Paradoxes of Precarious Sexualities: Sexual Subcultures Under Neo-Liberalism' Woltersdorff takes Sigusch's position as a starting point to discuss what he describes instead as a 'precarious' modern sexuality, which I regard as a productive way to move forward, taking into account the conditions that Sigusch identifies but also acknowledging that they are contingent and shifting:

Precarity refers to the juxtaposition of the gains in individualization and the increase in insecurity that arises through economic deregulation and the decline of social tradition. By using this term I am aligning myself with a critical analysis of

the conditions of neo-liberalism and political counter mobiliza-
tion, and it seems appropriate to use it to describe the contra-
dictions of neo-liberal restructuring. Using the term precarity
in relation to sexuality is furthermore a conscious intervention in this discourse in order to claim the sexual dimension of
capitalist socialization as an indispensable category for analysis
[...] Precarious gender and sexual subject positions transgress
traditional codices, constantly running the risk of failure and
collapse.

(2011:167)

In the Anglophone world,[13] this new context of a liberalised, de-moralised,
'precarious' sexuality has become a locus of anxiety, especially as these conditions manifest themselves in social attitudes and cultural expressions.
In recent years the associated commentary around sex and sexuality that
emerges under these conditions (often discursively framed in terms that
suggest a crisis) has coalesced around what has become known as 'the sexualisation debate', a rather catch-all term, marshalled by a disparate group
including journalists, politicians, policy-makers and lobbying groups as
well as academics to describe a succession of cultural and social developments that appear to diverge from (indeed to challenge) previously established social and, importantly, sexual mores. The evidence for what is often
described as the 'sexualization of culture' is various to say the least, with a
disparate range of artefacts and phenomena identified, ranging from:

Bratz dolls, pornstar t-shirts, playboy key rings, poledancing,
lads mags, push-up bras for teenagers, breast enlargement, breast
reduction, vaginaplasty, Viagra, the sexual self-representations
of sexblogs, sexting, Beautiful Agony and SuicideGirls, anime
and hentai, burlesque, *Cosmopolitan* magazine, a photograph
of Miley Cyrus in *Vanity Fair* and the photographs from Abu
Ghraib, Max Hardcore's prolific output, TV programmes like
*Girls Gone Wild, Sex and the City* and *Porn: A Family Business.*
(Smith, 2010:106)

The so-called sexualisation debate has been a fertile terrain for a range of
groups concerned about sexual representations and their 'effects' on society
and especially on young women, extending the anti-porn Feminist position
(already exhaustively discussed elsewhere) to a wider 'concern' about sexual

imagery/behaviours/attitudes in contemporary society.[14] Amongst the most vocal of these concerned parties is, inevitably, Gail Dines, who along with figures such as Karen Boyle, Julia Long and Pamela Paul, has colonised this territory and initiated an often divisive debate, that continues to this day, that feels distorted by contradictory (and sometimes dubious) motives. Few serious scholars would have very much to say about Dines' credentials as a researcher, indeed her hyperbolic media appearances, almost always used to make spurious claims, have often undermined her own arguments. For example, Ronald Weitzer's essay 'Interpreting the Data: Assessing Competing Claims in Pornography Research' (2015) includes a forensic analysis, questioning the credibility of Dines' research methods. Her many public appearances and aggressive promotional strategies are more suggestive of a personality interested in a career as a vituperative commentator and media pundit rather than in addressing the subjugation of women that sexualisation, we are told, represents. Whilst I would want to declare my support for at least some of the (Feminist) politics that underpin the interventions of Dines et al., it's much less easy for me to feel comfortable with the contribution that she and her anti-porn Feminist colleagues have made to a wider public debate that frames women (and especially young women) as objectified, victimised and without, it seems, any agency at all. Weitzer describes this with admirable concision as the 'oppression paradigm' (2005, 2010).[15] Furthermore, sexualisation is a term, as Clarissa Smith notes in her excoriating critique of Linda Papadopoulos' policy document, commissioned by the UK Home Office, *The Sexualisation of Young People Review*, that has rarely been adequately investigated:

> The term 'sexualisation' is one which has achieved a dubious currency – like its counterparts, pornographication and pornification – it's a term which benefits from remaining unexamined and untheorised. As with other authors' mobilisations of those terms (with the notable exceptions of Attwood, McNair and Paasonnen) Papadopoulos does not offer any significant discussion of her working definition of 'sexualisation' – other than to claim that 'sexualisation is the imposition of adult sexuality on to children and young people before they are capable of dealing with it (mentally, emotionally or physically)'.
>
> (2010b:176)

As Smith suggests, probably the most important and authoritative voice to be heard in the debates around sexualisation is Feona Attwood, whose essay 'Sexed up: Theorizing the Sexualization of Culture' remains one of the defining interrogations of both the term and the associated debates that have summoned it into existence (or that the term itself has brought into focus depending on your perspective). Attwood provides a starting point for defining (and problematising) the terms of reference by noting:

> 'sexualized culture', a rather clumsy phrase used to indicate a number of things; a contemporary preoccupation with sexual values, practices and identities; the public shift to more permissive sexual attitudes; the proliferation of sexual texts; the emergence of new forms of sexual experience; the apparent breakdown of rules, categories and regulations designed to keep the obscene at bay; our fondness for scandals, controversies and panics around sex.
>
> (2006:78)

Sexualisation and its corollary, pornification (and the rather more awkward pornographication), are terms that were not originally used in a value-laden way and in some cases were initially proposed to invite a rather more balanced and reflective consideration of the potentiality opened up by new ways of configuring, representing and exploring sexuality. Brian McNair, for example, used pornification to describe the ways in which new technology allowed sexuality to become democratised. However, as Clarissa Smith has observed, this terminology has been appropriated by individuals who would argue that:

> all right-thinking individuals must recognize the harms of 'pornographication'. Those who use the term pornographication do so precisely so that they can avoid any of the particularities of sexually explicit media. The obviousness of the term should alert us to the ways in which pornographication is not something that can be 'discovered', 'uncovered' and 'challenged', but instead it is a means of ensuring that behaviours, practices and actions can be labeled and assessed as problematic without addressing specific issues relating to their history, production and consumption; and that can suggest 'solutions' which are both intensely political and denuded of real politics at the same time.
>
> (2010:104–5)

As Smith succinctly puts it, sexualisation/pornification is now all too often regarded as 'a problem, not a description' (p. 106). The focus point of much of the concern, as Attwood, Smith and others observe, is, naturally enough, the pervasive reach and power of the internet. Questions of ease of access to limitless supplies of uncensored material with no regard for geographical or social boundaries, the privatised mode of consumption, sometimes in the home but increasingly via mobile devices anywhere, are specific qualities that mean that web-based porn can be thought of as simultaneously domesticated, personal and familiar and also insidiously invading the home, making sexual explicit material easy to find, readily available and thereby 'naturalized'. Whilst this is often the way public discourse around this so-called sexualisation is framed, there is also a critical mass of scholars who argue for the liberatory possibilities that the web opens up, especially for minority groups and alternative sexualities. As Anderson puts it:

> The internet provides anyone the ability to instantly access a display of sexual variety. Here bodies fuck (predominantly for straight and gay men's pleasures) in all combinations, styles, mixtures, manners and video quality. I am not necessarily critiquing this, instead, I think it provides what some feminists concerned with pornography have been calling for all along: not an abolition of pornography, but an explosion of the subjectivities of differing kinds of people in pornography.
>
> (2009:5)

Specifically, Anderson notes that gay men have been particular beneficiaries of this uncovering, or 'mainstreaming' of sexually explicit materials:

> The internet, I propose, has therefore been instrumental in exposing the forbidden fruit of homosexual sex, commodifying and normalizing it in the process. This, combined with a strategic and political bombardment of positive cultural messages about homosexuality through youth media, MTV, reality television, and other popular venues, has sent a message that while homosexuality is okay, homophobia is not.
>
> (p. 6)

Consequently, porn is no longer a paradigmatically abject and underground cultural commodity. Furthermore, I would argue that gay porn specifically

39

is also no longer a marginal obscurity, only accessed by, catering for and speaking to an ostracised minority group. In my view, therefore, gay porn instead becomes an instructive site for exploring the ways in which contemporary masculinities are constructed and (importantly) eroticised. Gay porn provides representations of a range of masculinities: 'passive' or 'active', hypertrophic, ephebic, even feminised, 'hegemonic' ideals or radical 'outsider' representations. We can observe masculinities that fundamentally challenge and undermine the very notion of a hegemonic masculinity. Gay porn produces masculinities that are sometimes dichotomous, but also masculinities that I would want to describe as 'spectrums' and it is this panoply of iterations of masculinities that are such a particularity of 21st-century popular culture and consciousness.

## Saturated Masculinity

It is this febrile contemporary context, described in this chapter – and which includes a radical reconceptualisation of the meanings, significance and function of *masculinity* – that has taken place in both critical and popular discourse since the late 1980s, alongside a concomitant set of technological developments in media and communications that have expedited access to a widened, perhaps more complex and ambivalent conception of plural *masculinities*.

These changes have occurred in a social and cultural context in which sex and sexuality are increasingly subjects of open debate both in public and in private and in which sexually explicit materials are widely accessible (and widely consumed) and therefore no longer regarded as beyond the pale. These changes, in turn, have also provided the conditions in which non-heterosexual and non-hetero-normative sexual identities, practices and representations (especially, though not exclusively, gay masculinities) have become more widely socially acceptable.[16] I would argue that sex and sexuality, in this contemporary moment, are increasingly regarded in public discourse as questions of personal choice and personal freedom rather than questions of morality. Furthermore, within the context of late capitalism, sex and sexuality are subject to the logic and demands of the market, and I argue that this concatenation of factors has resulted in a condition that I describe as 'saturated masculinity'.

The term 'saturated masculinity' owes a very conspicuous debt to the work of the social psychologist Kenneth Gergen, whose book *The Saturated Self*, written in 1991, anticipates (with eerie accuracy) a postmodern condition in which the individual is so overwhelmed and bombarded with opportunities for self-expression and communication that our very sense of our self becomes fractured, a condition that he describes as 'multiphrenia' (1991:73). Gergen sees the media and communications technologies, which he refers to collectively as 'the technology of social saturation' (ibid., 74) as playing an especially important part in this state of being. His ideas are based on the premise that technology is having deleterious effects on society and that the proliferation of information results in both a loss of the self and the ability for moral action. He expands on this theme in *Social Construction and Cultural Context*, arguing that:

> Given the potential dependency of conceptions of self on technological conditions, let us consider our contemporary ethos. In particular, what is to be said about the increasing insinuation of the technologies of sociation into our lives and the effects on our beliefs in individual minds? In my view this technological transformation is slowly undermining the intelligibility of the individual self and its function as a source of moral action.
>
> (2001:186)

I don't subscribe to Gergen's negative assessment of the (post)modern condition at all, and my focus in this work is on cultural expressions and representations rather than the construction of the self, so there is inevitably a limit to the usefulness of what he has to say. Nonetheless I do think that Gergen's description of the fragmented and complex ways in which a technological society is organised provides a useful grounding from which to develop a model for thinking about how representations of masculinities work and are circulated in such a context. So I am appropriating Gergen's terminology and freely adapting it for its value as a way of describing a complicated, contradictory range of masculine representations (especially sexual representations).

Rather than Gergen's pessimistic diagnosis of the consequences of multiphrenia, I instead draw inspiration from Zygmunt Bauman's rather more ambivalent conception of the 'liquid'. In *Liquid Modernity*, Bauman identifies the late-modern period, which he describes as 'liquid modernity', as one that is 'multiple, complex and fast moving, and therefore as ambiguous, fuzzy or plastic' (2000:117) and most importantly as constantly in flux. Likewise, contemporary masculinities, I would argue, can be regarded in this way. This perspective is one that is shared by Sofia Aboim, who, in *Plural Masculinities*, discusses the ways in which masculinity is figured in the complex social context that Bauman and Gergen delineate:

> In this perspective, masculinities must no longer be confined to the limited, though multiple, positions and ideologies that may be derived from material and structural relations. Quite the opposite, their polymorphous reality (which the French sociologist Christine Castelain Meunier [2005] calls the 'polyculture of Masculinity') should be based on the unlimited proliferation of discourses and symbolic references that construct fluid difference rather than fixed identity. Hence, categories that name 'men as men' and 'women as women' should be considered suspicious and ultimately dismissed.
>
> (2012:13)

What I am describing as saturated masculinity then describes a cultural context in which a vortex of proliferating representations of masculinity have emerged that suggest that the very notion of a 'dominant' or 'hegemonic' model of masculinity is problematised. Furthermore this suggests a set of cultural conditions in which the same dominant, patriarchal models of masculinity are only (and seemingly can only be) described in pejorative and negative terms. This is a context in which ridicule and satire or representations pointing to the oppressive or indeed the perverse are commonly deployed rhetorical strategies used to frame this previous hegemonic model of masculinity. It is a condition in which idealised, 'patriarchal' masculinities are sometimes marshalled, though they are used in representations solely in mythic, archetypical terms. Idealised masculinity becomes a chimera, constantly reappropriated, repurposed, hybridised, adapted, mutated and subverted. I would argue that these rhetorical techniques and representations – which are ubiquitous across popular culture, from advertising to popular music, the soap opera and reality TV – are surely the clearest indicators that the 'hegemony' that Connell had suggested was about the maintenance of the privilege of heterosexual and heteronormative masculinity, has been if not completely lost, then profoundly compromised. This has the potential to result in what social psychologists have recently described as 'precarious manhood'. This is, largely, an attempt to revisit and empirically evaluate what Arthur Schlessinger, in the late 1950s, described as the 'crisis in masculinity'; however, in this case, the crisis is ongoing and did not end in the 1950s.[17] I, however, do not regard what I see as a fluid, saturated masculinity as an indicator of gender crisis.[18] On the contrary, I see a necessary, and potentially liberating, expansion of the possibilities for the ways in which gender can be understood in this phenomenon. Instead of a static, monolithic masculinity that is singular, or, indeed, a hegemonic model that according to Connell is suggestive of a degree of continuity and stasis, masculinity is perpetually in flux and generative, producing new iterations and thereby replete with meanings. Contemporary, saturated masculinity is a fluid model that is contingent, contextual and reflective of (and responsive to) the demands of cultural conditions. Saturated masculinity is therefore discursive and iterative, and as I will observe in the second part of this book, the discourses at play in gay porn and the models of masculinity that the genre produces provide evidence for this phenomenon and illustrate the complex, polysemic and indeterminate nature of even the most apparently straightforward masculine ideals.

# 2

# History, Industry and Technological Change

*[T]he specific and unprecedented cinematic pleasure of the illusion of bodily motion emerged partly as a by-product of the quest for the initially unseeable 'truths' of this motion. At the origin of its invention, then, cinema is caught up in a technology that produces this body in its own image – as an infinitely repeatable mechanism.*

Linda Williams, *Hard Core: Power, Pleasure and the Frenzy of the Visible* (1989:39)

Linda Williams, discussing Eadweard Muybridge's 'Zoopraxiscope' and Etienne Jules Marey's *La Machine Animale* (1875), notes, in the above extract, that technology (in this case photography and its variants) results in certain types of knowledge and produces certain and very specific pleasures. Technology, then, is much more than a delivery mechanism for information; the nature of the information and our relationship to that information is shaped by technology which, as Williams puts it, acts as 'a "transfer point" of knowledge, power, and pleasure' (p. 36).

In the introduction and first chapter of this volume, I suggested that this study is situated firstly in the broader context of porn studies as an emergent field and the sub-field of gay porn studies in particular. Secondly, it is situated in relation to a wider set of debates around the social and cultural

**44**

construction of masculinities, the sexualisation of culture and the conflu-
ence of these two factors with the advent of what I describe as *saturated
masculinity* in the contemporary moment. In this chapter, I will present the
final context in which representations of masculinities to be covered in the
second part of the book need to be placed: an industrial context that has in
turn led to a series of generic characteristics that will be discussed here and
frame the representations explored in Part 2.

Firstly it is important to re-emphasise just how significant technology
has been in the development of the pornography industry, both gay and
otherwise. In *Hardcore: Power, Pleasure and the Frenzy of the Visible*, Linda
Williams argued that the invention of the cinematic apparatus was a key
contributor to the emergence of suitable conditions for hardcore pornographic representation to emerge:

> [A] cinematic hardcore emerges more from this *scientia sexu-
> alis* and its construction of new forms of body knowledge than
> from ancient traditions of erotic art [...] thus we can begin to
> recognize how the desire to see and know more of the human
> body [...] underlies the very invention of cinema.
>
> (p. 36)

I take Williams' position still further in this chapter as I argue that technological developments are not only fundamental to the development of
pornography as a genre; they are also central to the ways in which we experience, mediate and make sense of our own sexualities in contemporary
culture. Technology is in fact instrumental in the production and fulfil-
ment of our sexuality, and technology is a central mechanism through
which we gain access to the knowledge/pleasure of sexuality.[1] As Sarah
Schaschek notes,

> Pornography forces us to consider the relation between sexual
> pleasure and technology. Not only does the act of filming and
> screening audiovisual pornography involve technical instruments,
> thereby making the body of the actor and the viewer interact with
> the filmic apparatus, pornography is also said to be a driving force
> behind the technological development and deployment of media
> such as print, photography, cinema, video and cyberspace.
>
> (2014:54)

The media (and the producers of gay porn in particular) create models of sexuality and sexual desirability for our consumption, through the deployment of sign systems, iconography, mise-en-scène and narrative tropes as well as the models of masculinity that are the subject of this study and that I have described elsewhere as homosexual prototypes[2] populating the world of gay pornography. In this way technology is not merely an adjunct to sexual gratification via the consumption of the pornographic text: it is, in fact, central to our experience of sexual pleasure.[3] As Ken Plummer has recently noted in *Cosmopolitan Sexualities*, 'the decisive factor in the development of modern sexualities has to have been the gradual evolution of modern media from Gutenberg to Facebook' (2015:45).

## The Epochs of Gay Porn

It is not my intention to provide a detailed history of gay porn here, irrespective of how necessary that work is. In part, this is because a major portion of this task is already underway, most notably with the example of Thomas Waugh and the scrupulously researched *Hard to Imagine: Gay Male Eroticism in Photography and Film from Their Beginnings to Stonewall* (1996) and in a more populist way by Jeffrey Escoffier in *Bigger Than Life: The History of Gay Porn Cinema from Beefcake to Hardcore* (2009) and partly because this is work that will inevitably continue through the efforts of subsequent scholars and historians of sexuality, not least because, as I noted in the previous chapters, this has become a prevalent trend in research in the field. Instead I am presenting what might be described as a heuristic chronology that enables the discussion of the evolution of gay porn production, the connections to technological developments and their impact on form and content. In his essay 'Seen as a Business: Adult Film's Historical Framework and Foundations', Kevin Heffernan notes that much of the historical work on pornography 'falls somewhere on a continuum between Walter Kendrick, who [...] defines the object of study by its hidden [...] nature and Linda Williams who [...] outlines the textual features that constitute hardcore cinema' (2015:37). Heffernan poses the question, 'what happens if we place economics at centre stage in the historical narrative?' (p. 38) in order to suggest that shifts in production and distribution produce new institutions and, perhaps more importantly for my argument, that 'changes in distribution have major effects on the aesthetic conventions of adult films' (ibid.).

The chronology I offer here adds traction to Heffernan's argument as it points to instances where shifts in technology and culture result in shifts in style and format and to the establishment, over time, of a recurrent set of conventions that I will describe as a *demotic* mode of gay pornographic representation. This position can broadly be understood as falling within the somewhat indistinct ambit of what has been termed media archaeology. As Erkki Huhtamo and Jussi Parikka describe it in the introduction to their edited collection on the subject:

> When media archaeologists claim that they are 'excavating' media-cultural phenomena, the word should be understood in a specific way [...]. Media archaeology rummages textual, visual, and auditory archives as well as collections of artifacts, emphasizing both the discursive and the material manifestations of culture. Its explorations move fluidly between disciplines, although it does not have a permanent home within any of them.
>
> (2011:3)

In the spirit that Huhtamo and Parrika summon up, the chronology I describe here connects technological and cultural change to representational change, but it is neither entirely linear nor does it describe a progressive, forward trajectory. Whilst porn is often written about – both in scholarly and popular accounts – in terms that demonstrably emphasise what might be described as its 'epochal' nature, in fact, the organisation of porn history into neat temporal packets tends to overlook the overlapping and rather more circular nature of developments that, as Huhtamo and Parrika note, 'do not point teleologically to the present media-cultural condition as their "perfection"' (ibid.).

In this context, then, when I present a chronology describing the development of gay porn as a genre in epochal terms, I am doing so not to describe a facile linearity in order to suggest that the contemporary material that is my object of study is the apogee of this developmental trajectory, but instead to illustrate how changes in technology and conditions of production and consumption can be mapped onto shifts in form and content, style and modes of representation.

## Photography and Magazines

The first two epochs in this chronology ostensibly constitute the material that forms the substantial basis of Thomas Waugh's *Hard to Imagine*, the first one being the emergence of 19th-century homoerotic photography, the subsequent genre that Waugh describes as 'partouze' photography (1996:285) and the development (via physique magazines and photosets) of the beginnings of explicit gay magazine publishing. The time frame here is considerable, ranging from the 1870s to (in Waugh's study at least) the 1970s. Waugh presents a history in which social, cultural and (implicitly) technological change impacts on the material that is produced and circulated. He also usefully notes that there are 'visual and imaginary continuities' resulting in recurrent 'image constellations' (p. 41) that I would also see as framing the ways in which the sexualised male body is contextualised and presented for consumption in contemporary representations. The patterns, or more accurately dichotomies, that Waugh observes are 'looking versus being looked at' (p. 42), 'subject versus object, identification versus desire' (p. 44) and finally 'difference: culture, gender, and class (p. 48). It will be pretty clear to even the most casual reader that Waugh's identification of discursive regimes in this way has informed the structure of the research presented in the second part of this book.

## Stag Films and Gay Loops

The second epoch that Waugh also writes about in some detail is the period of 'stag film' production from about 1908 to the 1970s.[4] Waugh helpfully defines the stag film as 'an explicit sexual narrative, produced and distributed, usually commercially, to clandestine, nontheatrical male audiences' (p. 309). As Waugh notes, whilst the majority of the corpus of stag films depicts heterosexual activity, scenes of homosexual contact are sometimes included as components of group sex scenes and exclusively homosexual acts are not uncommon either.[5] These films are usually silent, monochrome, and range from a few minutes to ten minutes in length. For the sake of simplicity and because of the similar technological, production and distribution contexts, I would additionally include the emergence of physique (often called beefcake) shorts from the 1950s until the late 1960s and early 1970s during this epoch. Studios such as the Athletic Model Guild (AMG), the publisher of *Physique Pictorial* – virtually a one-man operation run by Bob Mizer – diversified from selling photosets and magazines into short films[6] for private consumption sold illicitly via mail order, ranging from posing and wrestling shorts to fantasy 'fancy dress' scenes, and even later, in the 1960s and early 1970s, short sexual vignettes. Like the stags, the 8 mm (and occasionally 16 mm) 'loops' produced by AMG and competitors such as Apollo, Bruce of LA, Kris and Zenith, were silent, mostly monochrome and a few minutes in duration.[7] Waugh describes these films as 'a unique and somewhat arcane body of work confined historically within a fifteen year period' (p. 254), an observation that I think, perhaps unintentionally, devalues the extent to which the settings, scenarios and, most importantly, the athletic physiques of the performers, have informed the gay erotic imaginary and the modes of representation that were to follow and can instead be understood as important precursors of what we now might describe as 'mainstream' gay representations. So, for example, films like *Talent For Sale* (dir. Bob Mizer, 1965) use the, now routine, cliché of the 'casting couch scenario' in which an 'agent' auditions three young street toughs who strip to posing pouches (curiously striped) for a gratuitous display and then wrestle with little pretext (or even logic) on the floor of his office. With even less narrative motivation, they proceed to attack the hapless agent, stripping him to the waist before they leave. The scene ends with a happy line-up of the cast smiling and waving. Similarly *Strip Poker* (1959) has a title that makes its content plain, as a group of leather-clad bikers play poker, strip and then wrestle in an all-male scenario that is now a familiar trope of contemporary gay porn.

It's also useful to note here the important connection that Waugh makes between photography, magazine publishing and the later emergence of pornographic film. Contrary to common sense logic, publishing was not initially a promotional vehicle for the moving image. By contrast, films, especially in the case of Mizer's AMG as well as Jim French's Colt Studios, were an expansion and diversification of a successful and established enterprise based on an established core business in the sale of still, rather than moving, images.

The loops made by AMG, Zenith and Kris largely featuring models in posing pouches, swimwear, towels or any other assortment of props and acoutrements – were replaced over time by loops that gradually featured nudity. So by 1967, *Physique Pictorial* was advertising Warhol's protégé, Joe Dallesandro, nude, in an AMG 'posing' film that was made some time between 1964 and 1966. With slicked-back hair, a smile, an oiled physique, and self-consciously gauche gestures, Dallesandro sits on a wooden bench before standing and performing a set of athletic moves, including a short set of shadow boxing moves, with the camera pulling back and tilting down in the process from a medium close-up to a mid-shot that reveals his nudity. The five-minute film, which for some time was considered lost, could scarcely be regarded as sexually arousing by contemporary standards and instead has a quaint recherché quality that suggests that (apart from the nudity) it could have been made ten years earlier.[8]

By the end of the 1960s and into the 1970s, the sexual stakes of the content of physique shorts escalated from nudity to hardcore sex scenes. There are a relatively smaller number of AMG films of this kind, with titles such as *Cyclist's Dream* (1971), *Chief Singletary's Willing Captive* (1971) and *Visit From an AWOL Sailor* (1972),[9] but this was ostensibly the territory of another group of small enterprises including Jim French's Colt Studios, Brentwood, Target and Le Salon and indicates the beginnings of what might be more recognisable as the gay porn 'industry' of later years. This altogether more sexually explicit material was, once again, sold via mail order and exhibited in adult cinemas and bars in 8mm or 16mm, usually shot in colour by this stage, and often by now had sound. These later loops tended to be between 15 to 20 minutes long following an embryonic structure of an initial 'set-up' moving swiftly into a sex scene.[10] Escoffier notes though that the later structural formula for representing the unfolding of a sexual exchange was yet to be established:

> They merely provided a setup that created a charged atmosphere in which the sexual action could unroll. The sex almost always involved fellatio and anal penetration. The cum shots were not yet formalized as the ending of a scene, nor did they always take place after fucking – but sometimes the performers might have several orgasms at different points in the film.
>
> (2009: 133–4)

## *'Cinematic' Hardcore*

The next epoch that I would identify is the period of quasi 'cinematic' production and exhibition, through adult cinemas and flea pits, which begins with relative precision with the first screening of Wakefield Poole's *Boys in the Sand* in December 1971 at the 55th Street Playhouse in New York and was to continue during the early years of the 1970s. Given that this was one of the shortest periods of gay porn production, it's notable that this is also the historical moment, context, group of personnel and texts that have been written about the most extensively. Waugh for instance describes *Boys in the Sand* as 'epochal' (1996:271) and Richard Dyer in *Now You See It* describes the film as 'Hollywoodian in both its camera work and its production of the first gay porn star, Casey Donnovan' (1990:171). Linda Williams notes that *Boys in the Sand* predates the release of *Deep Throat* (more customarily associated with the beginnings of the cinematic hardcore) by almost a year and offers a very detailed and sensitive textual and contextual analysis that extends to a full chapter of *Screening Sex* (2008). Jeffrey Escoffier provides detail about the production context for the film, as does Wakefield Poole's own fascinating autobiography, *Dirty Poole* (2000:145–65).[11] Though Poole's work has tended to dominate critical discourse, clearly in part due to the ambition and technical virtuosity on display recognised when *Boys in the Sand* became the first gay porn film reviewed in *Variety* and by its reputed commercial success, it was a film that was to be very shortly followed by further releases that were equally notable but to date have tended to elude the sustained critical attention devoted to Poole's opus. These include *L.A. Plays Itself* (dir. Fred Halsted, 1972); *Nights in Black Leather* (dir. Richard Abel, 1973); *Adam and Yves* (dir. Peter de Rome, 1974); *Do Me Evil* (dir. Toby Ross, 1975); *Sextool*, Fred Halsted's 1975 bid for a 'mainstream' success, shot in 35 mm; Joe Gage's 'Working Men Trilogy' *Kansas City Trucking Company* (1976); *El Paso Wrecking Corp* (1978) and *L.A. Tool & Die* (1979). These films lend themselves to detailed critical readings for a range of reasons: for the instances of imaginative framing and creative camera work, because of their (implicitly and explicitly) radical political intentions and frequent seriousness of purpose, but also because of their emphatically authored status: the dreamy quality of Wakefield Poole's work, the gritty urban feel of Fred Halsted, Joe Gage's storylines revolving around blue-collar men.[12] The distinguishing characteristics of these films are not just their conditions of exhibition and distribution but also the ambition to produce a cinematic hardcore that results in films that approach feature length, and are driven, more or less, by the conventions of narrative cinema whilst simultaneously at points deploying experimental stylistic and visual strategies. In addition, these films collectively constitute a stylistic source book for what is best described as the gay macho iconography of the period that was to be endlessly plundered and recycled in subsequent years: muscular, sometimes hirsute, bodies; facial hair (less frequently tattoos and piercings); and the 'uniform', figuratively and often literally of the blue-collar American male, which is typical in many of the films from this period and, as we will see in subsequent chapters, has found its way into the iconography both of the modern gay male and the eroticised representations of contemporary gay porn. However, in terms of the broader development of gay porn as a genre, this short period, whilst fascinating and a rich source of material for researchers, in fact indicates very clearly that any history of porn that attempts to produce a linear, evolutionary trajectory is misguided. A cinematic hardcore did not sustain itself because of a constellation of factors and similarly the strong narrative focus and experimentation with camera work and editing were to be replaced, relatively quickly in subsequent years, with a more industrialised set of formal and narrative conventions.

## VHS

In 1972, Chuck Holmes, a recently unemployed sales executive, loaned $4200 to buy three film loops, directed by Matt Sterling (whose reputation would be later established through his 'discovery' of Jeff Stryker), and a collection of adult mailing lists. In May of the same year, Holmes dispatched his first mailing to potential clients under the company name Falcon and the most recognisable name in gay video pornography came into existence. This, for the purposes of economy, ushers in the fourth major epoch in the development of the gay porn industry: the emergence of the home video market that provided the conditions for the commercialisation (latterly the professionalisation) of the industry and the establishment of a studio system of production and distribution dominated by the major players

Falcon, Catalina, His Video, Vivid Man and All Worlds Video during the early to mid-1980s.[13]

In 1978, capitalising on the success of the Falcon film loops and the emerging home video market, Holmes' commissioned *The Other Side of Aspen* – directed by Colin Myers. Starring Al Parker, Dick Fisk and Casey Donovan – the film was to be marketed as the first release in the Falcon Video Pac line and was to become their best-selling release to date. Originally conceived as a series of four separate loops, Holmes' innovation was the insertion of a narrative that connected the sexual vignettes together (Escoffier, p. 140). This narrative framing, sometimes referred to in industry parlance as 'webbing', was to become the standard format, not just for Falcon productions, but for the majority of material produced during the 1980s and onwards. With the success of *The Other Side of Aspen*, Falcon were to release the most popular of their back catalogue of over 200 film loops on video in the following years and increasingly to diversify into producing new material exclusively on video. As John Burger observes, Holmes' commercial acumen enabled Falcon to exploit a new technology and a burgeoning market for porn in a way that many of his competitors could not:

> Many smaller porn production companies were unable to meet the consumer demand for home video, which surfaced in the early 1980s (the June 1982 issue of Drummer contains an article entitled 'The Video Explosion' which hails the advent of this new visual home technology). Film-to-videotape transfer and the subsequent packaging, marketing, and distribution of videos is a costly procedure. Unable to compete in this new marketplace, many companies went out of business.
>
> (1995:15)

Holmes' creative ambition, famously, was little more than to produce porn featuring performers with clean feet. This apparent modesty belies the extent to which his personal vision would inform the commercial and aesthetic direction that Falcon Studios would take and much of his competitors would subsequently follow: towards an increasing emphasis on a vision of 'cleanliness', professional production values, a polished, generic, aesthetic and homogeneity in output. Escoffier notes that:

Chuck Holmes was known for the strict guidelines he imposed on Falcon performers: white, 'All-American' young men, no body hair, especially no chest hair, no body builders, and no tattoos. The approach was often called 'the Falcon car wash,' ensuring everything was 'clean' and hairless.

(2009: 262)

Out of the various phases in the development of a porn industry, this is perhaps the period of gay porn production that opens itself up most obviously to parody; a period often decried in popular accounts for its cynical commercialism, low production values, stereotypical scenarios, paper-thin set-ups, inept performances and (worst of all) bad hair. Little in this critique holds up to sustained scrutiny: indeed, it was exactly the perpetuation of this set of clichés about gay porn – how it looks and what it represents – that motivated my own early research interests into the settings, the types and the concept of the generic in gay porn.

So instead of a reproduction of the stereotypes of 1980s and 1990s gay porn, it is more accurate to point to the establishment of a recognisable industrial structure during this period and also the emergence of a quasi-studio system of major studios and smaller (often quite specialised) producers. Studios were to develop relatively recognisable house styles and rosters of directors and performers. In addition, a conventionalised format is established at this time: videos of around 90 minutes in total, featuring four to five scenes linked together by webbing that creates a sense of an overarching narrative or theme. More or less standardised norms of physical appearance and modes of performance are established and, as the AIDS crisis deepened, at the end of the 1980s and the early 1990s, this eventually included mandatory condom use.[14] In addition to these norms of format, VHS is established as the standard playback technology, and a distribution network of mail order and sales via adult video stores becomes the way in which gay porn is brought to market.

Aping the Hollywood model, the majors additionally developed a star system, with each studio associated with a particular performer; Catalina was initially the strongest player in this arena as it worked with both Jeff Stryker, far and away the biggest star (in more than one sense) of the period, and during the late 1980s and early 1990s Catalina also developed the career of Ryan Idol. Falcon was to adopt a more graduated hierarchy, once again imitating Hollywood's system of contract players, supporting actors and stars, with a pantheon of Falcon 'Exclusives' and 'Falcon Superstars' working across the various labels/divisions of the Falcon Group; Jocks Video, specialising, as the label suggests, in sporting scenarios and 'sporty' models, Mustang, used to release shorts during the 1970s, and subsequently lower-budget video titles and the Falcon Studios main brand. So performers such as Falcon Superstars Rex Chandler during the 1980s and Ken Ryker during the 1990s, both the epitome of the blond, muscular, Californian dream, were initially trialled in Jocks productions. The look that these and other performers embodied during the 1980s and 1990s has sometimes been attributed to the AIDS pandemic. I see this as a relatively facile connection (but one that has some resonance of course) that disregards a broader industrial context. What is certainly true is that the home video market blossomed during the early years of the crisis in a wider cultural context of paranoia and sex phobia as gay bars, saunas and sex clubs closed (Escoffier, 2009:197). In fact, the star system was to continue to become an even more prominent feature of the gay porn industry as the 1990s progressed, and its evolution is a subject that will be returned to in the second part of this book.

In essence, then, what emerges under these specific conditions of production, distribution and consumption is a body of material that has a very specific tone, setting and formal structure and a set of performative conventions and iconography. Though there are many examples that challenge this assertion, what is collectively summoned up is, most often, an American, and more specifically Californian, ideal of an affluent gay lifestyle: a world of luxurious domesticity, holidays and pool parties, peopled by young, tanned, toned, Caucasian men. There are almost too many examples to mention that illustrate this, including: *Splash Shots: Memories of Summer* (dir. Bill Clayton, 1984), *Spring Break* (dir. Bill Clayton, 1986), *Night Flight* (dir. Anon, 1985), *Cruisin' 1: Men on the Make* (dir. Steven Scarborough, 1988). The idealised consumerist fantasy of many of the videos from the VHS period was not, however, without its detractors, and the so-called Falcon 'carwash' or 'cookie cutter' look was particularly singled out for attention. By the 1990s and with the advent of the internet, commentators were increasingly identifying a degree of dissatisfaction with the dominant representational modes of the industry. As one of the many informed contributors to the ATKOL Video gay porn discussion forum notes in 1999, there are demonstrable connections between technological change, cultural context and porn production:

1. Changes in technology have certainly played a part in the changing visual trends in porn. I noted a significant shift towards the current 'buffed' look starting in the 80s, as exercise technology made that look available to more gay men, thus something more desired. This change seemed to coincide with the decline of porn on film and the rise of video porn. The sharper definition of the video format definitely shows off the body in greater detail, favoring the muscular and 'buff' body to better compared to the less toned physiques prevalent in the film years.

2. There has been speculation by various writers on gay culture regarding the impact of HIV/AIDS on gay men's body consciousness. Some have speculated that the 'buff' archetype that we see in porn today, and that is striven for by many gym-going gay men, is in part an expression of resistance/denial to the fact of the ravages of HIV/AIDS that flooded the community consciousness in the 80s. It's sort of like saying, 'How can I be affected by a life-threatening disease with a body like this?'

3. I think the rise of the career porn 'Model' or 'Performer' in the 80s has made a difference in what we see on the screen. I speculate that before the rise of marketing of the Porn Superstar (Idol, Chandler, Stryker, et al.), porn was often conceived and perceived as a filming of actual sex acts by gay men. I think that the motivations of men getting into porn in those times might have had as much to do with the sexually-affirming aspect of the work as with the money. This would mean that men more into gay sex would be likely to do gay porn, with a better chance that the sex acts being filmed were actually being enjoyed in a way that would register for the viewer.[15]

By the middle of the 1990s, the size of the home video market for gay porn was such that it was possible for new studios to present a challenge to the market share of the majors and to the cultural hegemony of clichés such as the 'cookie cutter' look of models that had become widely regarded as anodyne and hackneyed, even if they were evidently commercially viable. I would regard this as the late phase of VHS production and a transitionary moment between an old technology (VHS) and a new one (DVD and the web). During this period a new group of studios emerged, largely set up by personnel who had worked for major studios like Falcon and Catalina, as significant industry players. So Titan Studios, first releasing *River Patrol* (dir. Bruce Cam) and *Is Your Big Brother Home* (dir. Christopher Harris & Bruce Cam) in 1995, marketed itself as providing an alternative to 'mainstream' output with a focus of macho, muscular and often hairy men. Raging Stallion, set up in 1999, like Titan focused on hirsute, macho men but also specialised in 'niche interests', most notably the *Fist Pack* series of fisting videos. Hot House, established in 1994 with its first release *The Road to Hopeful* (dir. Steven Scarborough) focused on high production values and strong narrative themes, in effect producing commercialised films that harked back to the era of the cinematic hardcore. In addition, this period saw the rise to prominence of so-called 'Europorn'. In 1994, the market leader in this field, Bel Ami, released *Lukas Story* (dir. George Duroy) and with it cemented the status of its eponymous star (Lukas Ridgeston) as the embodiment of the Europorn performer *sine qua non*. Physically beautiful and aggressively marketed as 'natural', set up in opposition (and as an antidote to) the supposed primped artificiality of many US performers during this period, Ridgeston and his Bel Ami compatriots were at the vanguard of a massive growth in production outside of San Francisco in Central and Eastern Europe, especially Prague, Budapest and Bratislava.

## DVD and the 'Early' Web

Whilst it has become a truism to observe that porn is always the first industry to exploit new technological developments, several of the major gay porn producers were, in fact, quite reticent to invest in DVD and consequently came to the technology relatively late. For example, Falcon Studios were especially cautious about the commercial viability of DVD and did not issue a release (a collector's edition of *The Other*

*Side of Aspen*) until as late as 2001.[16] In many regards this period of production was a continuation of the late VHS phase and one that was dominated by the new studios, Titan, Raging Stallion and Hot House. The
higher resolution of DVD images inevitably demanded higher production values and fed a market demand for 'quality' product. The response
to this was variable, with some studios creating longer and more elaborate productions drawing on a cinematic filmic style and aesthetic. Titan
in particular became market leaders, making full use of the opportunities opened up by DVD for expanded content, and the enhanced picture quality that encouraged more elaborate production designs. A case
study here is Episode 4 of the popular *Fallen Angel* series of leather and
S/M themed films, *Seamen* (dir. Bruce Cam, 2001). Apparently inspired
by Fassbinder's final film, the homoerotic *Querelle* (1981), *Seamen* is
overtly cinematic in terms of its aesthetics and elaborately stylised in
its treatment of a loose narrative set around the docks of San Francisco
bay and their macho, and apparently sex crazed, denizens. The film was
promoted via a marketing strategy that drew on the hyperbolic rhetoric
of Hollywood with a teaser trailer and a promotional cover image that
in tone and style was rather more suggestive of an action film than a
gay porn release. The DVD for *Seamen* was sold in a variety of formats
including multidisc box sets, described as 'collector's editions' and was
to win five GayVN awards including Best All-Sex Video, Best Gay DVD,
Best Sex Scene and Best Gay DVD Extras.

Whereas the industry adoption of DVD had been slow, this was not at
all the case with the development of platforms for the access to markets
offered by the newest technology of the internet. As early as the late 1990s,
most studios had at least a basic website providing product details and the
ability to join mailing lists, and by 2001 Titan, alongside many of its competitors, was also selling online membership access to its entire catalogue,
which enabled customers to stream video. So *Seamen* was simultaneously
released via DVD and online was consequently a major commercial success as a direct result of this multi-platform sales strategy. According to
Keith Webb, Vice-President of Titan (2004), it was the first Titan release to
exceed $1 million in worldwide sales.[17] The adoption of this new technol-
ogy and the gradual move to pay-per-view and pay-per-scene access leads
us to the contemporary gay porn industry.

## The Web

The final phase in the development of the gay porn industry is the era of the internet, which is the primary (if not the sole) focus of this book. The immense and exponential expansion of the industry that has been facilitated by the internet has created conditions in which choice seems limitless and ease of access to material has bypassed most legislation and regulations at a local level and altered commercial models almost beyond recognition. The internet has enabled communities of interest to emerge – a vigorous culture of interaction and discussion via blogging, discussion groups and websites that collectively constitute a dynamic network of paratexts that surround the creation, promotion and circulation of contemporary porn.

This new context has presented radical challenges for the established studios of the 1980s and 1990s, and by the early years of the 2000s it appeared that many of the major players were in terminal decline. This situation was, in part, a result of a commercial failure to respond to the new market conditions, in part to do with online piracy and falling profits and in part to do with a new generation of online studios whose form, style and content were more clearly tailored to contemporary market demands.[18] In the contemporary context, what this means is that the old studios have been supplanted by a group of producers who constitute a new 'mainstream'. Men.com, Cockyboys, Corbin Fisher and Sean Cody have all become dominant players in this new industry through the development of clear brand identities and product that is made expressly with the intention of being accessed via streaming technologies. What has resulted in these conditions is that the concept of authorship that was so important during the early 1970s, and a studio style that was so important during the 1980s and 1990s have collapsed in on each other in a new context in which each producer has a more or less distinctive imprimatur. Furthermore, the two-hour blockbuster porn extravaganzas that Titan and Raging Stallion specialised in during the late 1990s and early 2000s have been replaced with a return to emphasis on the sale of individual vignettes of approximately 15 to 30 minutes in duration, which in terms of tone, style, setting and models are clearly signposted as Sean Cody or Corbin Fisher productions.

During this period there has also been a concomitant challenge to the hegemony of overtly 'commercial' representations and 'mainstream' practices. Probably the most radical response to the supposedly bland, 'vanilla' homogeneity of 'mainstream' porn has been the emergence of 'bareback porn', most notably with the establishment of Paul Morris' Treasure Island Media as the trendsetter in this nascent 'genre' that has subsequently, and paradoxically, bled into mainstream representation in recent years. The injunction to represent safer sex through mandatory condom use, which had become standard industry practice by the late 1980s, has slowly but surely given way to the marketing of bareback scenes, often now produced by mainstream outlets as an 'extreme' or 'raw' addition to the sexual repertoires of their performers, usually as a result of supposed popular demand and not without controversy.[19] A host of other small producers has been set up as the trend for niche, specialist and kink content has continued during the course of the 2000s, as well as the rise of 'amateur' porn in all of its manifestations; subjects that will be returned to in later chapters.

# The Demotic Idiom of Gay Porn Representation

What then are the results of what amounts to a century or more of cultural development and change, beginning with isolated and artisanal activity and resulting in the contemporary moment in porn production on an industrial scale and scope?

In the first instance we can see that technological developments have informed both the content and format of gay pornography. In terms of format we can observe the changes over the various epochs I have described in this chapter: a prehistory of still images that begins to provide an image bank of iconography and themes, a transition into moving images, starting with short softcore films, and moving into hardcore vignettes, a shift to a hardcore feature-length cinema, a transition to a new technology (VHS) and the establishment of a corporate studio system and a format of four to five scenes linked through narrative, to a more baroque cinematic style in the late 1990s with the arrival of DVD, to the emergence, and dominance, of the internet and a return to vignettes and short form films, once more, accessible online. The connections between technology, form and content are far from teleological, as a range of social and cultural factors have to be taken into consideration. What matters in the first instance, though, is to emphasise that these industrial developments have been evolutionary, and importantly that they provide evidence, over time, of a cyclical, rather than linear, development to the ways in which porn is produced, distributed and consumed.

Secondly, over time, and largely as a result of the technical and commercial changes that I have described in this chapter, a set of narrative and formal conventions and a lexicon of settings and types have emerged. These conventions, settings and types are, out of necessity, generic and repetitive. I am not alone in making this observation of course. One of the principle criticisms of pornography, gay or otherwise, is that it is relentlessly, monotonously, formulaic. Susanne Kappeler, for example, describes the 'eternal sameness' of porn (1986:130). Susanna Paasonen also notes that porn is 'largely repetitive and rel[ies] on conventionalised formulas' (2011:159), though she argues (as do I) that this repetition is, in fact, central to the working of porn and connected notions of plenitude and excess.[20] Furthermore, Paasonen argues that this is especially true in a consideration of web-based porn:

> The sense of abundance and indeed of excess has grown ever more acute due to the accumulation of images, videos, stories, links and sites [...] Online pornotopia is abundant and impossible for any single user to map completely. The feel of endless alternatives and opportunities plays no minor role in the attraction of online platforms where something new, exciting, extreme and titillating is proposed to be always just a click away.
>
> (pp. 160–1)

The result then is a plethora of representations, but ones that, I would argue, can still be organised into broad categories. Importantly then, what has emerged over time is what I would describe as three aesthetic/discursive modalities that all porn (in this case gay porn) can be described as using: firstly, and most recognisably, a *narrative mode* where a storyline motivates sexual play and what Linda Williams describes as sexual 'numbers'; secondly, a *thematic mode* in which a specific type of setting or sexual practice rationalises a sexual encounter and/or creates a link across a series of sex scenes; and thirdly, and most broadly of all, the *reality mode* that encompasses the notion of the amateur that I will discuss in the final chapter, but also an array of materials where a realist aesthetic or quasi-documentary strategies are deployed.

The contemporary social and cultural context discussed in the previous chapter, alongside the technological and cultural/historical contexts discussed in this chapter, results in a gay porn that marshals a spectrum of masculinities and discourses of masculinity across a wide range of materials, and which the second part of this book will deal with in more detail. It also produces a set of thematics and narrative concerns, an iconography and a constellation of types, a performative vocabulary and a repertoire of acts. In short, gay porn has a vernacular style of representation, scenario, performance and iconography that can be described as a *demotic idiom*. This is largely perpetuated through what is repeatedly alluded to in this chapter as the 'mainstream' of gay porn, but what exactly is this 'mainstream'?

## The Problem of the Mainstream

Given the regularity with which the term is used in both scholarly and popular writing on porn and will be used in this book, it is necessary, at this point, to note that the expression 'mainstream' is a vexed and potentially contradictory term within the context of this study. The mainstream and its various corollaries, including the mass market and the yet more emphatically class-inflected 'middlebrow', are all terms that have previously attracted the attention of scholarship. Especially within the context of an analysis of gay porn, as I have noted elsewhere, the very expression 'mainstream' seems something of a contradiction in terms (Mercer, 2013). As Susanna Paasonen notes, the idea of the mainstream in porn and the aligned term 'porn industry' that I use here is a 'totalizing notion where nuances and differences tend to disappear from view' (2014: 31), and that, in fact, this 'mainstream' porn industry (notwithstanding the attempts to professionalise it) remains ostensibly 'a loosely knit meshwork of agents, images, concepts, interests and commodities categorised under the title' (ibid.). Nonetheless, for the purposes of clarity, I have drawn together a corpus of materials that I have designated as 'mainstream' gay porn on the basis that they constitute a set of texts made by producers who are prominent in media reportage, blogs and discussion fora.[21] As noted in the first chapter, I have also chosen to focus my analysis on the work of studios that have attracted industry recognition through being nominated (or winning) accolades such as the GayVNs or the Cybersocket Awards. I am inevitably conscious that this is a rather arbitrary designation and that I am inevitably making my own subjective judgement as to what the term mainstreat mainstreat means and how to evaluate a mainstream of gay porn. In many ways what the mainstream 'means' in the contexts in which it is used, rather than some attempt at an objective definition, is what is at stake here, and that is the idea of a generic, commercialised mass-market product, designed to appeal to the widest audience. In industry parlance, for example, 'mainstream' tends to refer to a product that is stylistically conventional and ostensibly 'vanilla' in tone and content. In short, the 'mainstream' is the contemporary version of the slick, professionalised, standardised product that was supposedly epitomised by the output of Falcon in the 1980s and perhaps has a parallel in the kind of material that *Playboy* or *Private* are associated with in terms of the straight porn market. This is of course a stereotype but one that is routinely used in popular discussions, media commentary and debate on gay porn and provides a mechanism for demarcating a group of texts, producers and modes of representation that are recognised as representing a set of dominant/prominent sexual and cultural mores. Furthermore, in the industrial context of a fragmented, highly differentiated, and bifurcated, online market (as has been the case in the period from 2004–2005 onwards), it becomes extremely difficult to determine what anything that constitutes the mainstream might look like. In part, this is because the marketing strategies and business models of the gay porn industry have, out of necessity, radically changed with the collapse in market share and the cultural as well as financial monopolies exerted by the major studios of the 1980s and 1990s. This meant that for a period in the mid to late 2000s the very term 'mainstream', though still widely used, had become something of a non sequitur. Ease of access, streaming and the unfettered rise of piracy, as well as the increased specialisation and bifurcation of the market, meant that seemingly every interest was catered for and perhaps nothing (or everything) could be described as 'mainstream'. Indeed, as the mass market model that the mainstream presupposes had also disappeared from view,

the term had begun to lose purchase and could only be used in a pejorative sense to refer to the anodyne, the vanilla, the 'safe'. However, in recent
years there has been something of a retrenchment with the major studios
of the 1980s and 1990s undergoing a process of conglomeration. So, in
2010 Falcon Studios was acquired by the video-on-demand giant AEBN
who then merged Falcon with Raging Stallion, and then, in 2014, with
Hot House.[22] With the further acquisition of the website Nakedsword,
AEBN is now both a major producer *and* distributor of online gay porn.[23]
Mergers and concentration of ownership are not, however, confined
to older studios struggling to maintain market share in the digital age.
Men.com and Sean Cody have both been acquired by the porn conglom-
erate Mindgeek (Manwin), whose portfolio includes a long list of straight
websites as well as the Pornhub Network of tube sites.[24] This means, in
effect, that a new mainstream has come back into view, where 'mainstream' production is controlled by a relatively small number of very large
entities and, in a rather bizarre set of circumstances, not only production,
sale and distribution but also piracy and illegal sharing are all concentrated in the same hands.[25]

## Notes on Convention: Narrative, Typage and Performance

Gay porn produces narratives that situate a range of masculine types who
perform sexually for a viewer's consumption, and at this point mention
needs to be made of the rhetorical and narrative conventions that structure the representations of masculinities discussed in the second part of
this book. In *Coming to Terms: Gay Pornography*, Richard Dyer discusses
the narrative constructions of pornographic film and video. Challenging
the commonplace assumption that it is marked by an absence of narrative,
Dyer asserts that narrative is, in fact, a central feature and component of all
forms of pornography:

> Even the simplest pornographic loops have narrative. In those
> quarter-in-the-slot machines where you get a bit of a porn loop
> for your quarter, you are very conscious of what point (roughly)
> you have come to in the loop, you are conscious of where the
> narrative has got to. Even if all that is involved is a fuck between

two men, there are the following establishing elements: the arrival on the scene of the fuck, establishing contact (through greeting and recognition, or through a quickly established eye-contact agreement to fuck), undressing, exploring various parts of the body, coming, parting. The exploration of the body often involves exploring those areas less heavily codified in terms of sexuality, before 'really getting down to/on with' those that are (genitals and anus). Few short porn films don't involve most or all of these narrative elements and in that order.

(1990:125)

In the contemporary, commercial, mainstream gay porn discussed in this book, the formal characteristics and narrative conventions of the texts have, as I have already noted, become extremely conventionalised. This, of course, is not a new development but an evolution of a set of norms and practices that have emerged over time. In *Hard Core*, Linda Williams refers to Stephen Ziplow's unintentionally hilarious *Film Maker's Guide to Pornography*, a manual for would-be pornographers that itemises the generic conventions of pornographic film. According to Williams, 'Ziplow himself offers no description of narrative in the genre, but he is clear that it should exist; specifically, it should occupy approximately 40 per cent of the screen time and should serve as a vehicle to the sexual numbers represented in the remaining 60 per cent' (1989:131). Unlike Dyer, who is (importantly) discussing the *sexual* narrative of a filmed encounter and argues that the representation of sexual activity in gay porn always follows a fairly linear narrative progression, Williams here is referring, instead, to the narrative sequences that *link* the sexual numbers: the 'webbing' that I have already discussed. Though I can offer no quantitative analysis or evidence to back up the suggestion that 40 per cent of the average multi-scene film is taken up with narrative (my guess would be that this figure is rather high) and given that much gay porn is now viewed on a scene-by-scene basis, which has radically reduced the percentage of set-up that precedes any sex scene, the principle that underlies this percentage, based on the notion that storyline is subservient and serves to link sexual number, is overwhelmingly borne out.

Just as the relationship between what Williams describes as 'number and narrative' is a constant in commercial gay porn, so the presentation and staging of sexual numbers adheres to a fairly universally applied structural formula: the sexual narrative that Dyer describes in his article. This sexual narrative generally follows what Robert Kirsch of Titan identified as 'the jerk-suck-rim-fuck-cum category'.[26] This means that the choreography of sexual numbers usually commences with solo or mutual masturbation, leading on to oral sex, rimming (oral/anal contact), anal sex and finally masturbation to climax. The culmination of any sexual number, even those that do not follow this fairly prescriptive formula, is the so-called 'money-shot' – that is, the depiction of the externally ejaculating penis, which seemingly attests to the 'authenticity' of the sexual activities that have been depicted. Linda Williams, who argues, by reference to Foucault, that heterosexual pornography strives to 'speak the truth' of sexuality and its secrets, sees the money-shot as 'the very limit of the visual representation of sexual pleasure' (1989:101), for, in order to provide evidence of sexual climax, the male performer must remove himself from interaction with another (in this case female) performer and stage his ejaculation for the benefit of the (presumably male) viewer. I instead see Williams' argument as just one of the discursive modalities that gay porn can summon up. Just as I will demonstrate in later chapters that there are examples of gay porn that aims to speak some 'truth' of sex (though perhaps rather different truths to the rather more elevated ones that Williams had in mind), there are equally many instances where gay porn presents gay sexuality as spectacle, as fabulous, idealised and perfected, and the money-shot in gay porn, extended through editing techniques and slow motion photography, is not designed to document the reality of sexual exchange but instead constructs a hyperbolic fantasy world in which perfected men engage in perfected sexual exchanges and inevitably achieve the spectacular, perfected climax.

Gay pornography deals in types, as I have already established, and the types that populate this gay pornotopia can be categorised according to a variety of criteria. For the purpose of this book and conscious of the sheer range and volume of material that needs to be organised, I have chosen to focus on a clearly demarcated set of social categories and recurrent thematics to map out the terrain: generation, ethnicity, class, heterosexuality and hypermasculinity, celebrity and the amateur, all become discursive categories that act as axes around which models of masculinity are constructed and circulate, and this study has been organised accordingly. This is a subject, however, that I have written about on several previous occasions, especially in relation to the ways in which typologies were constructed during the VHS period:

> With the absence of gender difference as a discourse to organise and categorise behaviour, performance and role in gay pornography, a plethora of codified types emerge. During the 1980s and the Falcon era, the pre-eminent form of categorisation concerns itself with sexual performance and sexual role: performers who are assigned the 'active' *Top* role in sexual encounters and those who are categorised as 'passive' *Bottoms*. This form of organisation and assignation of roles is based on predetermined assumptions about the nature of gay sexual practice and normative conduct, assumptions that are based largely on the agendas and perspectives of the producers of gay pornography.
>
> (2006:152)

In the contemporary context it's clear to see that the rather static binary model that has been discussed previously, based on a relationship between physical type and sexual role/performance, is no longer tenable. Indeed, even as I was making these observations in 2006, the active/passive dichotomy was on the wane.[27] Consequently, the organisation of types that constitutes the chapter structure of the second part of this book illustrates some, though by no means all, of the types that gay porn produces and deploys. I have focused on what I see as the major types/themes in this book but am mindful that it is in the nature of porn to promiscuously draw upon (and produce) novelty, so, no doubt, new models of masculinity will emerge over time and join the repertory of types I describe here.

Finally we should note that performers are chosen because of their physicality and the representative characteristics that they might possess, but also because of their facility to enact sex. These performances of sex, as I have already suggested, have also become codified and the meanings and mechanisms of porn performance are the final element that I would like to consider before moving on to discussing the panoply of masculinities in gay porn.

# Performance

The generic, repetitious nature of porn as a mode of expression, as already noted, seems to lend itself almost uniquely to parody and stereotyping. The seeming fixity of generic conventions and the recognisability of the tropes, scenarios and set-ups deployed mean that it can be all too tempting to make totalising generalisations about the homogeneity of porn: always the same and always *doing* the same thing. Amongst the many stereotypes that circulate round porn, perhaps one of the most pervasive (and probably one that seems the least controversial) is the orthodoxy that porn performers are bad actors; indeed that porn acting is the epitome of bad acting. Of course this is in no small part given traction by the fact that there are many examples readily available online that act as evidence.

For example, the Falcon video *Splash Shots: Memories of Summer* (Bill Clayton, 1984) provides what amounts to a paradigmatic case study of what is regarded as the dramatic standard that we might expect from porn acting. The title sequence of the video, replete with recherché video graphics, editing techniques and an audio track that draws comic attention to a modest budget and fairly primitive production values by contemporary standards, is interspersed with talking head inserts of the key protagonists from each of the scenes in the video. This sequence is as likely to provoke laughter rather than anticipation (as it no doubt also did in 1984). The dramatic skills of the performers are of a very particular and limited variety, ranging from clunky innuendo in the case of the star Kurt Marshall's high-camp delivery of the line 'But gee, coach, I'm doing the best I can. I'm only trying to please you,' complete with a knowing glance at the camera/audience, to the somnambulant monotone of Tom Mitchell's performance as the aforementioned 'coach', to Giorgio Canali's heavily accented and almost indecipherable delivery of the line 'You work in the pool area, I work around cleaning the house.'[28] Examples of this sort are so commonplace and have become so much a part of an ironising popular sense of what porn, and especially the 'retro' porn of the 1970s, 1980s and 1990s, is like, that this perspective tends to frame all discussion of the 'performative' in porn to a greater or lesser degree. My contention though is that this facile generalisation, however affectionate or humorous in intent, tends to both dismiss any possibility of a more reflective or meaningful critical engagement with porn and also to demean the labor of porn performers. Additionally, it fundamentally misinterprets the 'work' that is taking place when porn performers enact sex on screen. The performances that porn professionals deliver are far from accidental or impromptu. On the contrary, they are blocked, framed, lit, directed, edited; in short, as controlled and constructed as any other filmed performance. Furthermore, I would extend this point to emphasise that, even in non-commercial (i.e. 'real' or 'amateur' porn) settings, the minute a recording device is used in the documentation of a sexual encounter (providing that the participants know that they are being recorded of course), the possibility of an audience transforms a sexual act into a performance. Sex that is being staged for an audience/viewer, through whatever system of distribution and exchange then, but especially in a commercial arena, draws on a repertoire of gestures and postures, camera angles, edits, movements that constitute a language of display. Clarissa Smith is one of the very few scholars who has made any attempt to take the performative in sexuality explicit representations seriously, in her essay 'Reel Intercourse: Doing Sex on Camera'.[29] Smith notes that a consideration of performance is a conspicuous blind spot in the field, observing that this is a topic that too many scholars have either failed to recognise or have chosen to ignore, arguing that it has become an orthodoxy when writing about sex filmed on screen to:

> sideline the specificity of many of the films [...] in favour of an approach which examines how that record is made. Sex becomes an inert property of the filmic process rather than an interaction between actors.
>
> (2012:197)

Smith notes, importantly, that this marginalisation of the centrality of performance is often most marked in considerations of porn and the work that porn performers (Smith describes them as 'actors') are doing. In part, she observes this is because the discourses of porn in fact elide between the 'real' and the 'performed' almost seamlessly (p. 198). In addition, Smith argues that an emphasis on 'the centrality of the body' (p. 199) paradoxically means that how bodies move has tended to slip from view. As she astutely notes, assumptions are made about the overt content of porn, what it is intended for and how it will be received, and this results in a critical discourse that 'occlude[es] any understanding of expressivity' (ibid.). In her essay Smith then goes on to provide detailed microanalyses of scenes performed by several female performers to indicate the variety in style and tone that such an approach can uncover and the methods needed to undertake this work. I agree with Smith and have been mindful in this study of the need to consider performance in my analysis of the iconography and discourses of saturated masculinity that are the focus of the second part of this book.

This presents a set of analytical challenges, as there is a need for an appropriate lexicon and vocabulary as well as a framework to analyse sex performances. Just as a set of narrative and rhetorical conventions has emerged over time, so a repertoire of performance styles has been adopted that can be seen in use across mainstream commercial representations. Consequently, there is a lexicon of positions, gestures and movement, in effect a 'choreography' of porn performance. What is lacking for the purposes of scholarship, though, is a vocabulary to describe this. It is therefore necessary to draw on an alternative vocabulary drawn from the study of dance, gymnastics and perhaps (as Smith suggests) wrestling, to analyse and describe what porn performers are doing in sex scenes. Approaches to the analysis of dance are especially useful as they focus on a repertoire of gestures, physicality and movement, the expressive and aesthetic qualities of a performance, the interaction with a partner (or partners) and technical aspects including posture, movement and anatomical detail. It's perhaps not an unimportant detail that many performers working in the gay porn industry owe their physiques to athletics or gymnastics training and many also come from a background in dance or supplement their incomes through erotic dancing. Consequently, I would argue that far from being mute puppets required to senselessly fuck while the camera rolls, many performers are clearly aware of their bodies and their physical and athletic abilities, how to respond to direction and how to present a performance.[30]

In addition to the specific set of physical demands that sex on camera makes on a performer, there is an additional set of skills that falls under the umbrella term of what we might describe as 'dramatic' register. This encompasses the performance of arousal, pleasure, passion, excitement (sometimes trepidation, fear or pain) and finally, usually, sexual satisfaction.

I am conscious that this could all too easily descend into comical worthiness, so it's important to recognise what is at stake here. In essence porn performance is a specialised field demanding a specific set of skills. This is performance that is highly choreographed in all but a minority of cases and therefore a type of performance work that requires a high degree of technique, over and above the basic and essential physical requirements of maintaining an erection for long periods, being able to engage in lengthy bouts of anal or oral sex and being able to ejaculate on camera at a given point. This means that it's a performance style that requires some degree of training or at least preparation, varying degrees of athletic ability and a propensity for exhibitionism. Anyone who has seen the scene in Titan's *Cirque Noir* (dir. Brian Mills, 2005) in which the gymnast Cobalt suspends himself upside down from two lengths of silk whilst felating Spencer Quest can be in little doubt that porn performers are doing more than just having sex on camera.

It's also important to acknowledge that the choreography of gay porn performance has evolved over time and has become a central element of the demotic idiom that I have identified. So, for example, one can compare the often frenetic movements and rapidity of the transition between various sex acts and positions that we can see in examples of early porn cinema and the so-called stag films, to differences in the work of figures like Fred Halsted or Wakefield Poole during the period of the cinematic hardcore where naturalised and romanticised sex, presented through montage editing of body parts, creates an expressive and impressionistic 'idea' of sex. In these films, hardcore close-up representations of anal sex for example, including shots of initial penetration, are not routine. By contrast, if we compare these representations to those of the industrialised, VHS/DVD phase, we can see that external ejaculation – the *sine qua non* of porn, gay and straight insertion scenes, close-up shots of penetration and a set of performative conventions – represented via rhetorical conventions that constitute this demotic idiom – have emerged.

In addition, the specifics of particular genres of gay porn make particular demands on performers, ranging from what might be described as 'acting' in the dramatic sense to a transition into porn performance that will often have a specific style and tone depending on genre, studio, director or theme. As conventions and modes of porn have evolved therefore, so performance style has to be modulated to reflect those differences: the demands of gonzo-style porn, for example, which often revolves around point-of-view filming and therefore frontal staging involves different performative strategies to the oblique staging that is more typical of narrative porn, as a few brief examples will illustrate.

In much mainstream gay porn, performers need to demonstrate some rudimentary acting skills in order to perform the set-ups that establish and provide some narrative motivation for the sex play that follows. This can range from the most basic set-up – meeting in a bar or on the street, entering a domestic environment and then commencing sex – or in some cases can be altogether more elaborate. For example, Men.com – whose output ranges from scenes using the most rudimentary set-ups already described in this chapter to higher-budget series of episodic scenes drawing on a cinematic rhetoric – has produced a lavish porn 'version' of *Game of Thrones* entitled, rather predictably, *Gay of Thrones*, cast with their most recognisable star performers. This series requires performers to have some dramatic ability as the introductory set-ups are usually at least several minutes long, are elaborately staged and involve lengthy sections of dialogue. In episode 6, Johnny Rapid plays a king who on his 'name-day' is visited by two servants (Darius Ferdynand and Gabriel Cross) sent by the king's uncle, who are charged with ensuring that he 'becomes a man'.[31] The set-up involves tracking shots, multiple edits and a long exchange of dialogue among the three characters in order to build up a sense of the arrogance of Rapid's character in contrast to the rather enigmatic compliance of the two servants. All three have to deliver lines written in a faux antique style, in keeping with the quasi-medieval fantasy setting and theme, and they do so with some degree of conviction. The 'acting' continues into the early part of the sex scene as the king demands that the two servants undress and fondle each other while he watches. This transitions, after about three to five minutes into the scene, into a more conventional sex performance, commencing with oral sex, analingus and then anal sex. When the sex scene has become fully established, acting is replaced altogether with sex performance and this results in a rather awkward transition. The performers move from sword-and-sorcery-style 'acting' to a decidedly (if incongruous) contemporary performative register for the sex scenes: grunts of pleasure, spitting on an exposed anus, groans of satisfaction and encouragement that are accompanied by emphatically Americanised (and accented) vocalisations, 'oh yeah', 'fuck yeah'. Whilst, as already noted in this chapter, sex performance is temporarily bounded, the unnamed director of *Gay of Thrones* has not opted for a 'period' sex performance in keeping with the fantasy subject matter, but has required performers to shift between modalities and registers.

Kristen Bjorn is a studio that will be discussed in some detail in Chapter 5. Specialising in models from Central and Latin America as well as Europe, the studio is also renowned for a distinctive, rigidly choreographed and stylised mode of representation, and this extends itself to the performance style of his cast. Models are usually carefully framed and placed in positions that are intended to produce aesthetic compositional structures and to draw attention to the sculpted physical perfection of their bodies. Sex performance in Kristen Bjorn's films is never less than perfected in its visual realisation. So, in Scene 4 of the *Bare to the Bone* series, Letterio Amadeo and Toffic encounter Raul Korso on the streets of Madrid and invite him back to their apartment for sex in a standard enough set-up.[32] However, the three-way that ensues as soon as they are ensconced in the domestic setting is choreographed with painstaking attention to detail and framed, for the most part, by a doorway in the background, with the use of oblique staging affording the scene a still more theatrical air. All three of the performers are tattooed and athletically muscular and adopt postures throughout the scene that draw attention to their taut bodies, broad shoulders and narrow hips. In scenes of oral and anal sex, for example, it is customary for the performer who is fucking or receiving oral sex to place the 'spare' arm and hand that might otherwise obscure the view of the action behind his back and the models do this either by placing a hand on their own buttock or hip or by creating a fist which they hold behind their buttock. This level of stylisation (sometimes criticised for being too staged and artificial) requires a controlled and rather detached performance style that is typical of Bjorn's output and this has become a marker of his studio style.

The website Menpov.com, as the title suggests, makes gonzo-styled point-of-view porn that requires an altogether different style of performance. The extensive use of close-ups and high-angle, point-of-view staging produces the need for an intimate style where micro-performative details become highly significant. The rhetoric of this type of porn, with its extreme close-ups and frontal staging (achieved via head sets and high-definition cameras) in 'real' domestic settings, is designed to create a heightened level of intimacy suggestive of an almost direct, physical interaction with the sexual play that is staged in the sequences. A sequence entitled *Running Hard* is an interesting example.[33] The scene opens with Huxley Houston and Lane Harris meeting on the street whilst Houston is jogging. The rhetoric of this set-up is rather confusing as it veers between the point of view of an apparently unseen viewer (voyeur), conventional continuity editing and an exchange of glances between the two performers. Once they have returned to the apartment setting for the sex scene, the point of view is more clearly established, even though it alternates between the two performers. Houston's desiring gaze at Harris (and therefore the viewer) as he is pushed into a chair and has his shorts removed, draws the viewer into the action and his soft, seemingly involuntary sighs and pants, along with this exchange of looks, produces a sense of proximity that is entirely unlike that either the performance style, or the effects that a Kristen Bjorn film might produce or, for the most part, the mixture of 'acting' and mainstream sex performance that we can see in the *Gay of Thrones* scene. This instead is a micro-performative style that aims for an approximation (indeed it summons up the chimera) of 'the real' that we will return to in the final chapter.

It is in the context, then, of an emergent field of porn studies, a dynamic popular cultural context in which masculinity is in flux and constant revision, and an industrial context in which a demotic idiom of gay pornography has emerged, that we can situate the masculinities that are the subject of the second part of this book, which focuses on the panoply of representations of sexualised and 'saturated' masculinity.

# PART II
# Models, Patterns and Themes

# 3

# Generation: The Boy-Next-Door, the Twink and the Daddy

*Basically, if you are under 30 or over 45, but not quite 55, you're the right age for the job [...](I know an early 30-something performer whose small stature and youthful demeanor have allowed him to carry off being in his 'early twenties' for his entire career, and thus far no one has done the math.) Porn is not strictly for the young.*

Benjamin Scuglia, *Sex Pigs: Why Porn Is Like Sausage* (2004:188)

In a short piece on the experience of working in the gay porn industry, the journalist and blogger Benjamin Scuglia, who writes about the porn industry under the *nom de plume* J. C. Adams, is keen to foreground the work-a-day realities of porn professionals and to reveal that working in porn, like any other industry, is, in fact, rather mundane.[1] Amongst pragmatic considerations that Scuglia lists, he notes that age matters, profoundly, in the world of the porn industry and is therefore inevitably one of the primary considerations in an analysis of the iconography of gay porn. This chapter then looks at the ways in which age is eroticised in mainstream gay pornography, how age is foregrounded through narrative, setting and performance and what this can tell us about how generational masculinities are eroticised. In order to do this, I will look at both 'ends' of the generational spectrum, but primarily, in this chapter, I will focus on youth and then latterly on representations of intergenerational sexual encounters through a discussion of the figure of the 'daddy'. My field of view, therefore, is those instances where age, primarily youth, is hyperbolically summoned up as the focus of erotic attention and investment, and the next chapter will engage with the dynamics and deployment of mature masculinities in more detail.

In the first part of this book, I suggested that the themes that have dictated the chapter structure of this second part of the book (age, heterosexuality, ethnicity and so on) are based loosely around the categories that commercial websites and aggregators tend to favour. They should not, however, be understood as a mechanism for the discreet categorisation of types. I am not suggesting here that representations of either youthful or mature masculinities can be considered outside of any further engagement with the themes explored in subsequent chapters – for example, sexual orientation (such as the figure of the gay-for-pay performer) and celebrity are both discourses that explicitly connect to generation. On the contrary, the themes I have identified that map on to the use of specific physical types, scenarios and styles of performance, constantly overlap, and nowhere more so than when generation is concerned. As noted in the previous chapters, these themes should, instead, be seen as organising axes that enable discussion of a vast array and variety of representations. This model allows for, and is designed to accommodate, the mutable nature of the ways masculinity is exploited in gay porn and new iterations and articulations of masculinities regularly emerge; this is not merely a taxonomic 'listing' of types. As Susanna Paasonen notes, there is a need to do more than simply describe porn's iconography:

> Analyses of pornography's lexicon or iconography should not be limited to literal cataloguing [...] since the circulation of standard types and stock characters is the stuff that porn is made of.
>
> (2011:159)

Instead she argues that a discussion of the repetition and conventionality of porn needs to be connected back to an understanding of the genre as a modality; that the use of stereotypes and clichés are in fact central to the working mechanisms of porn. I would argue that in the specific case of contemporary gay porn, the repetition of this legion of masculine types provides evidence of the saturated masculinity discussed in Chapter 2.

# Gilded Youth

Whilst the intention of this book is to indicate that the range of representations and the manifestations of masculinities that gay porn offers are far more various than commonsensical accounts might suggest, if there is any over-riding constant at all, it is the prioritisation of youth, and consequently youth is the discourse that we will consider first and that will occupy the majority of the discussion here. An anglicised version of the French *jeunesse dorée*, also known as Muscadins for their fondness for dandyish dress and musk perfume, the term 'gilded youth' refers to gangs of fashionably dressed young men who roamed the streets of France as fighters in the bloody aftermath of the French Revolution.[2] The term has come to symbolise the paradoxical desire and threat that the beauty of youth can represent and is therefore especially apposite as a way into thinking about how male youth is presented as an erotic spectacle in gay porn.

Of all of the versions and visions of masculinity that I discuss in this book, which have been chosen because they are freighted with homoerotic significance for one reason or another, no category is truly more saturated with meaning than youthfulness. It is so overburdened, so prized, so laden with value and seemingly so various and generative that this book could easily be devoted to gay porn's cult of youth alone. This, of course, maps onto wider cultural preoccupations that reflect a contradictory mixture of desires and anxieties concerning youth as a period of exploration and potential, transition and upheaval, carrying with it the threat of dissolution and criminality (Gabriel, 2013; Best, 2007; Roche, Tucker, Thompson, Flynn, 2004, Campbell, 2004, Muncie, 2004).

This presents quite particular challenges for this study, which aims to map the masculinities of gay porn, as the category of youth contains, seemingly, legions of youthful types, all with their own particular iconography. These draw, variously, on archetypical masculine ideals dating back to antiquity (the athlete, the student, the object of beauty) as well as a vernacular that repurposes contemporary stereotypes and is firmly grounded in a popular culture that is constantly generating new 'versions' of youthful masculinity that can be put to use within the pornosphere: so the poolboy, the surfer and the beach boy of 1980s gay porn have been joined by the skater dude and the emo. Perennial figures such as the schoolboy, the college kid on spring break, the trainee athlete, the raw recruit and the houseboy have been joined by the circuit party boy, the go-go dancer, the intern and the geek. William Higgins' *Pizza Boy* (1986) (who, we were told in the 1980s, 'delivers') is joined, in the 21st century, by a panoply of young men using dating apps and hook-up sites to arrange sex from home with or without the need of the pretext of fast-food delivery.

In addition, we need to note that youth is also an elastic category and it is this very plasticity and adaptability to a range of sexualised settings that, in part at least, accounts for its ubiquity. There is a need then for at least a putative definition of youth as a starting point, and in this chapter I am referring to what is generally understood, as Ben Scuglia observes in his essay mentioned at the start of this chapter, as what might described as the *gay porn industrial standard*. This refers to performers between the age of 18 and 24, 'under 25s' being the commonly used industry term, as well as to contexts where 'youth' is very explicitly and hyperbolically foregrounded in the physical appearance of performers and the settings in which they are situated; the elements that collectively construct the discourses of youth (the narrative and rhetorical apparatus that situates and contextualises youth) and provide the conditions in which performances of 'youth' are eroticised, overdetermined and exaggerated (Paasonen, 2011:160).

It's also important to note here that there are probably three conspicuous contributions that the major studios of the 1980s and 1990s – such as Falcon, Catalina and His Video – made to what I have described as the demotic idiom of gay pornography. First, as noted in the previous chapter and elsewhere, the output of studios like Falcon resulted in the eventual establishment of the orthodoxy of the active/passive binarism in the representation and performances of gay sex that was both extremely pervasive and highly prescriptive (Mercer, 2012). In short, performers were identified as either *active* tops or *passive* bottoms and these were categories that were essentially fixed and unchanging. Second, the orthodoxy of this binarism was inscribed onto the physicality and iconography of the performers; so, petite, ephebic bottoms paired with muscular, athletically built tops.

Third, this process of inscription resulted, finally, in the identification and idealisation of a specific (and relatively new) type of gay masculinity: the 'twink'.[3]

## The Problem with Twinks

The slang term 'twink' has become so over-used and carries such a range of connotations, many of them largely pejorative – referring to so many disparate articulations of a type of gay masculinity ranging from teenage 'jail bait' to young, effeminate 'scene queens' – that its utility as a category must inevitably be questioned. Nonetheless, it is a term that has currency for gay porn producers and consumers, and is used with such regularity that it usefully points to further evidence of the ways in which masculinity, even of a very particular sort, has become saturated with meanings.[4]

It's something of a curiosity, given both the pervasiveness of youth across all aspects of gay porn and the popularity (and ubiquity) of twink porn in particular, that so little has been written about the figure of the twink and about twink iconography. I think this is in large part due to the widespread sense that the twink is a type that is already 'known' to readers and therefore beyond (or beneath) critical attention. For example, in Mickey Weems' analysis of gay circuit party culture, a scene that might be regarded as the natural habitat of the twink, we are given little more than a footnote that describes a 'twink' as 'a thin young man' (2008:99). Peter Hennen's study of responses to effeminacy across the gay community discusses the twink as an oppositional figure within bear culture; in effect the opposite of how bears wish to self-identify. Here the twink is 'dismissively known in Bear culture' as 'the feminized, hairless, and gym-toned body of the dominant ideal of gay masculinity' (2008:117). For Hennen, then, the twink, a figure who is seemingly central to the research presented in his book, becomes an absence, summoned up and dismissed with the scarcest of mentions.

In the specific context that I am using, the term *twink* in this book describes both a specific physicality and a performer who is cast in quite particular settings to perform an equally specific repertoire of sexual acts. This is the way gay porn producers usually use the term. The physicality of the twink speaks emphatically of youth, and specifically, more often than not, describes a particularly Caucasian, Anglo-American or European iteration of youth: smooth, hairless, boyish bodies (often devoid of the overdetermined muscular definition that characterises the partners that they are sometimes paired with), fair skin, boyish looks and blond hair are characteristics that recur. The twink is frequently positioned as the younger and less experienced partner in a sexual encounter, almost always (in the films of the 1980s and much of the 1990s at least) performs as a bottom, and is often socially located within the domestic sphere. The specificity of these domestic locations tends to emphasise the passive, receptive and sexually available qualities characteristic of the twink. As Zeb Tortorici (who performs in twink porn) notes, *twink* refers to 'a young, white, and performed masculinity that can be fetishised, consumed, and appropriated by both viewer and performer alike' (2008:207) and also 'the production and performance of a consumable and visually/anally receptive masculinity' (p. 206). Whilst the sexual binarism of tops and bottoms that underscores the role and iconography of the twink is no longer the relentless standard it was during the 1980s and 1990s (indeed, as Tortorici goes on to argue, and, as we will see in this chapter, there is plenty of porn in which twinks assume both the top and bottom sexual role), a vestige of this dichotomy is always in place and partially accounts for the charged nature of many twink-based encounters, especially those that play on the 'taboo' notions of intergenerational sex discussed later on in this chapter, for example, the fantasy of a petite younger man 'serving' or being overpowered by an older and stronger man, as in the Men at Play videos *Papi Rules* (2014) and *Boylust* (2014);[5] in short, power relations eroticised in, and through, sexual play.

Furthermore, the figure of the twink is more various and nuanced than this initial sketch might suggest. Even during the 1980s and 1990s, where the specifics of the twink iconography and performance were formalised, the twink can be seen as a type that draws on ideas of youth as symbolising energy and vitality, innocence and potency, and the glamour (indeed the danger) of transgressive erotic desire. For example, the blond, smooth-bodied and baby-faced Kevin Williams, the archetypical twink for many fans of the porn of the 1980s, was routinely cast as the cute but also the hypersexual and predatory teenager, always on the look-out for sex, as in *Out of Bounds* (dir. Bill Clayton, 1987) and *In Your Wildest Dreams* (dir.

Bill Clayton, 1987). The statuesque and toned Kurt Marshall was cast in scenes that emphasised his startling physical beauty and the aloof hauteur that such perfection suggests, as in *Night Flight* (dir. anon, 1985) and *The Other Side of Aspen 2* (dir. Bill Clayton, 1985). The dark-haired Joey Stefano, prized for his enthusiastic performances, punctuated with expletives, was by contrast positioned as the rebellious bad boy or the spoilt rich brat, as in *Revenge: More than I Can Take* (dir. Steven Scarborough, 1990). Stefano's persona and performances were clearly the inspiration for later figures such as Tristan Paris, who as I have noted elsewhere was identified as a 'power-bottom' to describe his aggressive performance of the so-called 'passive' role in anal sex (Mercer, 2012:219).

Drawing on these various articulations of the twink, and partially inspired by John Muncie's description of the ways in which youth is positioned as 'either gifted, dangerous or innocent' (1988, 2004:10), my analysis in this section identifies three broad models of youthful masculinity that are mobilised across a range of texts with a considerable degree of regularity: first, the figure of the 'sexy kid' or 'boy-next-door'; second, representations of what I collectively describe as 'disruptive' youth; and third, the altogether more rarified and highly idealised model of the beautiful boy.

## The Boy-Next-Door, the 'Sexy Kid' and the Ingénu

Perhaps the most commonly used eroticised versions of youth to be found in gay porn are those that refer to a set of related types: the fantasy boy-next-door, the 'sexy kid' and the slightly more ambiguous figure of the male ingénu who, in some respects, acts as a bridge between the domesticated, sanctioned and 'safe' notions of sexuality that the former two types epitomise and the altogether more risky and disruptive types I will discuss later on.

All of the types that populate the pornosphere are necessarily marked by discourses of class, region and ethnicity and consequently these are subjects that will be returned to repeatedly in the chapters to follow. This specific set of types is usually fairly unambiguously marked out as Caucasian, often suburban, often provincial and middle-class iterations of youthful and overwhelmingly North American masculinity. The market-leading purveyors of contemporary twink porn are notably a group of studios that include Helix, Staxus, Dominic Ford, Boy Crush, Spank This and Raw Lads; however, this is a sizeable and an especially vibrant segment of the overall gay porn market and one in which the notion of the ordinary and the everyday are consistently invoked. For example, sites such as Next Door Male clearly market themselves through a label that draws very explicit attention to the specific appeal of the everyday and the ordinary and the implicit attainability of the boy-next-door. In promotional videos for solo performances on the site, we are told that Ivan James is a 'good ol' country boy from West Virginia who has got the right attitude and a nice package to boot',[6] that (the presumably unrelated) Wes James was 'raised by the beach, this sun kissed, soft-eyed hunk has plenty of confidence, and when he loosens up his shorts and exposes his meaty cock, it becomes obvious why'[7] and that Ken Riley 'is a tanned, cocky Florida guy brimming with confidence and a sexy smile. Originally from Tampa, this lax [sic] playing bro is comfortable out on the field or in front of the camera.'[8] In fact, all three of these performers only in part deliver on the promise of Next Door Male, as whilst their regional and largely suburban origins are foregrounded, their bodies are perhaps too overdeveloped and athletic to conform to the dream of the lithe-bodied twink. So whilst sites like Next Door Male market the fantasy of the boy-next-door, they also indicate that the summoning up of this fantasy, through words, is almost as important as the realization of the fantasy in images; that, in fact, a fundamental tenet of the porn is that desire cannot ever be fully satisfied. Mindful of this, I have chosen to focus my analysis here on performers who possess a specific physicality that embodies a heightened and eroticised version of the boy-next-door and a performance style that ranges from naïve passivity to a more playful, cheeky sexuality to a knowing self-awareness, rather than on this broader, more generic, notion of the boy-next-door. This means that my focus is on a relatively narrow number of performers chosen not for their remarkable qualities but in fact for the exact opposite. Instead, they have been chosen for their 'typicality', as typicality is at the heart of the type discussed in this chapter and also at the heart of the ways in which porn is structured and organised.[9] In particular, I will analyse three performers associated with the conflation of ideas laid out in this section: Justin Owen, another Next Door Male performer earlier in his porn career, identified as 'a California cutie, easy going and easy on the eyes',[10] Johnny Rapid, an especially prolific porn actor,[11] and the Spanish performer Allen King. All three epitomise the specific physicality and aesthetic of the boy-next-door and the sexy kid. They are petite, all have a 'swimmer's' taut and toned rather than heavily muscular physique, all have light brown natural hair, and the youthful fresh-faced look of an idealised teenager. They all embody a look that is meant to be read as overtly sexually attractive but one that is unself conscious and not about conspicuous displays of sex appeal. This is also a look and a type that speaks perhaps of a rather 'banal' conventionality (often subverted in the scenes that they perform, in for 'surprise' effect). In terms of performance, then, they demonstrate an interplay between innocence and calculating 'self-awareness' and this is often played on their videos, as they seem to oscillate in terms of casting choices and performances between the rather more suburban conventionalism of the boy-next-door and 'sexy kid' and the altogether more disruptive notion of types such as the hustler or the ambitious ingénu.

## 'Natural' Urges

Unsurprisingly, in porn, as elsewhere in popular culture, youth is connected with freedom, a lack of responsibility and an equally carefree attitude to sexuality. Adolescence (and irrespective of the official age of the performers discussed in this section, *it is* adolescent youth that is being invoked here) is governed by what Bill Osgerby has described as 'the ethic of fun' (2002:22), noting that from the 1960s onwards 'teenage culture was essentially the culture of a leisure class' (p. 24). In the pornosphere, and under the logic of this rubric, sex is a 'fun' leisure activity, is positioned as natural, and the urges and responses of the boy-next-door emphasise the naturalness of those desires.

So in a solo scene filmed for Dylan Lucas, a site featuring surfers and skateboarders, Justin Owen is filmed at the beach cavorting in the surf, playing with a football and subsequently masturbating.[12] The copy for the scene tells us that 'I took some pictures of him at the beach and Justin got so turned on he just wanted to jerk off right then and there.' Owen has a taut swimmer's body that indicates both youth and a physique acquired through outdoor 'natural' pursuits rather than a more self-conscious investment in gym culture. His complexion is sun kissed and his hair is wavy, tousled and fair. His fresh face and perfect teeth draw to mind the archetypical teen of Disney movies, or indeed (and I do not think this is inconsequential) the young Donny Osmond. In short, his looks, his demeanor and even his 'stage' name all signal that he is the all-American boy-next-door. The use of shaky, panning camerawork, designed to suggest an impromptu capturing of the moment and also a photo shoot, turning into horseplay and then a sexual display, is used to organise the unfolding of the scene and to situate Owen's smiling and uninhibited display of his lithe naked body and unself-conscious masturbation.

In a scene for Randy Blue, the same Owen meets Billy Taylor in a suburban park.[13] The scene is marketed as Taylor's 'first time fuck', drawing on another perennial set of discourses of youth surrounding the 'first time' and the 'loss of virginity', and is in effect the boy-next-door meeting a sexy kid on the street for sex. The scene opens with bold graphics superimposed over a sunlit Californian setting and the two performers entering from opposite sides of the park, seemingly oblivious to each other. An electronic music track and time-lapse editing creates a generically 'youth oriented' atmosphere and both performers are dressed in shorts, vests and trainers, wearing headphones and a backpack: the uniform of the American teen. An elaborate and heightened rhetoric, including the use of slow motion and big close-ups pulling into focus, sets up the dramatic effect of the encounter as Owen and Taylor pass by, each transfixed by the other. Owen decides to seize the opportunity to follow Taylor and they shortly relocate to an apartment replete with monochrome decorative features that speak, in the broadest of terms, of the contemporary tastes of the young (and single) adult male. In the sex that ensues, both Owen and Taylor are presented as enthusiastic performers, flushed and excited by the sexual play. It is Owen, though, as the performer who initiated the encounter by pursuing (the 18-year-old) Taylor, who is seen here as directing the action, asking Taylor if he enjoys the sexual repertoire that they enact with choreographed precision: kissing, undressing, oral, 69 with analingus, anal sex in four positions, climaxing with oral cumshots. Whilst it is Owen who is the receptive partner in the anal sex in this sequence, it would be hard to read this as a 'passive' performance in any meaningful sense. Furthermore, Taylor's 'first time' demonstrates a rather surprising degree of sexual sophistication, made even more surprising by the post-coital interview that has become a familiar feature of online porn. In this section of the film we discover that this is purportedly Taylor's first experience of anal sex with either a male or female partner. Owens and Taylor cheerfully, and without any apparent misgivings (given their bisexual status), discuss how 'laughter' and 'bonding' are important components of a sexual encounter, with Taylor advising us that 'it felt super natural'. I would argue that during the course of this vignette, lasting 29 minutes in total, Owens and Taylor perform three 'versions' of the youthful boy-next-door: first, a performance of two boys meeting on the street drawing on a broadly realist dramatic register; second, a sexual performance veering between flushed-faced energy and the rather more controlled delivery of the porn professional; and third, an impromptu interview style, where the smiling and laughing 'real' boys-next-door reminisce about the positive experiences that they have had.

The 'youthful' tone and style of this Randy Blue scene is partly in response to and attributable to the success, commercially and critically, of the most prominent exponent of this idealised and romanticised material: Jake Jaxson of Cockyboys. Jaxson's Cockyboys, like the work of his other East Coast rival, Michael Lucas, has garnered a great deal of media coverage, in part because of the high production values and statements of the elevated ambitions of the company to produce porn that can attract mainstream attention, and in part because of a media-savvy marketing strategy that positions Cockyboys as the acceptable, even hip, face of gay porn that has a widespread appeal.[14] As a corollary to this, Cockyboys is reputedly especially popular with female audiences and has even been recognised in a feature in *Cosmopolitan* for its 'smorgasbord of hot foxy men'.[15]

Though Jaxson rather disingenuously rejects the idea of using 'types' in his productions (the Cockyboys 'manifesto' states 'you are not a type, you are you'),[16] his constellation of performers includes many who would comfortably fit into the categories of the boy-next-door and the sexy kid, as well as the 'beautiful boy' that I discuss later on. Subsequently it's perhaps no surprise that Cockyboys has established a collaborative arrangement with Bel Ami, the longstanding market leaders in this territory.[17] Indeed, Jaxson's roster of 166 Cockyboys can be seen as sexy boys par excellence: the boys-next-door that audiences, male and female, might hope to meet.

Cockyboys has popularised a distinctive aesthetic that draws on stylistic reference points ranging from art house, independent and experimental film (harking back in a knowing fashion to the ambitions of Wakefield Poole) to the rhetoric of reality TV formats, pop music videos and commercials.

This hybrid style constitutes what might be described as a 'naturalistic' verité aesthetic balanced artfully somewhere between a youth-oriented fashion or fragrance commercial and the structured reality TV show. It is an aesthetic that is more conspicuously stylised than has been the norm in commercial porn until recent times, but it's also a distinctive style that has been widely imitated by competitors. The style emphasises (in a self-consciously mediated fashion) a sense of the 'naturalness' of gay sex alongside an aspirational image of romanticised encounters between fashionable, often metropolitan, young men.[18] The production standards, including arty, cropped framing and natural, rather than studio, lighting alongside an absence of the stock set-ups and blocking of shots of much mainstream porn, have become an influential trend across the industry. This stylised, 'realist' aesthetic, using natural lighting and a minimum in the way of heavy makeup, body shaving and so on, inevitably demands the use of performers with a 'natural' youthful body and a clear complexion, in short the kind of good looks that need little in the way of technical assistance.

So, for example, in a scene between Gabriel Clark and Allen King, a setting is established that presents the possibility of a carefree, romantic encounter between two young men who could become lovers.[19] In a chic, white room, loft location, Clark discusses his experiences as a bisexual man, revealing intimate pictures on his mobile phone to King, who in turn teaches him Spanish phrases for specific sex acts. The camera work focuses on faces and the interactions between the two performers rather than on body parts, and the principle of 'maximum visibility'. The tone is playful and lighthearted and moves seamlessly and seemingly 'naturally' into the sex scene, which is filmed in medium close-up for the most part, rather than the more customary longer shots interspersed with intrusively subjective close-ups. The decision to maintain a consistent rhetorical proximity to the action emphasises a sense of intimacy rather than the 'spectacle' of the sex act itself.

It's possible to argue, then, especially if we are to take Jaxson's account of his working practices and motivations in interviews at face value, that Cockyboys material is implicitly political as it foregrounds quite overtly the 'naturalness' of gay sex and gay desire, in part by reframing ostensibly heterosexual discourses of romance and the romantic. The use of romance is, of course, not at all new in gay porn *per se*; however, Jaxson's strategic use of romance is qualitatively different to the use of over-determined signifiers of the romantic, such as soft music and lighting, candles, drapery and so on (often feeling evacuated of meaning) that have become porn clichés. Instead Jaxson summons up the idea of a romantic masculinity that is produced by the rhetoric and performances in these scenes. This romantic masculinity connects a youthful masculinity with friendship, emotional connections and often (with the most *soto voce* echoes of Thoreau) to the outdoors and to nature.[20]

## 'Performing' Sex

I have already discussed the idea that the 'first time' is one of the key discourses of youth that is summoned up in gay porn. An altogether different type of 'first time' that is deployed with great regularity is the audition and the debut performance. As noted in the previous chapter, porn performance is a subject that has tended to elude critical attention, and therefore it's hardly surprising that scenarios where 'performing' sex, in the context of an audition, a casting or a screen test, have been given so little attention. This is a major absence, given how common this trope is and indeed how central it is to the structural workings of the industry.

The solo 'audition' video has often been used as an entrée into the industry and is an effective way of market-testing new performers. Audition material ranges from the more established rhetorical conventions of the 'audition tape', to more elaborate showcase solos. The conventional setting of the audition is most commonly an anonymous apartment location, featuring a couch (and an unseen director/camera operator) with a model in casual dress addressing the camera, before proceeding to undress and masturbate to climax. The aesthetic of these scenes is usually one that foregrounds the amateur nature of the performer and an absence of any stylisation or elaboration in terms of cinematography, lighting and editing. The rhetoric speaks of documentation of the performance act (and therefore visibility) rather than aestheticisation of the subject/performer.

So for example Max Andrews' audition for Boycrush makes minimal concession to aesthetic considerations, production design or performance, with an especially pale-skinned and young performer filmed on a dark leather couch, in a room with equally dark terracotta walls that collectively work to emphasise his pallor. Andrews strips to nothing more than his black socks and masturbates without acknowledging the camera/viewer in a scene that is relatively typical of this material. The lack of context or an overt attempt at a performance for an assumed viewer, is compensated by hyperbolic website copy that strives to suggest that this callow youth is indeed a hypersexualised 'sexy kid':

> Boys get into porn for various reasons, but all of them love sex. Max takes things further than this though, he's a self-diagnosed sex addict who can't stop thinking about cock! The sweet and versatile boy is pretty experienced, having enjoyed plenty of action including locker room fucking, DP and outdoor sex too. There's more we can teach him! Check out his jack off and that amazing squirting cum shot![21]

The solo audition format, which is a standard of the industry, has evolved, naturally enough, with the advent of the web, and Next Door Male for example features altogether more technically polished presentations of the debut that act as promotional packages for new performers.[22] Studios with more substantial resources and commitments to enhanced production standards, such as Helix and Bel Ami, similarly film solos or shorter sex scenes marketed as 'introducing' a new performer, often through the quasi-documentary device of a seasoned performer showing the debut performer the ropes.[23] In all cases, these scenes equate youth with a mixture of potentiality and inexperience. Even in the most basic of audition set-ups the plasticity and malleability of youthful masculinity is presented as key to its appeal.

Of course, the audition also has a dramatic potential, as it carries another set of associations relating to the exploitation of naïve and ambitious youth via the cliché of the 'casting couch' scenario. So 'acting' and 'audition' scenarios are used for their dramatic possibilities as they explicitly expose the power differentials inherent in the working of the entertainment business (adult or otherwise) and also because they eroticise the dismantling and destruction of the ideal of youthful masculinity that might potentially lead to the 'disruptive' models of youth that I will discuss subsequently. So for example the Randy Blue series *Welcome to L.A.* draws on the all too recognisable trope of the so-called 'Californian Dream' with a series of scenes about young men, effectively male ingénus, who pursue ambitions in a city that is synonymous with sex and sexual exploitation. The series charts Justin Owen's rise to fame as a model (we see him emblazoned on a billboard in Venice Beach) and also as an actor.[24] In episode 2, *Burbank*, Owen auditions for a film role in the studio of an executive (played by the muscular Austin Wolf).[25] Owen demonstrates a genuine degree of dramatic acting talent as he performs the role of the male ingénu, in this case an aspiring actor auditioning for a part who is then seduced by the predatory casting director. The scene culminates with Owen delivering the inevitable line, 'Does this mean I get the part?'

## Troublesome Youth

The dichotomy of youth, expressed across popular culture and given its most sustained and potent expression in the figure of the teenager, is that it is simultaneously a golden era of optimism, realisation of potential and the blooming of romance, and also a time of familial and social conflict, sexual confusion and tension and a period marked by disruptive 'acting out' and antisocial behaviours. Even whilst the teenager is a contemporary invention, this conflicted, dualistic view of youth, as Philip Graham notes, has a long history (2004:27) and the connection between youth and sexual experimentation is equally long lived (Eyben, 1977). This inevitably means that the eroticised visions of youthful masculinities found in gay porn range from the idealistic and idealised discourses of youth as a life-stage marked by carefree fun embodied by the fantasy boy-next-door – an innocent but a figure with an awakened sexuality and prodigious, unlimited sexual appetite – to a set of more troublesome or disruptive youthful masculinities, sometimes connected to ideas of youthful rebellion, to subcultural identities, and at the most extreme, drawing on Muncie's expression, to 'depravity'. This then is a set of masculinities that encompasses the street tough, the skater boy, the emo and also figures more directly related to gay subculture such as the hustler, the voracious 'cumslut' and the yet more marginal figure (in the pornosphere at least) of the effeminate young male. Performers cast in these roles often exhibit physicalities that less easily conform to classical ideals, are distinguished by markers of class, ethnicity, social groupings or subcultural affinities and are also often positioned as urban. This constitutes a pool of masculinities that firmly belong to a domain of production distinctly less mainstream in its mode of address and aesthetic decisions. Nonetheless, as is the way in the promiscuous world of pornography, mainstream producers often also draw from and flirt with the vernacular and tropes of troublesome youth with some degree of regularity.

## Transactional Sex/The Hustler

The trope most commonly appropriated by mainstream producers is the fantasy of street pick-ups, sex work and the erotically charged figure of the hustler, working the streets for money or, just as likely in the fantasy world of porn, merely for the excitement and irresistible draw of anonymous sex. This is a scenario often used for marketing and promotional purposes, to reveal another, perhaps more rebellious or sleazy side of a popular performer. It's striking that whilst the scene discussed earlier with Justin Owen and Billy Taylor began with an encounter in a suburban park and then moved to an apartment location, it's much more common for hustler scenarios to be located in urban settings, on the street (the natural habitat of the fantasy sex worker), and often to stay in quasi-public locations such as bar settings rather than being relocated to a domestic environment.

In a Randy Blue scene with the minimal title *Justin Owen*, we are provided with an example of the street pick-up trope being used as a showcase for Owen to extend his range beyond the role of the boy-next-door to encompass the altogether more transgressive figure of the hustler. The scene is in all respects a rather striking and imaginative take on both the solo masturbation scene and the fantasy of picking up a hustler on the street for transactional sex, with or without the exchange of cash.[26] Owen acts the part of a young kid hustling on the streets of LA, and here, as elsewhere, he demonstrates a dramatic skill that rather emphatically undermines the commonplace perception that porn performers can't act. The scene in fact makes very significant demands on Owen's dramatic range and improvisational skills as he performs the sexy kid artfully posing his lithe young body as he 'waits' on the street and then struts towards a car that has pulled into a parking bay and procures his unseen client. Driven to a luxurious home, which excites him so much that he needs to 'jack off', Owens leads the viewer, placed in the position of his trade, to the bedroom, where he masturbates, uses several sex toys and then ejaculates, ending the scene by winking at the camera/viewer and telling us, rather gnomically, 'I guess it's time to hang out now.'

Street pick-ups and hustling scenarios are also a popular trope in material made outside of the USA that features European, Hispanic and Latin men in particular. Kristen Bjorn, for example, a producer who will be discussed in Chapter 5, uses this kind of scenario routinely.[27] Such material also extends beyond the kind of glossy professionalism with which Bjorn is associated, to the quasi-amateur 'gonzo' porn of studios such as Czechhunter where supposedly straight young men are picked up for sex with financial incentives.[28] Early in his career, Allen King appeared in several scenes for the now defunct Spanish producer Locuragay, in which he performed in the *City Boys* series as a young street hustler, picking up older men on the streets of Madrid and having sex with them either on the street or in sex bars such as Boyberry, a sex club famed for its young clientele.

## The 'Other' Boy-Next-Door

Whilst mainstream, mass-market producers summon up disruptive, rebellious figures like the hustler on a fairly consistent basis, this is, more often than not, a repositioning of existing performers in new settings and part of a strategy of raising the sexual stakes (and performative range) of figures such as Justin Owen, who have already been positioned in the market place as the fantasy boy-next-door. There is, however, a qualitatively different and perhaps more troublesome type of boy-next-door that is eroticised, usually by niche producers. The youthful masculinity that results from this context is consequently qualitatively different at both an aesthetic and discursive level.

For example, the website Citiboyz, with a title already suggestive of an urban setting and therefore the tantalising potential of rebellious, sexually confident young men, describes itself as 'Home of the all American

boy-next-door'. However, this is indicating something qualitatively profoundly different to the articulations of the similar youthful archetype
summoned up by Cockyboys, Randy Blue or even Next Door Male.[29]
Instead, the Citiboyz roster of performers exhibits a range of physicalities,
ethnicities and identities, all of them seeming to point to something other
than a suburban ideal in favour of a sexual fantasy that is inflected more
clearly by class, race and urbanism. So whilst Justin Owens and Billy Taylor
met on a sunny day in a pretty suburban park in the scene discussed at the
start of this chapter, by contrast Billie Ramos and Timmy Tyler, both slim
and petite, both pierced, meet in a leaf-strewn alley whilst smoking, and
consummate their encounter in what appears to all intents and purposes to
be an authentic domestic bedroom in a scene entitled, tersely and literally,
*Smoke Break Leads to Sucking Cock*.[30] The casual pragmatics of both the
title and mise-en-scène are far removed from the heightened eroticism of
the Owens/Taylor encounter.

A sizeable proportion of the material produced by studios such as
Citiboyz, Staxus, Helix and others, features adolescent (or adolescent-
looking) models, frequently with slim, ectomorph physiques that appear
to be deliberately cast on the basis that they appear to be on the cusp of
teenhood, clearly flirting with more overtly taboo desires. Indeed, this is a
porn that self-consciously plays with the transgressive potential that such
youthful bodies (and the attendant naïveté of the models) presents in videos that eschew the cinematic styling and glossy sheen of the mainstream
studios in favour of minimal narrative set-ups and the most basic production values (HD picture clarity being the usual marketing boast). In this
context I would argue that youth is not romanticised but instead fetishised.
The promotional rhetoric of these sites draws attention, in the most hyperbolic terms, to the status of the performers who are 'barely legal', 'just 18',
or 'barely turned 18'.[31] For example, the promotional copy for the website
Boycrush advises us that:

> our models are fresh young men who have just barely turned
> 18 and love twink porn. They exude their natural personality,
> and each person brings his unique talents to each video we
> produce [...] Our young men models are rarely experienced in

filming before they come to our website [...]. Our videos lack
any music, and our boys fuck fluidly without stopping for special camera shots.[32]

It is tempting to draw easy, judgmental and negative conclusions about
porn that seemingly presents callow youth in such explicit terms for
sexual consumption and it's equally easy to overstate the transgressive
nature of this kind of material. Instead I think it's more useful to acknowledge that transgression, in its broadest sense, is, as Susanna Paasonen
has it, 'pivotal to the inner dynamics of pornography' (2011:162). The
thrill of porn, or, drawing on Paasonen, the 'affective power' of porn, is
connected, intimately, to seeing what is ordinarily not seen, including
taboo practices and desires and these transgressions are 'painted with the
broadest of brushes and presented with exclamation marks' (pp. 162–3).
In addition it is important, I think, to note that these rather more 'marginal' representations offer what might be described as 'recognizable'
bodies, types and articulations of youth to audiences that must com-
prise, in some part, young men of a similar age, and with similar physicalities, to those represented on screen. Whilst it is notoriously difficult
to obtain any kind of accurate commercial data about the porn industry,
for a host of reasons, the website Alexa, which gathers commercial web
traffic data, provides some intriguing clues, if not definitive evidence, as
to who is watching gay porn online. For example, a search for data in
August 2015 revealed notably that whilst Cockyboys appears to attract
a particular demographic in terms of educational profile (which is in
part an indicator of consumer age) that includes college-educated and
grad-school level (as well as the much discussed constituency of female
viewers), Helix attracts a preponderance of graduate-school-educated
viewers and Boycrush traffic appears to be exclusively male and also
exclusively college educated.[33] I want to make no claims here about the
reliability of these statistics. However, what can be deduced from such
limited data is that it is perhaps reasonably safe to suggest that this kind
of material is not accessed exclusively by much older men wanting to
look at much younger 'boys'. We might therefore assume that it is at least
a strong possibility that the audience for sites like Boycrush comprises a

proportion of young men who want to see bodies, indeed *desire* bodies, that look like their own.

## The Beautiful Boy

I have left discussion of the discourse of the beautiful boy towards the end of this chapter because in many respects this is a masculine ideal that represents the apotheosis of youth, and whilst youth is consistently overdetermined across gay porn, this is the most hyperbolised model of youthful masculinity of all, for Western producers and consumers at least. It is of course almost impossible to talk about idealised youthful male beauty without reference to classical precedent, as this is, in large part, the origin of these ideas. Consequently, the connections with the kinds of representations of the beautiful boy that are found in gay porn and the figure of the sybarite, devoted to a life of luxury and the cult of the beautiful and unattainable Adonis, are easily made (Burkert, 1985). The beautiful boy also figures, via this antique route, in art and literature connected with homosexuality, in, for example, the character of Dorian Grey (1890) or Tadzio in Mann's *Death in Venice* (1912). The beautiful boy in such contexts is positioned as the object of passionate (and almost always) unrequited desire, often oblivious to his effects, or even (*à la* the female archetype, Helen of Troy) unconcerned about the destructive powers that his beauty contains. In addition, and certainly since the late 18th century, this kind of beauty has often been connected not with the natural, as in the figure of the boy-next-door, but instead with decadence and depravity, as in the case of Wilde's *The Portrait of Dorian Grey* (1890) and Huysmann's 1884 novella, *A Rebours* (Against Nature). So, once again, embedded in this exemplar of masculine beauty is a paradox: that the idealised standard of beauty brings with it the potential of danger and degradation. It may seem an extravagant claim that the representations of masculinity produced by commercial gay porn carry with them the burden of such a long and complex history of culture and tradition, but this would be not only to relegate the status of this material but also to misunderstand the rather prominent place that the sexually explicit and the homoerotic has within 'legitimate' culture, that porn is a feature of that wider culture, and also to disregard that the masculinities that porn draws upon largely originate in that wider culture.

So, then, if there were a hierarchy of sexualised masculinities in gay porn, the beautiful boy might not be at the zenith but would certainly occupy a very prominent position. Like the previous discourses identified in this chapter, this is not a discrete or fixed category. For example, the attribution of this status is sometimes a marker of what might be regarded as a transitional stage in a performer's career as he graduates from 'twink-dom' to a new career phase, as in the case of Kevin Williams in the mid 1990s, Lukas Ridgeston during the late 1990s and Brent Corrigan in the 2000s. Furthermore, many of the producers who work with the iconography of athletic masculinity and its most strident and overdetermined expression, the jock, discussed in the next chapter, such as Randy Blue and Sean Cody, can also be seen as in the business of presenting visions of the beautiful boy. Nonetheless, the studio that is primarily regarded as the key purveyor of the iconography of the beautiful boy is without question Bel Ami, the producers who have become the gold standard in this field over two decades.

As discussed in a later chapter, in the early 1990s Bel Ami was at the vanguard of the so-called Europorn phenomenon, featuring young, athletically built and exceptionally handsome performers drawn from Central and Eastern Europe. It would, however, no longer be accurate to describe the company or its output as constituting 'Europorn' in any meaningful sense. Instead I would suggest that what Bel Ami produces is a transnational, 'International Style' of gay porn. I am deliberately referencing what has become known as the International Style of architecture here, as I will explain in Chapter 5, as it is usually characterised as concerned with form and aesthetics and in opposition to the social purposiveness of the Modernist movement (Scully, 2003). Whereas the early Bel Ami productions were often set in quasi-rural idealised settings, a homoerotic idyll where beautiful boys had carefree sex in equally beautiful locations, the latter Bel Ami output has evolved an aesthetic and vernacular that has become progressively homogenous, corporate, consistent and extremely commercially successful. Bel Ami makes no secret that their performers are cast for the uniformity of their physical characteristics and because they have a particular Bel Ami 'look'.[34] The Bel Ami boys no longer live in the idealised Ruritania of the early films but, instead, in a world of luxurious resorts and glamorous, international locations: a consumerist fantasy of travel and tourism, in essence. Usually devoid of any social context, the performers are presented largely as sybaritic playboys, living for pleasure and perpetually on holiday.

For example, in a scene entitled *Jack, Jim and Roger*, in a modishly appointed apartment setting, Roger Lambert takes a brief respite from sunbathing to undertake some minor household chores.[35] These consist of polishing a mirror, providing an opportunity for Roger to admire himself and the viewer to admire him. He proceeds to vacuum carpets but is soon distracted by Jack Harrer and Jim Kerouac who sit on the bed mocking his investment in homecare and instead invite him to join them for sex. All three models are smooth, toned, tanned, pretty and fair haired, their bodies are almost interchangeable and their sexual performance is playful in tone and abandoned (the scene is sold on the basis that it is 'condom free'). Bel Ami situates the beautiful boys as figures who are playful and without responsibility and in pursuit of pleasure at all costs.

Bel Ami, as already noted, is not alone in this territory – Sean Cody and Corbin Fisher (discussed in the next chapter) and Randy Blue and Cockyboys (discussed in this chapter) all operate in a similar field – but there are key differences, I think, that result in the particularly heightened and 'glamorous' (in the true sense of the word) tone of Bel Ami productions. For instance, the rhetoric of Cockyboys material is concerned with a certain personalization of performers, creating a sense that, through the extensive use of talking head pieces to camera to establish a sex scene, we 'know' who Tayte Hanson, Jake Bass or Darius Ferdynand are through hearing them speak as 'personalities' in their own right (and usually in advance of seeing them perform as porn professionals). By contrast, we know much less about Bel Ami models (and the term 'model' is pretty consistently used in media reportage and marketing materials to indicate once again the physical beauty of the performers rather than their identities as individuals). Whilst Bel Ami scenes often feature tourist trips, boyishly impromptu horseplay and reality TV-styled fly-on-the-wall footage, the performers are rarely presented as representing anything other than a generically youthful and carefree persona that is similarly interchangeable.

This creates a distance (often enhanced, for Anglophone viewers at least, by the fact that they rarely speak English) that is very clearly scrupulously managed, between the viewer and the viewed: the beautiful boy needs to be kept at a distance and remain unattainable, existing in an equally distant, utopian realm.

Furthermore, the connections between the beautiful boy, idle pleasure and decadence emerge in the taboo subjects and practices that are also familiar territory for Bel Ami. Schoolboy scenarios, for instance, have been a fairly consistent trope for Bel Ami, and the most dramatic twist on this must surely be the film *Scandal in the Vatican* (dir. Marty Stevens, 2012). Filmed, in part, at the Vatican and featuring an unauthorised (and obscured) walk-on performance by the then Pope Benedict, the story of a group of young missionaries who consummate their pilgrimage to the Holy See with an orgy with their priest, was inevitably designed to cause a furore. The spectacle of the group sex scene (a Bel Ami speciality) featuring seven luminously beautiful boys is set in a suitably antique Roman setting, flooded with light that provides a heightened mise-en-scène that turns this ecclesiastical transgression into an instance of glamour and luxury.

Perhaps even more controversial, though, is Bel Ami's flirtation and in some cases explicit depiction of incestuous acts. This is once again not an uncommon trope and Bel Ami was keen to promote their 'discovery' of the first gay porn triplets, with the Visconti brothers in 2009. However, in 2010 the stakes were raised yet further when the identical Peters twins were filmed having sex with each other as well as in group scenarios. The hyperbole surrounding this transgressive scenario was further amplified by the revelation that the brothers were also lovers in real life.[36] Notwithstanding the challenging nature of this kind of sexual relationship, real or fantasised, it is in the nature of the operation of porn that a theme, an aesthetic, a narrative device or a sexual practice should be taken to its ultimate extreme: the largest dick, the biggest gangbang, the most sexual partners, the most extreme form of sexual play. In many respects, then, the Peters twins represent a logical step in Bel Ami's production of the discourse of the beautiful boy by elliptically referencing another figure from classical mythology: Narcissus, the beautiful boy in love with his own reflection.

# The Daddy

At the other end of the generational spectrum (which in the mainstream of the pornosphere is in fact a relatively limited spectrum ranging from 18 to about 45) we find the figure of the daddy. The term, like its youthful counterpart, the twink, is another slippery one, freighted with connotations of taboo desires and sexual practices that are sometimes literally invoked, as we will observe shortly. Increasingly the term is used merely as a value-neutral label for the older partner in a sexual encounter. In *Homos* (1995), Vito Russo uses the term daddy in the context of an interrogation of S/M practice and relations of dominance and submission. However, in contemporary gay parlance (and consequently in gay porn) the term has lost at least some of these connotations and is more familiarly a generic descriptor that is used quite loosely, sometimes referring to generation, quite often to a particular physicality and to a performance style or type of sexual play that might be read as 'dominant'. Providing traction to this, Peter Nardi notes, the terminology of gay culture is particularly pliable and descriptors are fairly routinely repurposed, adapted and reappropriated:

> Rather than an older man who supports a younger lover [...] the contemporary terms 'daddy' and 'son' reflect physical types, intergenerational interaction, and sometimes sexual relation-ships of dominance and submission.
>
> (1997:58)

So for my purposes, and in this context, the term *daddy* simultaneously refers to a broad generational category (men over 30), to a physicality (frequently mesomorphic and sometimes herculean in stature) and to a style of performance (usually, though not always, the dominant and 'active' partner in a sex scene).

I should also make it clear here that the figure of the daddy is not the sole model of mature masculinity available to audiences, though the lack of precision in the ways in which this language is applied means that an iconography that celebrates maturity and the bodies and desires of 'older' men (and I'm conscious to use this term advisedly) can slip from view. A further complication is that the term daddy is sometimes used inter-changeably with, indeed sometimes as a synonym for, the figure of the bear (the term daddy bear is used) and is part of a wider culture of hypermasculinity discussed in the next chapter. As I have noted in an earlier essay (2012:313–26), the mutability and ambiguity of a term like daddy in part at least indicates the limited vocabulary that is available to make sense of and to situate the sexualised older man within a wider culture that is fixated with youth. This is not to say, though, that it is not possible to do so, and in the next chapter I will discuss a range of mature masculinities that have become recurrent features of gay porn, either through sites that specialise in mature masculinities, such as Hot Older Male and Butch Dixon, but also through instances where the mainstream, mass-market producers make use of the older man, the most common trope being intergenerational encounters, which will be the focus of discussion in the final section of this chapter.

## Intergenerational Sex: the Amorality of Desire

I have previously written about intergenerational sex scenes in gay porn and have argued that whilst it seems axiomatic that these scenarios are fairly simple and uniform in their manner of address and their narrative constructions, they are, in fact, far from straightforward representations of 'taboo' sexual acts and instead rather complicated and often ambiguous enactments of fantasies that draw on a range of cultural reference points. This includes at one extreme idylls of man–boy love, to, at the other extreme, scenarios where domestic abuse is presented as an erotic fantasy.

In part, the apparent simplicity of such scenarios relates to sexual performances that are often routinely locked into an active/passive binarism, with the daddy as the 'active' top and a twink as the 'passive' bottom. Consequently, it might seem in such scenes that generational power dynamics (Sinfield, 2004:115) as well as an implicit gendering (feminisation) of the 'passive' (and therefore by extrapolation the submissive) nature of the 'bottom' sex role is dramatised and emphasised; in short that this kind of porn is largely about an older man fucking a younger man and therefore about celebrating the potency of hegemonic masculinity and objectifying and feminising youthful masculinity and passivity. However, whilst there are many examples to endorse this analysis in the round, I would argue that this would be too reductive a reading in many cases and would fundamentally disregard both context and conditions of consumption: who this porn is made for and who, based on narrative and rhetoric, we might assume is positioned as the viewer for this material is often complicated in this specific subgenre. So, for example, there are several 'amateur' sites that overtly eroticise the predatory desires of what I have described elsewhere as the priapic 'dirty old man' (p. 320). Daddymugs, for instance, revolves around the sexual exploits of the eponymous paunchy, middle-aged everyman who has a body that does not meet the standards of the hypermasculine ideals that will be discussed in the next chapter. Instead he represents an idea of an 'authentic' and therefore 'average' man; not muscular, not handsome, not exceptionally endowed but nonetheless rapaciously sexual. Describing himself as a 'lucky man' in his online biography, Daddymugs tells us that:

> We are your premiere site for exclusive content of the boys you want to see plowed by a real man [...]. I was born and raised in Ohio. I love sports, travelling and of course boys. I drive a Dodge truck and my business partner has an H3 that I drive sometimes or you have seen it in some of my scenes [...]. As for boys, I'll get right to the point, I LOVE THEM. I love to fuck their brains out, have them suck on my thick daddy cock and I love sucking and rimming them.[37]

Daddymugs' roster of performers, 'Daddy's Boys', largely conform to the model of the boy-next-door described earlier in this chapter, with the rather unexpected addition of two female dominatrix performers.[38] Whilst Daddymugs emphasises his 'love' of boys and in some scenes he adopts the accoutrement and elements of leather iconography associated most closely with gay subculture, in most respects his performance, appearance and demeanour are marked out as that of an ostensibly straight-identified man who through, through a combination of personal preference and coincidence has sex with boys. Daddymugs has attracted a fairly consistent degree of negative feedback, including in 2008 an especially vigorous discussion over the ethics of an older man 'taking the virginity' of the reputedly 18-year-old model, Justin. The furore was, notably, not about the taboo spectacle of intergenerational sexual congress, but instead was ostensibly about the unattractive physical appearance of the older man, commonsense logic seemingly dictating that no 18-year-old could possibly have a sexual interest in him.[39]

By contrast, Jake Cruise, who like Daddymugs produces amateur porn (perhaps more accurately described as amateur 'styled' porn, given that Cruise often works with professional porn performers), presents himself much more unambiguously as a middle-aged gay man who uses his website as a mechanism for having sex with attractive, athletic and younger men:

> I find my friends in all sorts of places: from ads placed in local magazines; by referral; in the gym; sometimes just walking down the street [...]. Sometimes I only get to watch from behind the camera. Some guys let me 'play' with them a bit, touching, and sometimes sucking. Every once in a while I get lucky and get to have hardcore sex with a hot stud. But my favorite movies are the ones in which when I get to give a hard, muscular man an erotic massage, rubbing his meat until he shoots his load onto his belly.[40]

Unlike Daddymugs, Jake Cruise's site features a range of performers and body types involved in intergenerational scenes and though Cruise himself is usually the star turn, he also casts the hirsute and hypermasculine Brad Kalvo[41] and the sculpted and equally macho Bo Dean as proxy daddy figures.[42] Cruise, like Daddymugs, is also middle aged, with white hair and a recognizably 'average' untoned physique for his age. Cruise is presented, again like Daddymugs, as priapic, engaging in body worship, oral and anal sex in which he performs in both the 'active' and 'passive' role depending on the model he is working with. It is notable that in this case, Cruise's pleasure is marked out as one that is about the visual and metaphorical consumption of youthful bodies that are unlike his own mature body and young attractive men we are to once again infer would not be interested in him were it not for financial reward. A scene with the blond and athletically built professional performer Brady Jensen is described in terms that indicate the tone of many similar encounters:

> Brady Jensen is almost too good to be true. Visually, as you can see, he's stunning. Tall, blond, tan, impossibly well-built, with a smooth body, sculpted ass and large cock, he's the fantasy of many men. On top of being incredibly sexy, his ability to laugh

and have fun in bed makes servicing him a total pleasure. His see-through cotton briefs immediately drew my attention (and my tongue) to the head of his cock. He was instantly erect as I drew his dick all the way down my throat. But a body like Brady's has many parts that need to be tasted, including his armpits, manhole, feet and toes [...]. Just wait till you see his expression as he cums into my mouth. It's the next best thing to being there![43]

In the scene, Cruise presents Jensen to the viewer with his arm around his shoulder. He fondles his body and strokes his chest, describing the younger man to his audience in a manner that encourages us to 'look at his eyes and that face', advising us that he is totally smooth, before going on to point out minute elements of muscle definition. He then moves on to undress the model, masturbate and perform oral sex on him, lick his feet and anus, culminating in an oral cum shot. Throughout this sequence Jensen does not (and is not expected to) reciprocate; he is merely there to be admired for his exceptional physical beauty and to be consumed by Cruise and the audience alike. If Cruise is meant to be read as an everyman, this strategy has not always been especially successful. Indeed he has consistently attracted even more negative comments about his appearance than Daddymugs, with commentators and bloggers routinely disparaging his age, looks and demeanour and complaining that his mere appearance is enough to distract from an erotic engagement with the younger and much more physically attractive models that he tends to employ.

Just as intergenerational sex scenes do not signify a homogenous set of power relations or even represent the same sequence of sexual acts in the realm of 'amateur' porn, so across mainstream narrative gay porn, sex that eroticises differences in age is structured, performed and makes meaning in a range of ways. The Helix Studio *Man on Twink* series, probably unintentionally referencing the narrative of Sade's *120 Day of Sodom*, presents a succession of scenarios linked through the conceit of a group therapy session, in which a room of twinks reveal their deepest fantasies. Helix specialises in twink porn, and since most of their output is focused on scenes with men in the 18-to-25 age bracket, it's therefore safe to assume that the majority of audience members for this material are primarily interested in the twink type. The fantasies of the young men in the series all involve sex with an older daddy figure, with the exception of a scene with a younger tennis coach, jock type. All six scenes in the series pair three of the younger performers with two older models who figure as stand-in fantasy ideals of maturity: 'a smart guy who was really into art' in Kyle Ross's fantasy of romance and sophistication, *The Art Gallery*,[44] and a professional photographer played by the dark, muscular and hirsute Tommy Defendi in Max Carter's 'fantasy realized' scenario in which the erotic display of a photo shoot turns into a sex scene.[45] The blond Landon Conrad plays a 'big muscular and hunky' daddy in Jessie Montgomery's doctor's waiting-room fantasy scenario,[46] doubling up as a hyper-macho, car mechanic teacher (a rather complex conjunction of social types) in *Anything to Pass*.[47] Finally, Landon is cast again as a 'hot muscular jock' in Andy Taylor's dream scenario *The Lunch Date*,[48] and the dreams of an individual twink leak into reality as Taylor's 'fantasy' is witnessed by the rest of the group, who masturbate whilst watching him and Landon have sex. In this series we see that the older man is a relatively flexible concatenation of the anonymous hot stranger, the 'paternal' sophisticate and the authoritarian teacher, and in all cases a figure desired by the twink because of his ability to overpower the younger man and take charge of the sexual play.

By contrast, the *Daddy Hunt* series, produced by Hot Older Male, constructs narratives that alternate between older daddy figures cruising the streets of San Francisco looking for young men for sex, as in *Daddy Hunt 3: The Boy in the Window*[49] or *Daddy Hunt 4: The Boy on the Chaise*[50] and scenes in which the younger man actively pursues the daddy figure, such as *Daddy Hunt 5: Hot Daddy on the Roof*.[51] The site specialises, as its title suggests, in mature performers, and consequently, unlike the relatively flexible notion of maturity that is constructed in the *Man on Twink* series, physical maturity is emphasised here through the use of performers of an age (and sometimes embodying a physicality) that falls outside of the mainstream norms (i.e. the site features models who are over 45). In all cases, though, it is the body of the older male that is the primary focus of erotic attention, whether in scenes between two (or more) mature performers or in representations of intergenerational sex. In these films, the younger performers tend to be far less overdetermined, whereas the older performers have evidently been chosen for their bulky masculine physiques and their enthusiastic performance of 'manly' sex that is often marked by its mutuality, as will be noted in the next chapter. It is not, for instance, uncommon that sex roles switch, with the younger performer fucking the older daddy figure. Even whilst a site like Hot Older Male explicitly sexualises mature bodies and the appeal of sex with an older man and overtly trades on the term daddy to ascribe an identity and role to performers, there are very few instances in which the most obvious taboo that the term suggests is drawn upon. In fact, ironically, in order to find instances where incestuous or domestic sexual abuse scenarios are most routinely played with, we have to look no further than to the most mainstream and mass market of all contemporary gay porn producers: Men.com. Even whilst they go to great pains to provide narrative rationalisations that operate as an alibi for material with titles such as *Stepfather's Secret*, *Make My Son a Whore*, *My Mom's New Husband* and *Son Swap*, it is clear, as commentators have noted, that the transgressive potential of taboo familial sexual relations has become a particularly recurrent (and presumably popular) theme. The exemplar daddy performer at Men.com is Dirk Caber: bearded and greying but also muscular, squared jawed and conventionally handsome, Caber in many respects is the epitome of the 'hot daddy' and sexy older man. Caber is also a sexually versatile performer and in many scenes that foreground and eroticise 'abuse' scenarios the sexual play works to undermine and dissipate simple, and literal, interpretations. For example, in *Big Bro Part 1*, Caber plays a mentor to a troubled urban youth (Will Braun) and abuses his position by attempting to seduce the younger man (who is clearly amenable to these advances). The sex that ensues involves Braun topping Caber, confounding our expectations of this kind of scenario and according to the rubric of the rhetoric of gay porn at least thereby altering the dynamic of the sexual play.

At the end of this chapter, I come to what is perhaps a rather surprising conclusion. The discourse of the daddy, as it is deployed across gay porn, is far from the definitive authority figure and the concrete, immovable, monolithic archetype, but instead is chimerical and indistinct. The daddy in contemporary gay porn has become a flexible container for a range of models of masculinity, including the rapacious everyman, the gay-for-pay porn professional, the over-determined gay 'he-man' and the fantasy 'father figure'. Furthermore, as previously noted, in much intergenerational gay porn the annunciative position of the text is constantly shifting and unstable. Across specific sites and even within individual scenes, we can move between a narrative and rhetoric that encourages us to identify with the sexy kid or the herculean daddy: by turns desiring to be overpowered by the weight of masculinity that the daddy can bring to bear and also desiring to possess these markers of hypermasculinity. In almost all cases, though, the one constant is that the daddy, who is frequently positioned as a straight (or straight-identified) man, is someone who embodies a specific model of macho masculinity, and it is the iterations of this often paradoxical version of masculinity that is the focus of the next chapter.

# 4

## Straight Acting? Heterosexuality, Hypermasculinity and the Gay Outlaw

> *Gay porn was never dominated by gay models [...]. Gay porn should be more accurately called 'all-male porn'. [...] I know some gay models in the U.S. who claimed to be straight to get a job with some of the American Studios. [...] We live in a world where traditional labels don't apply anymore, partly as a result of gay emancipation. Being gay is not taboo anymore, and I'd say at least thirty per cent of city boys in the Central European region happily experiment with their sexuality. Many enjoy it, but they wouldn't think of themselves as being gay. They simply mingle freely, going with their girlfriends to gay bars and fondling other boys in front of girls. And now tell me – what is their orientation?*
>
> George Duroy, *The Porn Game: An Interview with Bel Ami's George Duroy*[1]

One of the key markers of the contemporary phenomenon that I describe as saturated masculinity, is that the signifiers of dominant, patriarchal and heterosexual masculinity have been reappropriated, hybridised and eroticised. I will argue in this chapter that this condition is especially evident in the themes, discourses, iconography and performances of gay porn where any sense of a dichotomous distinction between hetero- and homosexuality exists merely to be played with, complicated, questioned and satirised.

In this context, traditional binary distinctions between sexual identities and orientations are presented as mutable, ambiguous, porous and open to question. Even whilst Bel Ami's founder George Duroy poses a rhetorical question rather than offering a critical perspective on the subject of sexual identity in the extract from the interview cited above, he is pointing to an important consideration: that sexuality, like class or ethnicity, is not a fixed universality, that it is, in fact, socially and culturally constructed and equally specific. This is especially important when thinking about the ways in which the figure of the 'straight man' is eroticised in gay porn, not least because as the French critic Louis-George Tin argues, 'heterosexuality is assumed to be ever present as a matter of course and has escaped analysis as if it is transparent to itself' (2012:8). One of the perennially fascinating paradoxes of gay porn is that it presents the potential to interrogate the construction of heterosexuality as the 'exnominated' normative position. In this light, Duroy's use of the term 'all male porn' becomes especially interesting as a way of (albeit unintentionally in Duroy's case) radically rethinking what gay porn is and what it does. Although I am not proposing to dispense with the term 'gay porn' in this book, I am conscious that in previous studies, including my own work, it has become orthodox to argue that gay porn (especially the gay porn of the 1980s and 1990s), for better or worse, constructs a heteronormative vision of masculinity and sexuality in terms of sexual conduct, body types and settings. In the contemporary moment, however, and in the context of a saturated masculinity, this simplistic formulation becomes increasingly less tenable.[2] Instead, I am arguing that gay porn offers multiple masculinities, iterated through a network of settings and themes, and furthermore that, even within the parameters of the prescriptive demotic idiom of the commercial mainstream practice that is referenced in this book, there is considerable diversity and variety. This is particularly true of the ways in which the heterosexual male is eroticised and the ways in which the signifiers of a specific, strident, macho masculinity, writ large, have become the markers of what is described in this chapter as the hypermasculine gay male.

## Straight Acting/Acting Straight

What it means to be 'straight acting', or indeed to enact straightness, is a core consideration in this chapter. The spectre of straightness looms so large over an understanding of masculinity and 'manliness' that I am folding a set of issues into one here by focusing on the problematically prised 'straight acting' gay man and the heterosexual male performance of straightness in gay porn. This means that I am specifically interested not just in the category of gay men who invest in the idea of 'passing' as heterosexual (itself a vexed category and the one that has been the primary focus of such scholarship as does exist) but also, critically, in the ways that the signs of heterosexuality are performed in gay porn. The two are closely related, bleed into each other at points, and certainly benefit from consideration alongside each other, but they are not equivalent.

'Straight acting' is yet another term that is core to understanding the eroticised representations of masculinity in gay porn, a term loaded with significance for gay men and that has motivated a range of critical interventions encompassing popular debate[3] and scholarship across disciplines (see Martino, 2012; Lanzieri, 2011; Eguchi, 2010; Clarkson, 2006). For several of the scholars who have written on this subject in recent years, the website Straightacting.com has been alighted on as an especially rich (if relatively obscure) resource and has formed the basis for their analyses of the category of 'straight acting'. The site has also, I think, been an object of study that has been mined in order to provide evidence in a rather selective fashion, in effect to 'speak the truth of sex' that researchers have wanted from it rather than the much more complex, fractured and uncertain level of discourse that actually is evidenced, for example, on its discussion board.[4] Martino, for instance, suggests that 'straight acting functions as a compensatory mechanism for displacing an already internalised sense of inferiority that is attributed on the basis as identifying as gay, constituted as failed masculinity' (2012:43) and furthermore that straight acting has the express function to 'dispel the abjected and feminized Other' (p. 46). Eguchi proposes that 'the rhetoric of straight-acting may play a dual role in both producing and reproducing homophobic and anti-feminine communication among gay men' (2010:194). The model of straight acting that scholars suggest is produced here is one that is fundamentally heteronormative in the sense that Michael Warner and Steven Seidman originally used the term.[5] In essence, then, these arguments are uncontroversial enough; however, they provide a narrowly deterministic perspective from which to analyse the layers of complexity and ambiguity that gay porn trades in and exploits on a routine basis. It is therefore insufficient to argue that straight acting or, indeed, that heterosexuality is eroticised in gay porn because gay men are self-loathing or complicit in their own oppression. This kind of analysis is not especially useful for understanding the workings of fantasy and what goes on in porn where, very often, the idea of 'straight acting' and the straight man are undermined even as they are celebrated. Instead, I see gay porn as playing with (and picking apart) the very notion of the heteronormative. As Rob Cover astutely observes, this provides the conditions for 'a form of fluidity that allows for a certain kind of "play" around the fringes of what masculine heterosexuality might mean, and how it might be articulated otherwise' (2015:3). In fact in much commentary on the subject there is nothing said at all about the transgressive nature of fantasy. This rather literal interpretation of straight acting is also curiously ahistorical, suggestive of a singularity of meaning that does not hold up to scrutiny. By contrast, David Halperin (1990:9) and Peter Drucker (2015:163), for instance, both see the fantasy of the straight-acting gay male as a late 19th- and early 20th-century phenomenon in analysis that places such ideas in their social and cultural context, mindful that models of homo and hetero-masculinity change over time. In keeping with this, an altogether more nuanced perspective is offered by Bryant Keith Alexander, who notes that:

> The subject of straight acting always begs the question of the performative nature of gender [...]. Straight acting invokes what I have described elsewhere as heterotropes, reoccurring patterns of expected heterosexual behaviour that become signifiers of masculine performativity.
>
> (2011:64)

Whilst I don't necessarily agree with Alexander's argument in its entirety, what matters is the connection that he draws between heterosexuality and a masculinity that is posited as monolithic (and mythic). I would argue that the eroticisation of the signifiers of this supposed monolith that takes place in gay porn, involves an unpicking and dismantling of an iconography that always carries with it at least a vestige of heterosexuality and is suggestive of, as Cover describes it, 'performances and practices of heterosexuality that disrupt its overall coherence without dismissing heterosexual identity altogether, and thereby extend the possibility for a broader set of understandings of sexuality as complicated, diverse, and sometimes illogical' (p. 2).

Secondly, and equally importantly, straightness (which in this case tends to refer to a very specific, largely Anglo-American, Protestant and Caucasian version of straightness) is 'performed'. In *Bodies That Matter*, Judith Butler points to the complexity of this relationship:

> Performativity describes this relation of being implicated in that which one opposes, this turning of power against itself to produce alternative modalities of power, to establish a kind of political contestation that is not a 'pure' opposition, a 'transcendence' of contemporary relations of power, but a difficult labor of forging a future from resources inevitably impure.
>
> (1993: p. 241)

Consequently, the spectacle of the straight man or even 'straight acting' gay man performing male-only sex acts is a complex performance that unravels a fixed and singular model of heterosexuality set up in opposition to homosexuality.[6] As Jay Poole observes, then, in gay porn that eroticises straightness, 'the viewer is challenged to disrupt the traditional heterosexual binary' (2014:289). Furthermore, I would argue that the condition I describe as saturated masculinity, which has emerged alongside, and in tandem to, an increased social and cultural acceptance of homosexuality in the developed world, contributes to an environment in which the very notion of a binary model can be questioned.[7] Whilst it is self-evident that gay porn establishes ideals of appearance and behaviour, I see these as plural orthodoxies that evolve and mutate, and not binaristic norms; a contemporary example here being the orthodoxy of the athletic, straight-identifying jock type (discussed below) who enjoys receiving anal sex seemingly without regarding this as an *a priori* index of a 'failed masculinity'. Additionally, it is easy to overlook porn's facility to satirise and subvert convention (Paasonen, 2011:146). For example, the straight man 'fooled' into gay sex is a common trope, discussed later on, that operates based on the assumption of a complicated viewing position, where viewers allow themselves to be complicit in a shared fantasy; the straight man performs his 'shock' or reticence at the prospect of engaging in gay sex whilst viewers engage with a performance of the undoing of unreconstituted heterosexuality at the same time as being conscious of the constructed nature of this fantasy. It's hard, I would argue, to regard this complex set of relations as straightforwardly reducible to gay self-loathing impulses.

## Gay for Pay: The 'Jock'

Gay culture more broadly (and gay porn specifically) has often been fuelled with erotic fantasies about straight men. It is important for my purposes to distinguish between material in which the performer's heterosexuality is explicitly eroticised, as in the case of *Getting it Straight* (dir. Michael Youens, Jocks, 2004), *Straight Boy Seductions* (dir. Nica Noelle, Icon Male, 2015), *Str8 from the Gym* (uncredited, Next Door Studios, 2014) and instances where textual, paratextual and contextual referents are suggestive of the heterosexual credentials of the so-called 'gay for pay' performer. So there are things to say here about the straight man as an icon of gay porn as well as heterosexual performers in gay porn. In a previous essay on this subject, I argued that gay porn deploys a range of 'alibis' to rationalise 'gay for pay' performance (Mercer, 2011). These alibis are the financial alibi (entering into some kind of financial transaction to justify the performance of gay sex acts), an amoral alibi, situating gay sex as inconsequential fun, and the exploratory alibi, where a curious, straight man 'tries out' gay sex. Whilst distinguishing here between the eroticisation of straightness in gay porn and the gay-for-pay performer who may not play straight in a scene, I am also conscious that these distinctions are increasingly less clearly defined and also increasingly ambivalent; indeed the change in tone of the content analysed in my earlier essay and the contemporary context is quite marked.[8] The slippage between these two categories is perhaps most vividly played out in the summoning up of the iconography of the contemporary jock figure.

The jock is an icon of youth that maps onto and intersects with, but is qualitatively different to, those discussed in the previous chapter. The jock represents an athletic masculinity that is in many respects the apotheosis of American youth culture, embodying athleticism, physical perfection and (usually) immaculately grooming. As Eric Anderson notes, the jock is an American archetype that traditionally 'embod(ies) what orthodox masculinity entails [...]; thus, masculinity and athleticism are interlinked, providing for a cornerstone of contemporary gender ideology in which patriarchal and heterosexual privilege is maintained' (2009:44). Anderson's description of the jock as the epitome of a culturally (and ostensibly nationally) specific model of heterosexuality accords to a greater or lesser degree with many of the ways in which the jock (and the authority figure of the coach) is deployed, through the routine use of overdetermined sporting iconography and locker-room scenarios across all genres of gay porn. There are almost too many examples to mention here, including narrative films such as *The New Coach* (dir. Chi Chi Larue, Jocks, 1997), *Team Players* (dir. Chris Ward, Raging Stallion, 2005) and *Playbook* (dir. Brian Mills, Titan, 2008), which all use American sporting iconography and the erotic frisson of the all-male environment locker-room as providing the mise-en-scène for gay sex. This scenario is so ubiquitous that it is expressed in a variety of sometimes quite attenuated, even satirical ways. Randy Blue's *The Coach* series, for instance, pokes fun at the hackneyed convention of jock/coach scenarios in a trilogy of videos in which Chris Rockway and Reese Rideout perform camp parodies of the kind of earnest, gung-ho enthusiasm and unself-conscious display of physicality that is associated with the cliché of the 'dumb jock'.[9] The jock and sporting tropes are also referenced in examples of thematic rather than narrative porn such as the stylised *Score!* films from Hot House: *Score! Game 1* (dir. Steven Scarborough and Christian Owen, Hot House, 2011), *Score! Game 2* (dir. Steven Scarborough and Christian Owen, Hot House, 2011) and *Play Hard* (dir. Christian Owen, Hot House, 2014), in which the locker-room setting becomes an abstracted porn set and the iconography of the jock (football boots, chest pads, sporting apparatus, jockstraps) in effect becomes drag that the models sport to draw fetishistic attention to the signifiers of jockdom.

However, the figure of the jock is also the most prominent feature of the quasi amateur 'American college' websites, including Sean Cody and Corbin Fisher who present a contemporary version of jockdom that is more nuanced than merely an unquestioning veneration of American, heteronormative values. As Ron Becker observes:

> Although there is a long gay-for-pay porn tradition, SeanCody. com's amateur-video style establishes the 'reality' of the models and their sexual pleasures in ways that differ from the fictional

narratives of porn films [...] the site destabilizes the notion that sexual pleasures match up neatly with sexual identities – that just like some gay guys, certain straight guys physiologically enjoy the sensation of anal sex and others don't. Such a view profitably exploits gay fantasies of course, but that fact doesn't negate its ability to shift constructions of gender and sexuality.

(2009:138)

The content of sites like Sean Cody, Corbin Fisher and their many imitators, and the popular reception to that content, illustrates what I regard as the neuralgic core of the contemporary 'straight acting', straight and gay-for-pay conundrum. These sites offer, through the rhetoric of reality porn, representations of a 'new jock' signifying a conventional masculinity at a superficial level that is problematised by sexual performances that speak directly of a degree of ambiguity and complexity that I think is an indicator of saturated masculinity.

Evidence of the 'alibis' that I have previously argued are deployed to make sense of the straight man's performance in gay porn are, in this context, no longer alibis to justify sexual behaviour, as no justification or mitigation needs to be provided for the sexual conduct of this uninhibited and sexually liberated 'new jock' who engages in all-male sex performances on screen for both pleasure and profit. Consequently, performing in gay porn becomes, rather than a marker of a fixed sexual identity, a pragmatic question of choice. For example, in media accounts and interviews, Corbin Fisher, a key purveyor of the 'new jock', have promoted the level of workplace care that is extended to their models, including health insurance and the payment of college fees for students in higher education, support for charitable work and donations.[10] This reportage works in two ways: to emphasise the social responsibilities and professionalism of the company and, secondly, to foreground what might be described as the 'pro-am' status of Corbin Fisher models, who are seen under the logic of this rubric as employees, performing ostensibly for financial gain and workplace benefits. Gay-for-pay porn then becomes a rational and viable career decision for athletic and attractive college students.

The discourses that frame the performers, however, are themselves mutable and ambiguous. In quite marked contrast, whilst the studio makes no secret that it works with and actively casts straight men,[11] financial gain is never explicitly mentioned in Sean Cody promotional materials or porn content. It seems axiomatic to assume that profit is a motive for choosing to appear in porn, but Sean Cody takes pains to foreground pleasure, of a particular, vigorous and 'natural' variety, as the principle thing that encourages models to work with them. Sean Cody therefore constructs a world and set of sexual scripts revolving around carefree, harmless, amoral sexual play[12] and additionally a space for sexual curiosity and experimentation.[13]

These performers then are not 'acting the part' of the jock, as in the narrative porn that I have identified, nor are they assuming jock drag, as in previous examples. Instead, this is a meticulously constructed, and even whilst it might seem a contradiction in terms, an *emphatically naturalised* and embodied jockdom. The Sean Cody models are presented as 'real' exemplars of this 'new jock' persona and this reality is insistently foregrounded through introductory interviews and behind the scenes footage that links athletic physicality to sexual prowess.[14]

Sean Cody's performer Brandon offers an example that in many regards epitomises the 'new jock' masculinity that the studio presents. As in the previous chapter, I have not chosen this specific performer as a case study on the basis of exceptionality even though he is regarded as one of the most popular Sean Cody models and has been the subject of a mass of online comment, gossip and speculation.[15] He is, instead, singled out for attention here because he typifies the essence of this specific 'new jock' masculinity and functions as a metonym for the values of the studio. The breathless prose of the copy on his profile page at the site, telling us that 'no one defines summer perfection like Brandon' and emphasising his pansexual appeal – 'a guy that can make anyone want to sleep with him just by looking at them' – accompanied by a picture (dating back to 2011) of a young, bare-chested and smiling Brandon in track shorts in a meadow-like rural setting, sets a very clear tone. His body conforms to the Western aesthetic criteria established, by using the terms 'beauty' and 'perfection'. He has an athletic, muscular physique and is conventionally handsome with a clear complexion and an open, fresh-faced appearance. His developed musculature, especially the musculature of his highly developed chest, is a particular focus of fan appreciation. He perhaps has what is often described disparagingly in the US as a 'corn-fed' appearance;

he is certainly unaffected, neither primped not pierced nor tattooed. He has none of the signifiers of a narcissistic sexualised masculinity and like almost all Sean Cody models he has clearly been cast because of this apparent lack of contrivance. Brandon is evidently sporty (an axiom of jockdom) and this is a distinctively American version of sportiness associated with boundless energy, jocularity and good humour.[16] Far from the comparable stereotypes of the inarticulate British footballer, or the surly and obsessively focused professional athlete, Brandon represents a genial and playful 'new jock' who enjoys laughter and horseplay, summoning up the discourses of carefree fun sex associated with youth as discussed in the previous chapter. The video *Brandon and David: Bareback*, for example, opens with the two performers showering and playing suggestively with a can of shaving foam.[17] In the video *Brandon and Dean: Bareback* the performers go water-skiing and spend time discussing the most effective techniques for staying afloat, as a prelude to the sexual play that ensues.[18] Brandon's sexual performances are also marked by this sense of play and a comfort in his own body and physicality. The rhetoric of the sex sequences strives to create an impression that the sexual encounters between the performers are largely impromptu rather than blocked and choreographed. In the scene *Coner and Brandon: Bareback*, sex begins in the shower and moves by way of an edit to one of several lounge settings that are used across all Sean Cody videos.[19] The camera is mobile, in part to remind viewers that we are to understand that Cody himself has orchestrated and is now filming this encounter, sharing his own sexual tastes for young, straight jocks with his audience, and secondly, to foreground the authenticity of the passion and energy of the sexual play. Brandon's performance is about the manifest and enthusiastic demonstration of sexual excitement and the scene involves gymnastic positions and multiple climaxes from both performers. The video ends with Coner and Brandon in the gym engaged in a post-coital workout, joking about Coner's ability to fellate himself. Whilst Brandon has famously refused to be fucked in videos, his performances are not, as this boundary setting might suggest, about a disengaged enactment of gay sex. In fact, he performs fellatio, demonstrates no sign of squeamishness at the sight, touch or taste of another man's ejaculate, routinely allows analingus to be performed upon him and, perhaps most conspicuously, kisses his partners passionately. This especially intimate exchange is always a key feature of his performances. Indeed, Brandon's success as a Sean Cody model for over four years must in part be accounted for by his ability to so fulsomely perform his enjoyment of sex with the succession of handsome young men with whom he has been paired. What might be described as the homosocial atmosphere of collegiality and male bonding that Sean Cody takes great pains to foreground, connects, in an overt sense, to the more traditional ideas of the jock as jocular, whole-some and an 'all-round good guy'. This makes the sexual performances that emerge from these set-ups especially interesting, not merely because they depict the fantasy of the athletic, straight-identified jock engaging in 'gay' sex but also because of the specifics of the rhetoric of the scenes and par-ticularly the performance of that sex. Sean Cody has established through casting choices, through the interview segments that bookend the sex scenes and through the direction of the sex scenes themselves, a relatively distinctive house style. These are not mechanical performances of athletic sexual positions, and neither are they aggressive in tone. Instead the scenes are often notable because of the rather affectionate and intimate exchanges between the performers, akin to lovemaking between boyfriends rather than animalistic sex between hyper-sexed athletic young men. Scenes that begin with two young athletic jock types passionately kissing somehow seem startling, even unsettling, as the cliché of the straight jock feels as if it is profoundly undermined by such demonstrations of tenderness and affection. Perhaps, then, the huge popularity of Sean Cody is a result of this vision of the 'new jock' offering a fantasy for older viewers of a contem-porary masculinity that is not hidebound by the fear of physical intimacy and male affection, and for younger viewers (perhaps) it offers a utopian blueprint of a fluid, ambiguous, modern masculinity.

At this point I should emphasise that I am conscious of the temptation to overstate the importance and distinctiveness of the representations that I am discussing here, and that, even whilst I see the work of studios like Sean Cody and Corbin Fisher as providing evidence of a 'new jock', this kind of output (which in the case of Sean Cody is rigorously managed through the aesthetic vision and sexual taste of an individual) could just as easily be connected back to the work of figures from the physique photography era in the 1940s. In many regards, Cody's proprietorial impulses are very simi-lar to those of Bob Meizer, the idiosyncratic publisher of *Physique Pictorial*.

This might then suggest that rather than a 'new jock', this kind of material is actually rather regressive and provides traction to the argument that these sites are in fact heteronormative after all. The popular response to Sean Cody in particular has often been ambivalent and in some instances the site has attracted a degree of negative comment and discussion amongst bloggers, gay media and occasionally porn performers.[20] I think it would be too narrow an understanding, though, to write off this kind of material and the deployment of the straight man in gay porn in this way. Instead, I see the reservations expressed by commentators, fans and performers as an indicator of the ways in which interested parties struggle to make sense of the ambiguous and complex, contemporary representations of saturated masculinity that can be found in this material.

## The 'Fooled' Straight Man

An alternative, though increasingly common, trope that has become an especially distinctive feature of web-based gay pornography, and one that I have written about previously (Mercer, 2011), is one in which the straight man is fooled, compromised and derided in one way or another. Whilst the 'new jock' performs an unrestricted and uninhibited sexuality, material that presents the figure of the foolish straight man in gay porn constructs a straight masculinity that is rather brittle and unstable; the unreconstituted (and therefore often provincial, arcane and unsophisticated) straight man is subjected, as noted in the first chapter, to mockery, humiliation and even in some cases contempt. Whilst saturated masculinity is associated with play and fluidity, it should also be seen as a phenomenon that carries with it anxiety and ambivalence.

So in the case of the website Bait Bus, the narrative conceit is that a rapacious straight man is picked up on the street on the promise of sex with a buxom, female porn performer. The straight 'trade' is blindfolded and the female is substituted for by a gay male whom the duped straight is then persuaded to fuck for money (the so-called bait-and-switch tactic). Once the straight has performed his duties, he is unceremoniously dumped by the side of the road without payment and sometimes without his clothes.[21] Similarly, Ungloryhole uses the device of a fake booth set up in a sex shop where yet more horny straight men can be persuaded to be filmed receiving oral sex from a female through a glory hole. The 'girl' on the other side of the glory hole is always replaced with a male performer, and through an innovative use of split screen, we are encouraged to be simultaneously aroused and amused by the spectacle of the straight man's enjoyment of fellatio (based in part on his own supposed fantasy of the girl on the other side of the wall) whilst he is 'obliviously' receiving oral sex from a man.[22] The Casting Room, with the strapline 'Thousands of men want to become models. Would YOU take advantage of them?', uses the audition scenario discussed in the previous chapter as a setting to make explicit use of the implicitly exploitative nature of the power dynamics in such settings. Here men who have aspirations to become models in heterosexual porn are interviewed about their sexual histories and then instructed to display themselves in a variety of compromising, homoerotic positions, revealing their anuses and so on.[23] Sites such as Fraternity X eroticise the homoerotic overtones of the hazing rituals that are associated with membership of American university fraternity houses.[24] Here initiates are 'humiliated' by performing sex acts for the benefit of fraternity members and, as in the case of Ungloryhole, this and other comparable sites create a sexual atmosphere of voyeuristic desire and 'gross-out' dark humour. However, by far the most extreme examples of this discourse of humiliation are to be found in sites such as the notorious Straighthell, now rebranded as Breeder Fuckers (produced by the same team as The Casting Room). The ritualistic and often violent scenes of sexual degradation metered out to the 'straight' performers on this site take place because, we are told, 'they fucking deserve it'. The site advises us that:

> Straight young athletes are seized, stripped naked, bound, tormented, degraded and fucked [...] and it's all captured on video. The torment is fiendish and relentless. It's high time these straights were taken and used greedily for our own pleasure don't you think?[25]

The racist, the homophobe, the fascist, and the arrogant all get their 'comeuppance' at the sadistic hands of the abductors of Breeder Fuckers. Over the course of time, Straight Hell/Breeder Fuckers content has evolved.

When the site was first set up, the verité aesthetic of the material was scrupulously maintained. However, more recently (largely due to an increased need for legal disclaimers and protection due to the sadistic nature of the sexual play) interviews and commentary have been added to the site to make it clear that these challenging scenes of sexual abuse and degradation are actually performances acted out for an audience's consumption and not documentation of 'real' acts of abduction and sexual assault (as was previously suggested through the rhetoric of the earlier Straight Hell output). Notably, even whilst the site now acknowledges that the videos are fantasy enactments, Breeder Fuckers continue to assiduously maintain the illusion with regards to the sexual identities of the performers. So the heterosexual credentials of the performers are insistently reiterated, indeed the homosexual practices in which the models engage are sometimes positioned as 'ordeals' that might be considered as part of a macho rite of passage.[26]

Here we can see that even an apparently straightforward mockery/subversion of the signs of heteromasculinity are, once again, altogether more complex than they might seem and not least because of the ways in which these sites situate the audience in relation to the acts and the performers as depicted. The reception of this kind of pornography elicits a fluid and shifting point of view that moves beyond the mere suspension of disbelief that underpins our engagement with most fictional narrative forms. Instead, here we are encouraged to shift between accepting the 'authenticity' of sexual incidents sold on the basis of their realistic aesthetic and modes of representation at the same time as being complicit in (and tacitly acknowledging) the illusion that is presented as a reality. Fraternity X, for example, makes no secret that performers are cast through a commercial adult entertainment agency[27] and performers increasingly traverse genres, working with a range of studios from the mainstream to the marginal and the niche. This means that when a performer such as John Magnum, who regularly works for studios like Randy Blue or Hot House, appears as a gullible straight man for Bait Bus – persuaded to have gay sex and then stranded on a highway – audiences, who will have seen him many times before across a wide range of material, are both buying into and encouraged to enjoy the fantasy of the 'easily persuaded' straight man at the same time as understanding that this is a contemporary trope performed by professionals for our enjoyment. Whether we are discussing the straight man, the straight-acting gay man or straightness as a performative act, the discourse of straightness has multiple significances and is used in multiple ways in the world of gay porn and is strongly suggestive of the multivalent nature of saturated masculinity.

## A Man's Man: The Hypermasculine Gay Male

In Kimmel and Aronson's *Men and Masculinities: A Social, Cultural and Historical Encyclopedia*, Kirby Schroeder (2004) provides an albeit brief summary of literature and also describes the ways in which the term hypermasculinity has been used in scholarship:

> *Hypermasculinity* describe[s] 'an exaggerated ideal of manhood linked mythically and practically to the role of the warrior' [...].
>
> Hypermasculinity refers to sets of behaviors and beliefs characterized by unusually highly developed masculine forms as defined by existing cultural values.
> What is hypermasculine, then, is always hyper*not*-feminine.
> (2004:418)

This orthodox definition of hypermasculinity is useful as a starting point in the consideration of the figure of the hypermasculine gay male in porn, but the summary that Schroeder provides, which is largely designed to summarise the ways in which heterosexual hypermasculinity is expressed, is perhaps too limiting and too much of a simplification to describe the avowedly homosexual masculinities that I am referring to when using this term. It's also important to clarify at this point that the figure of the straight man or even the 'straight acting' gay man are neither synonymous with nor do they often have a close relation to the idea of hypermasculinity in gay porn. On the contrary, as already indicated in this chapter, the straight man in gay porn often tends to be an articulation of a new, metrosexual, masculinity, a figure who might be popularly described as 'comfortable with his sexuality' rather, than the unreconstituted, monolithic figure of the 'real man'.

Instead, hypermasculinity is routinely and emphatically associated with a homosexual identity and homosexual practice in gay porn. In this context, then, it's rather misleading to read gay hypermasculinity as merely being about a phobic disavowal of the feminine (even whilst this is a tempting conclusion to draw). I would argue instead that it's more meaningful to focus on what hypermasculinity *is* rather than what it *isn't* in gay porn, and that is an emphatic and hyperbolic amplification and eroticisation of the masculine at its most axiomatic. Varda Burstyn (1999:151) draws a parallel between the hypermasculinity of competitive body building and porn, which are both about providing 'an influential source of masculine sexual ideals', and these comments, I think, make an important connection. Hypermasculinity in gay porn is about the construction of the masculine as extreme and excessive: the hypermasculine gay man as resolutely macho, hypertrophic and hypervirile, as, in essence, a 'fucking machine'.[28]

Additionally, we should note that this is not a new (or even an especially recent) development in the sexual lexicon of gay porn. On the contrary, the hypermasculine gay man is a figure whose signification is closely connected to the gay liberation movement and to the emergence of a gay macho identity during the late years of the 20th century (Luther Hillman, 2015). Martin Levine's classic study *Gay Macho: Life and Death of the Homosexual Clone* (1998) is an invaluable source here and in many respects a forerunner to Tim Dean's *Unlimited Intimacy* (2009), providing both a description of the social and cultural context in which a hypermasculine gay identity emerged, and, just as importantly, his analysis of an iconography and set of behaviours that have informed the ways in which the gay pornographic imaginary has been represented on screen in the intervening years. Levine notes that the gay clone 'was the manliest of men. He had a gym defined body [...] his physique rippled with bulging muscles. He wore blue-collar garb [...]. He "partied hard" taking recreational drugs, dancing in discos till dawn, having hot sex with strangers' (1998:7–8). Levine's ethnographical work uncovers findings that retain their currency in terms of understanding the ways in which the hypermasculine gay man is represented in gay porn and the performative specifics of that deployment. He observes, for instance, that the clones 'masculinized their sexual scripts' and 'actualized this script in their sexual activities [...] for the clone sexual activity was the primary way of validating his masculinity' (p. 92). Levine advises us that 'The script set the standard for sexual activity. Defining "hot sex" as "butch sex", it led clones to "take it like a man"' (ibid.). Furthermore he

Gay Pornography

observes that clones draw upon what he describes as 'hot rhetoric' to construct an overtly sexualised masculinity:

> Clones used butch fashion and stylization to express hotness
> [...]. Moreover this fashion was displayed in a particularly
> sexual way. Form fitting Levis and T-shirts typically hugged
> the body, revealing the contours of their genitals, buttocks and
> musculature [...]. Clones wore this clothing differently from
> heterosexual men again so there could be little doubt about
> whether someone was a heterosexual macho man or a gay
> macho man.

(p. 65)

Although the iconography of the clone was especially distinctive and belonged to a very specific moment in gay history, as we will see in the subsequent examples in this chapter, this sexualised stylisation and rhetoric continues to inform the ways in which the hypermasculine gay male is eroticised in contemporary gay porn.[29] I think, therefore, that there is perhaps an element of something akin to nostalgia in the investment in the cult of hypermasculinity. As a poster to an ATKOL discussion forum in 2015 notes:

> Aggressively virile performers are the ones who push my
> button. There's a special thrill and satisfaction I get, when
> viewing that type of man in porn. The butch factor is actu-
> ally more important to me, as to whether a star is handsome,
> muscular, or well hung [...]. I admit it might be a genera-
> tional thing. When I was young, it was constantly drilled in
> one's psyche, that homosexuality was tantamount, to weak-
> ness and effeminacy. So it was very reassuring and somewhat
> empowering, to view macho porn in the late 70s. I actually
> credit porn, with helping me become more at ease, about my
> sexuality.[30]

A range of contemporary producers specialise in hypermasculine gay male porn, ranging from the relaunched Colt and the major studios of the 1990s, in particular Titan and Raging Stallion, who have been most closely associated with eroticising this kind of masculinity. In recent years they have been joined in this marketplace by online competitors such as

Men.com, Alphamales, High Performance Men, Menover30, Men at Play, UKnakedmale, which all either specialise in, or regularly produce, videos featuring macho, muscular, tattooed and bearded performers engaging in 'manly' sex. The remit of Butch Dixon, for example, is to offer, as their promotional copy suggests, 'Big Hung Men' and the site caters to the full gamut of attributes, types and behaviours associated with gay hypermasculinity discussed in this chapter, including overdetermined muscles, bears, leather and bareback sex. This hyperbolic masculinity is succinctly summarised by Butch Dixon's sloganeering, pointing to the value invested in 'being hung' (having a large penis), which, whilst it is not an absolute prerequisite for the hypermasculine gay male, is certainly a significant benefit. Indeed, models who tend to become most closely associated with the idea of hypermasculinity tend to be those whose physicality, including their genital endowment, most emphatically speaks of the signs of hypertrophic muscularity: the bulging bicep, the swollen pectoral and the turgid penis all connected as one.

In a scene from 2011 for Butch Dixon, Ted Colunga and the idiosyncratically named U-John are paired in a scene that illustrates the qualities that constitute gay hypermasculinity and the performative characteristics that are valued according to this rubric.[31] Colunga, a Hungarian performer who has had an especially long career in porn and has been known by several names (including 'Fred Fele' in his early career),[32] is described as 'a massive bodybuilder with a huge nine-inch dick with a bulbous cock head' and U-John as 'a professional body builder and he loves showing off his hard muscled body. When he strips down to nothing, you'll be awestruck by his beautiful, uncut cock.'[33] The scene opens, in the house style of Butch Dixon, with a teaser montage of the sexual highlights of the scene that follows. Set to a throbbing electronic beat and accompanied by the sounds of sighs and hard muscles being slapped, the rapid edits and close-ups of these opening shots work collectively to produce an impression of interchangeably pulsing, muscular bodies, culminating with U-John on his back masturbating whilst repeatedly encouraging Colunga to 'Fuck me harder.' The sequence then commences with Colunga adopting body builders' flexing poses whilst U-John fondles, kisses and admires his body, working his way from Colunga's chest to his crotch in quite short order. Once the sexual play commences, the music track drops (a standard rhetorical convention) and the scene is initially conducted without words, Colunga's herculean physique being the focus of U-John (and the audience's) attention. Throughout this scene, Colunga is an impassive performer and the anal sex that follows the initial period of muscle worship, oral and then analingus, is designed to be read as robust, macho fucking rather than an intimate exchange; a type of sex divorced from emotional connections, that Levine describes as a 'depersonalized erotic encounter' (p. 92). Here Colunga (even whilst he has a putative 'star' status) represents a fantasy ideal rather than an individual personality; he is the silent, hyperpotent and hypermasculine fucking machine. By contrast, in a scene from the Michael Lucas film *Eye Contact* (dir. Michael Lucas, 2011), Dirk Caber (another especially popular and prolific performer discussed in the previous chapter) and Alessio Romero are cast as macho lovers in a film whose unifying theme is that couples invite the viewer into their bedroom to watch them have sex.[34] In this instance the rhetoric of the scene and the sexual repertoire of the performers are both designed to implicate the viewer in the action. Caber and Romero exchange glances with each other and with the implied voyeur/viewer. The mutuality of the sexual performance is signalled with both partners taking turns at oral and anal sex which is accompanied by a running paralinguistic 'commentary' of manly grunts, groans, chest slaps, affirmations and instructions. Here, as Levine observes, 'macho sex is rough, phallocentric, and uninhibited [...] [concerned with] deep throating, hard fucking and heavy tit work' (p. 93).

Any number of performers easily fit into the category of the hypermasculine gay male, including titanic body builders such as Ted Colunga or older masculine and versatile performers such as Dirk Caber. However, I would suggest that the logic of hypermasculinity is that it reaches towards extremes, and in contemporary gay porn, the epitome of this type is represented by Rocco Steele, breathlessly described in reportage as having the biggest cock in gay porn, who, in large part, represents the apotheosis of the hypermasculine gay man. An article by Mark Beische for *Vice* describes Steele (who had been crowned Mr International Escort of 2015) as 'Gravel-voiced and naturally dominant, he's covered in tattoos' and as 'a 45-year-old Ohio native with a rugged physique, a great hair cut, a law degree [...]. Oh, and a ten-inch dick'.[35] His heavily muscular physicality, his rugged features, his modishly tattooed body and extremely deep voice (as well of course as his thick and equally muscular penis) mean that he has been used by a wide range of mainstream producers as an older 'daddy' figure as well as by studios that specialise in hypermasculine performers and scenarios. Steele has also, with some degree of ease, transitioned between working on a consistent basis for bareback studios such as Treasure Island[36] and Bareback That Hole[37] and mainstream producers such as Men.com,[38] indicating, as I will note subsequently, that in gay porn the distinction between mainstream and niche practitioners has eroded considerably. This means that Steele has been cast as the fantasy daddy in videos such as the Lucio Saints scene *The Little Prince* in which he is awoken from his dreams by an aesthete Allen King who reads poetry whilst Steele sleeps, and rouses him (in more than one sense) by caressing his naked body with a red rose.[39] The ersatz, 'romantic' mise-en-scène of soft furnishings, drapes and reproduction art here only amplify the rather overpowering macho presence of Steele in contrast with the petite physicality of King. Throughout the scene, low-angle, eye-level shots that play with perspective draw attention to the size and girth of Steele's endowment, with King appearing to struggle to felate and be penetrated by him. In a rather more extreme example for Breed Me Raw, Nick Tiano is caged, on his knees, naked and masturbating, whilst he felates a mystery abductor, introduced, through framing in the first instance, as reducible to his thick, priapic penis.[40] The metonymic penis that we initially encounter is attached to a bulky and heavily muscled body that moves around the cage so that Tiano can provide oral sex from a variety of angles and then anal sex whilst the abductor groans with pleasure and encouragement. It is not until 12 minutes and 35 seconds into the scene that the camera tilts upwards from a shot of Tiano being fucked through the bars of the cage, and pulls into focus to reveal Steele as the abductor. Steele is routinely paired with younger and physically much slighter performers like Allen King, but is also cast as the 'man's man' in many videos, as in the Raging Stallion productions, *Bang On!* (dir. Steve Cruz, Bruno Bond, 2015), the group sex scene in *Clusterfuck 2* (dir. Steve Cruz, 2015) and *Guard Patrol* (dir. Bruno Bond, 2014), in which security guards sexually assault men who break into a warehouse at night. Steele's fashionably retro macho appearance, alongside his resolutely contemporary macho sexual performances, have meant that he has attracted a sufficient fan base to establish his own production company, Rocco Steele

Studio, which is promoted with the legend 'Rough, Rugged, Realness', sum-marising his appeal.[41] As the epitome of the hypermasculine gay male, the paradoxical nature of Steele's professional and 'private' persona, revealed via his porn appearances, his website and Twitterfeed and a host of inter-views – the supremely macho porn performer, sex worker, law graduate, middle-class professional, non-smoking, non-drinking, bareback sex prac-titioner – provides further evidence of the complicated ways in which con-temporary, saturated masculinity is figured.

Hypermasculinity, then, in the context of gay porn, is a discourse of mas-culinity that draws on, and can be located in, the emergence of gay liberation and one that references (and reappropriates) attenuated and exaggerated ele-ments of the iconography of macho heterosexual masculinity, recasting them in unambiguously homoerotic terms. It's a masculinity that is more inclusive than it might seem, at first appearances, and one that speaks to a wide con-stituency, perhaps especially older gay men, not least because this is a model of masculinity that very clearly places a positive emphasis on maturity as connected to and signifying both masculinity and sexual potency. This is a version of gay masculinity that I would argue reaches its zenith in the iconog-raphy of the muscle-bound 'he-man' discussed here, but also encompasses the bear subculture and the distinctive iconography found in porn that can be collected under the generic banner of kink and these are, therefore, the examples that I will use to focus the analysis in the remainder of this chapter.

## Bear Culture/Bear Porn

Bear subculture, with the figure of the stocky and hirsute gay bear at its centre that is its most vivid cultural expression, is a relatively contempo-rary development, emerging during the 1980s (Hennen, 2008; Manley, Levitt and Mosher, 2008) in part, according to Wright (1997) as a resist-ance to the highly codified organisation of clone culture and the atten-dant body fascism and sexual consumerism of that particular version of gay hypermasculinity. As Peter Hennen remarks, 'in staking their claim to gay masculinity, Bears challenge hegemonic assumptions about male sexuality by introducing what feminists have identified as an "ethic of care" into an objectified sexual culture perceived as alienating' (2008:98). Whilst the organisation of international bear events, the publication of magazines such as *BEAR* and any number of websites devoted to bear culture suggest a sense of community and a cohesive bear identity that is in large part articulated as a commitment to a celebration of masculinity writ large but also about rejecting standardised physical ideals, as Hennen again suggests,

> the very undecidability of identity is a prominent subcultural feature of the Bear community. Just what is a Bear? Responses to this question reveal a variety of answers, but almost all reference the Bear body, either in an attempt to describe what the typical Bear looks like or to refute the idea that Bears can be defined exclusively by their bodies.
>
> (p. 96)

This indeterminacy, unsurprisingly, then translates itself into the ways in which the term 'bear' is used in gay porn and the types that are presented as representative of the bear aesthetic or the values of bear culture. The most basic Google search will provide examples of specialist niche sites, such as Bear Films,[42] that cater to this market by producing or hosting 'authentic', often amateur bear porn which very often focuses on models with hairy and/or overweight bodies. There are also any number of tube sites that promote themselves as purveying bear porn, largely by recycling a mixture of amateur found footage and clips from commercial porn releases. It is, however, much harder to find bear porn that overtly or intentionally articulates a politics that is antithetical to masculinist body fascism.[43] Consequently, whilst we can note that the figure of the gay bear has become part of a broader cultural landscape relatively quickly over course of the past 15 years, the consequence of this is that specific elements of bear image/identity have been equally quickly assimilated into mainstream gay porn representations and some have just as quickly fallen by the wayside. Furthermore, even whilst bear culture was, in part at least, initially a reaction to the pervasive clone culture of the late 1970s and 1980s, the mainstreaming of the bear has resulted in the production of a gay porn bear who often, ironically, now very closely resembles the despised clone of an earlier age. This means that in the context of gay porn, the bear, like the daddy to whom he is closely related, is a hybridised hypermasculine ideal, with a relatively flexible iconography that can be deployed across a range of contexts. Hypermasculinity, the gay bear and the appeal of the 'older man' are then tethered to each other within the gay pornosphere. I have noted in a previous essay on the subject (Mercer, 2012) that mature bodies, albeit within the fairly narrowly prescribed parameters of gay hypermasculinity, are brought into view and situated as objects of desire across a range of mainstream and marginal material. Whilst this is not a new development in and of itself (the daddy, as we have already noted, is a staple of the vernacular of gay porn), material that focuses on mature bodies, desired in and of themselves, and sexual encounters between mature men has become increasingly prominent. What, for some audiences, might be regarded as this relatively positive development, is to some extent due to market demands from older men who now want to see erotic representations of men in their own age group. So for example Pantheon Productions, who own the sites Hot Older Male, Pantheon Bear and Pantheon Men, claim that their objective is to 'combat ageism in a youth-obsessed society' and:

- To celebrate the physical, intellectual, emotional and spiritual attraction of older men.
- To overcome ageism in our society.
- To provide a forum for older men and their admirers to converse and meet.
- To produce top-quality adult-entertainment that meets the needs of our niche.[44]

Just as I noted in the previous chapter that twink porn is consumed by young men who desire the bodies of their peer group, so we need to be mindful that mature men also desire other mature men and that the market for 'hot older men' constitutes in part at least a sizeable proportion of baby boomers who have grown up with, and contributed to, gay cultural life and now demand a porn that reflects their interests, bodies, sexual practices and generation. The gay porn bear then serves a range of interests and represents a contemporary vision of a gay hypermasculinity that can envision and eroticise maturity and simultaneously contains nostalgic references to previous eras and speaks to an equally various constituency. This mutability is, as already noted, a feature of contemporary saturated masculinity and it is also in the nature of the workings of porn, which is a cultural form that feeds from repurposing, reappropriation and bricolage. The term *bear* therefore becomes, in gay porn, an adjective to describe a physicality, a type or a style, rather more often than it is used to denote any affiliation to a subculture. Consequently and particularly across mainstream gay porn production, performers who fall outside of the 18-to-24 age bracket (Butch Dixon for example advertises a casting call for models between 24 and 45),[45] performers with hairy rather than smooth (or shaved) bodies and performers with mesomorphic physiques but also bodies that might be regarded as connoting maturity (solid rather than toned and gym trained, muscular, heavy set and, to use an Americanism, 'husky' bodies) make up the group most commonly nominated as bears. As I have observed in the previous chapter, this physical type is fairly routinely situated in intergenerational 'daddy' sex scenarios that effectively conflate the signifiers and iconography of the authoritative daddy figure and the hirsute, macho bear into the hybridised daddy bear. Although intergenerational play scenes are not at all uncommon, I would argue that it is in the nature of the ways in which hypermasculinity is structured and performed in gay porn that its potent essence is concentrated and amplified when the focus of sexual play, the settings, mise-en-scène and narrative framing is exclusively and emphatically (perhaps hysterically) macho in tone and orientation. So, for example, the performance style in a Butch Dixon scene between Jose Quevedo and Felipe Ferro is one in which the sexual frisson of 'man on man' action is emphasised through passionate kissing and grappling body movements. The promotional copy for the scene draws attention to the erotic values of the hybrid gay porn bear:

> Jose is a hairy, ripped stud with [...] a big dick, beard, foreskin, and great hairy body, whilst Felipe is bald, hung, ripped, mean looking, uncut and hung [...] these two rampant studs are versatile so I can watch them both as nasty tops and cock-hungry bottoms [...]. Its all nasty, slippy, spunky [...]. And when they've finished slam fucking each other's hairy, musky, raw holes it's time to blow a load all over Jose's hairy abs.

Throughout the scene both performers, who are 'handsome, hung and totally masculine', vocalise their sexual pleasure, drawing attention to their bass 'manly' voices.[46]

Butch Bear, a now defunct website and production company in opera-tion between 2004 and 2008, has left us with what might be colloquially described as a 'capsule collection' of DVD releases that, whilst not a com-prehensive list of every particularity, fairly succinctly illustrate the general style, setting, themes and tone of the bear porn that is now released by contemporary producers such as Pantheon Bear or Butch Dixon, which specialise in this genre.[47] Initially the studio focused on releasing DVDs of solo performances and compilations from especially popular models such as Blake Nolan, Eric Evans and Danny Mann (who also worked with major studios such as Titan and Raging Stallion), and Steve Parker and Clint Taylor, who were eventually to go on to appear in bareback films for Treasure Island, amongst others. However, perhaps the most significant of the models who Butch Bear was to work with was Jack Radcliffe. The sub-ject of an interview in Ron Suresha's *Bears on Bears* (2002) rather histrioni-cally entitled 'What Makes a Bear Porn Legend?', Jack Radcliffe is in many respects the paradigmatic example of what the gay bear should look like, and, as his interview with Suresha reveals, he was firmly embedded within the bear culture of the late 1980s and onwards into the early 2000s. As Les Wright notes in *The Bear Book II* (2001), Radcliffe was to become the top model for *BEAR Magazine* and performed in porn for both Brush Creek and Butch Bear (2000:lviii). Radcliffe's hairy, bulky body, muscular but without the kind of overdetermined development that was to become *de rigeur* in later years, his fuzzy and untidily natural haircut and facial hair, are all suggestive of the he-man lumberjack type, which is itself a rather particular version of 'natural' American manhood and the quintessence of the eroticised bear image. Radcliffe as the axiomatic gay bear, then, is a man who is represented in reportage, photo and video shoots and even academic accounts as sexually potent and attractive, almost in spite of him-self, appearing to pay little in the way of narcissistic attention to grooming and fashion.[48]

From 2005 Butch Bear began releasing more elaborate, feature-length productions and this small number of films describe a set of heightened fantasies that situate the bear as firmly within the hypermasculine milieu. In the first instance the bear is connected to 'manly' leisure pursuits and sports, as in *Tap Out* (dir. Steve Labutch, 2007), a wrestling-themed video, wrestling being a trope that is used routinely across gay pornography.[49]

Secondly, the bear is situated within the world of the fantasy blue-collar worker and specifically the world of the uber-masculine trucker in *Muscle Bear Hotel* (dir. Steve Labutch, 2005), *Muscle Bear Motel* (dir. Steve Labutch, 2005) and *Muscle Bear Truck Stop* (dir. Steve Labutch, 2006), all three films clearly in part referencing Joe Gage's 1970s 'Working Man Trilogy' of *Kansas City Trucking Co.* (1976), *El Paso Wrecking Company* (1978) and *L.A Tool and Die* (1979). Once again, these are routine scenarios across gay porn, from the margins to the mainstream. Finally, as illustrated in the especially lavishly marketed and produced *Cabin Fever* (dir. Steve Labutch, 2007), the bear is situated (as his epithet might suggest) in a scenario that I describe here as the 'log-cabin fantasia'. This scenario contains within it the idea of a return to nature, the rural location and the rugged epitome of masculinity represented by the lumberjack, the farm labourer or indeed the country bumpkin, and whilst this is nothing new, it is this disparate mixture of cultural and gender stereotyping, nostalgia and romanticism with which the bear is perhaps the most closely associated. Even within the context of the log-cabin fantasia, there is a wealth of variety. This ranges from the rather prosaic visions of hiking holidays and suburban retreats offered by the Pantheon release *Backwood Bears* (dir. Chris Roma, 2008), the glossy stylisation of the Colt Studio releases *Bear* (dir. Kristofer Weston, 2011) and *Fur Mountain* (dir. Kristofer Weston, 2012) and the comedic vision of the cabin retreat in *When Bears Attack* (dir. Chi Chi LaRue, 2007), in which a group of bears – including Blake Nolan, Arpad Miklos and Damien Vincetti – is tempted out to the woods (due to a misguided directorial decision perhaps performing rather more like zombies than voracious animals) by the 'scent' of sexy twink, Johnny Hazard.

I see a fundamental irony in the rather compromised ways in which the gay bear has been incorporated into the repertoire of types that populate the gay pornosphere. I would argue that there is an apparent mismatch between the supposedly 'inclusive' subcultural bear identity and its appropriation by porn producers and incorporation as part of a wider cult of hypermasculinity in gay porn. So whilst the rejection of twinkdom and the prioritisation of youth in gay culture, which was part of bear culture's development, is replaced with a positive celebration and eroticisation of maturity in bear porn, the resistance to body fascism and purported inclusivity and diversity of bear culture is replaced (and transfigured) instead with an emphasis on a rather more narrow and exclusive vision of hirsute, over-determined muscularity and hypermasculinity rather than an eroticisation of non-conventional bodies and standards of sexual desirability that, as we will see in the final chapter, have been relegated instead to the domain of 'amateur' porn.

## Aristocrats and Outlaws: 'Kink' and Bareback

There is already a wealth of productive scholarship addressing kink, covering BDSM cultures and practices (for example, Barker, 2013; Beckman, 2009; Califia, 2000; Langdridge and Barker, 2007; Newmahr, 2011; Rubin, 2011; Sullivan, 2003; Taormino, 2012). Furthermore, the politics, aesthetics and practices of bareback (including bareback porn) have become one of the major preoccupations for a sizeable number of scholars in the field of porn studies, due, in no small part, to the intervention of Tim Dean in these debates and the responses that his book *Unlimited Intimacy: Reflections on the Subculture of Barebacking* (2009) has provoked.[50] However, within the context of this study, with its focus on the ways in which masculinities are constructed in gay porn, my field of view is necessarily narrowed down to representations of sexual fantasy rather than all of the attendant debates around the cultures that produce those fantasies. My argument in this chapter, then, for the sake of economy, is twofold: that in gay porn, kink/BDSM practice is bound (appropriately figuratively) to the wider discourse of the hypermasculine gay male, and secondly, that the iconography and rhetoric of bareback porn refers to and draws on the mise-en-scène, iconography and performances of kink, but adapts and mutates kink styling for its strategic value and for the connotations of taboo and excess that it affords. Kink, perhaps more than any other subgenre of porn (gay or otherwise), is dealing with fantasy in the most vivid of terms. When Martin Barker (2014:155) proposed his five orientations of fantasy in porn (as a magnifying glass, a mirror, an emporium, a journey and another self), he could have easily argued that kink speaks, to a greater or lesser degree, to all of them. Kink summons up an arena of transgression, and a mise-en-scène and style of performance that entails an excessive 'opening up' of the body through acrobatic positions, the use of paraphernalia, sex, toys and sex acts such as fisting and sounding that require training, perseverance and endurance (qualities often ascribed as 'masculine'). So for reasons of economy, as much as any other motivating factor, in this final section of this chapter, I am establishing a heuristic dichotomy here for the sake of clarity, and that is that kink is represented as an essentially theatrical, refined, controlled and aristocratic performance of sexual play in commercial gay porn and that by contrast (and even whilst bareback porn draws on the rhetoric of kink) it is instead essentially represented and performed as concerned with sexual abandon and expressivity, qualities that are about a loss, or release, of control.

## The Leatherman

A discussion of the distinctive iconography and significances of the leatherman could easily form the basis of a book in its own right. Indeed, Peter Hennen devotes a third of *Faeries Bear and Leathermen: Men in Community Queering the Masculine* (2008) to an analysis of the status of the leatherman and, just as importantly, to the relationship between this very particular style, and to fetish and kink. As Hennen notes, these relationships are in fact not at all straightforward (2008:135). As I have already suggested, the milieu to which the leatherman belongs has been the focus of some degree of academic attention, with recent work building on the important earlier contributions of Pat Califia and Gayle Rubin, amongst others. Rubin, for example, conducted anthropological work into the gay leather scene of San Francisco, in a similar vein to Martin Levine's ethnographic study of the gay clone, mentioned earlier in this chapter. Jack Fritscher, who was for several years the editor of *Drummer* magazine, has also written extensively on the subject of gay leather fetishism.

As with the previous category of bear porn, the contemporary gay porn industry caters pretty extensively to a specialised market for kink with a wealth of sites featuring BDSM, fisting, water sports and so on. However, once again my focus here is on the ways in which kink/BDSM has become incorporated into the discourses of mainstream gay porn. This is an area in which the distinctions between the mainstream and the niche are especially hard to establish, partly as a result of the significant popular success (and high visibility) of commercial gay porn franchises such as Titan's *Fallen Angel* and *Kink* series Raging Stallion's *Sex Pack* series, Hot

House's *Skuff* and *The Urge* series, as well as the emergence of Kink.com, with its scrupulously realised fetish fantasies, catering to a range of audiences, including gay men, with subsidiary sites such as Bound Gods, Naked Kombat, Bound in Public, 30 Minutes of Torment and Butt Machine Boys.[51]

The leatherman, then, in his classic (if now rather quaint) uniform of military cap, chest harness, chaps and jockstrap, and his contemporary reimagining as the kink performer, is a version of gay hypermasculinity that regularly makes an appearance across mainstream gay porn. This is a masculinity that is often located in liminal fantasy spaces: the dungeon, the S&M club or an abstracted, imagined space that gives free rein to the imagination of the director and production team as in the stylised dungeon/fetish club sets for the Hot House productions *Sektor 9* (dir. Christian Owens, 2011) and *The Urge: Huntin' for Ass* (dir. Tony Dimarco, 2015), the Raging Stallion extravaganzas *Animus* and *Dominus* (dir. Steve Cruz and Bruno Bond, 2011) and the later release *Heretic* (dir. Bruno Bond, 2013). It is also a masculinity that signifies a set of sexual practices (usually about power play), a style of performance (usually about ritualistic and theatricalised sex) where, as Mark Thompson notes, the leatherman is a 'daring symbol of cultural transgression and personal transformation' (1991:xvi).

In comparison to the examples of gay hypermasculinity identified in this chapter so far, the leatherman is a singular figure inasmuch as his iconography is perhaps the most overtly linked to an autonomous gay identity and lifestyle and equally almost exclusively linked to a specific expression of sexual activity; the leatherman is unequivocally and unambiguously *about* sex. The very distinctive iconography of the leatherman is constructed out of a bricolage of militaristic, authoritarian and subcultural motifs. Hennen notes that 'the literature on this community reveals a general consensus that gay leather culture first emerged as a recognisable part of the queer cultural landscape in the United States in the decades following World War II' (2008:136). It certainly seems evident that this specific model of masculinity had no representational existence until the emergence of biker and leather bars during the 1950s, the appearance of biker styling and iconography in physique magazines and Tom of Finland's illustrations in these magazines in the 1950s onwards (this is an often overlooked phenomenon) and Etienne's illustrations of the early 1960s, which were, in turn, to inform the clone iconography of the post-Stonewall era. Tom of Finland in particular, creating images that Waugh describes as 'grotesquely overstated and stylised models of masculinity – muscular, active, upright, potent, square-chinned, broad-shouldered, bursting-crotched' (1996:228–30) was to articulate and epitomise this specific form of hypermasculine homoeroticism in his drawings, eliding biker iconography with militaristic motifs, effectively conflating the signification of the rebel with that of the authoritarian figure (Ramakers, 2000). The specific iconography of leather chaps, thongs, studded armbands, chest harnesses, cockrings, chains, aviator glasses and leather caps were repeatedly deployed and were to become integral components of the leatherman's signification in gay porn.

As I have already noted, saturated contemporary masculinities are not static categories or entities; they evolve and transform themselves over time and between texts according to the dictates of contemporary tastes and mores. This is perhaps best exemplified in the changing nature of the leatherman's iconography and deployment in commercial gay pornography. This change, at a straightforward level, could be identified as a historical evolution: from the conflation of fascist and biker imagery that was articulated by Tom of Finland and Etienne, during the 1950s and 1960s, to the inclusion, during the 1970s and 1980s, of leather and rubber fetishism concomitant with the emergence of an increasingly sophisticated and developed gay leather culture. This, however, would provide only a partial understanding. Leather iconography and leather themes have, since the early films of Bob Mizer, been an integral part of gay pornographic film and video. By the late 1970s to early 1980s, films such as *A Night at Halsted's* (dir. Fred Halsted, 1980) were marketed by drawing on the distinctive clone and leather iconography of biker's caps, aviator glasses and black leather. Only a few years later, the emerging Falcon Studios was to begin to draw on the iconography of the leatherman. In the cover image for *Biker's Liberty* (dir. Bill Clayton, 1982), a collection of early film loops, the Californian blond Tim Kramer adopts the leatherman's accoutrements to signify that he is the eponymous biker of the video's title as well as to suggest a particular, perhaps rather more extreme, form of sexual play. This strategy adopted by Falcon of using leather iconography to signify the potentially more extreme theme of a specific video is a technique that would be regularly deployed by any number of producers. So during the mid to late 1980s and early 1990s, performers would be depicted as adopting the prototypical leatherman iconography as a form of drag to indicate the theme of the text or as a way of indicating the sexual scenarios that would form its basis, whilst the performers were not specifically identified or marketed as leathermen *per se*, a category perhaps too specific for commercial marketing purposes and certainly, by that point, too closely linked to older, pre-AIDS sexual practices.

During the late 1990s and into the 2000s, the 'classic' leatherman iconography deployed in commercial mainstream video was to undergo something of a transformation and this neo-leatherman, refigured as what I describe here as the kink performer came fully into view. This is in many respects a reimagining of leather, foregrounding and exaggerating the masculinist focus of this particular version of hypermasculinity. Hennen notes in his research into the subcultures that inspired the iconography of gay porn that 'The vast majority of leathermen I encountered identify themselves first and foremost as men and, in some cases, men who understand themselves as actually more masculine than heterosexual men (p. 144). He also notes Daniel Harris' critique that leather had become nothing more than a style of dress and that its radical potential had been lost (p. 141). The neo-leatherman kink performer, I think, simultaneously provides traction for this argument and also offers evidence of a response to it. There is, for example, a quite markedly different nature in style, tone and casting choices between the films in Titan's *Fallen Angel* series beginning with *Fallen Angel 1* (dir. Bruce Cam and Robert Kirsch, 1997), with its cast ostensibly sporting 'classic' leatherman drag – which itself was pitched as an updating of leather-themed porn – to the altogether more stylised and exotic representations and practices of *Fallen Angel 5: Horse* (dir. Bruce Cam, 2004), a mythologically inspired fantasy with a muscle-bound cast of hyper-macho gay men. The neo-leatherman kink performer is cast, I would suggest, because he possesses the muscular physicality that is an index of gay hypermasculinity; he is often tattooed, has a shaved head, facial hair and body piercings, all elements of urban gay male style, but, at the same time, he almost always performs across a range of sub-genres. On the one hand, it's possible to see this as merely the appropriation of kink drag by performers who need to diversify their sexual and performative repertoires to sustain a career, but I think it's also possible to argue that this is further evidence of a saturated masculinity in which porn performers enact versions of hypermasculinity, at varying points playing a muscular body builder in a gym-themed scene, a macho bear in a log-cabin fantasia and a leather-and-rubber-clad kink performer in a dungeon scene.

## What Bareback Means Now

I have left bareback porn until the end of this chapter and have provided only this relatively compressed discussion largely because bareback as a practice and the eroticisation of that practice in porn has dominated discussions around gay porn in recent years, for obvious reasons. This means that there is already a wealth of research and publications on this subject that will continue to grow and that does not need revisiting here. In part I have limited discussion here because much bareback porn belongs to and continues the lineage of leather and kink, and in part because as bareback has infiltrated the mainstream, the term progressively refers increasingly to a sexual practice rather than to a distinctive iconography associated with a subculture. Notwithstanding these provisos, the material that I am referring to as bareback porn continues to matter because this is subgenre often eroticises the performance of hypermasculinity through sex acts that foreground danger, risk and abandonment. The status and prominence of bareback porn has changed pretty fundamentally between the late 2000s and mid 2010s. Whilst it was initially a relatively specialised porn niche that attracted a storm of controversy, apparently reflective of, and catering to, a marginal subculture of gay men who engage in unprotected and 'unsafe' sex, I would argue that this is no longer the case. Indeed, as Mowlabocus, Harbottle and Witzel note, bareback porn has moved from the 'margin to centre', noting that 'recent forays into bareback pornography by larger commercial studios such as Sean Cody, Corbin Fisher and Chaosmen are good examples of this "normalising" of bareback pornography, with UAI being incorporated into the existing aesthetic of these studios' (2013:525). This context of a 'mainstreaming' or 'normalizing' of bareback porn (which is perhaps symptomatic of the status of bareback practice within the wider culture) inevitably complicates a discussion of the aesthetics of bareback and the models of masculinity that bareback porn produces. For the purposes of clarity, therefore, I am making a distinction here between bareback as a *sexual practice* that has become, in recent years, part of the performative repertoire available to mainstream studios, and a distinctive *iconography, setting and rhetoric* that has become associated with a smaller group of producers who ostensibly specialize in the production of 'bareback porn'.

The culture of barebacking has inevitably provoked a great deal of discussion and this has extended to a consideration of the ways in which this culture is represented in gay porn and the associated ethical, moral, social and medical implications. Whilst he did not initiate a debate that was already well under way, Tim Dean's book *Unlimited Intimacy: Reflections on the Subculture of Barebacking* (2009), as I have already indicated, has become a foundational text on the subject. An ethnography with an extended section on bareback porn, largely, though not exclusively, focused on the work of Paul Morris of Treasure Island, Dean's work has been the subject of fairly sustained critique with scholars ranging from Linda Williams (2014) to Michael McNamara (2013) to Casey McKittrick (2010) all questioning his insistence that bareback porn can be regarded as appealing 'not to the standard rationale of fantasy for its justification but to the opposite, documentary realism' (Dean, 2009:xi).

Partly in response and as a corrective to this argument, Christien Garcia provides an extremely thorough and considered critical analysis of some of the output of Treasure Island and the pronouncements of Paul Morris, the self-styled pioneer of bareback porn. He notes that:

> Morris advocates a mode of representational authenticity. This notion of authenticity or honesty has recourse to pseudo-ethnographic axioms of the 'how gay men really have sex' variety, but also to more nuanced configurations of truth, affect, and social justice.
>
> (2013:1038)

A foregrounding of 'realism' and authenticity then is central to Morris' justification for his work and is a key feature of the representational and marketing strategies that Treasure Island deploys in a very deliberate and self-conscious manner. This encompasses an aesthetic, camera work, editing and sound that is highly suggestive of (an albeit studied) impromptu

'capturing of the moment' in one anonymous hotel room and apartment setting after another. However, I would argue that, irrespective of Morris' pro-
testations, to regard this as realism is a simplification in the first instance
and is to misunderstand what is fundamentally at stake in the kind of bareback porn for which Treasure Island has become recognised. In 1977 John
Rechy, author of the infamous novel *City of Night*, published his first non-
fiction work, *The Sexual Outlaw*. The book, described by Rechy notably as a
'documentary', has a fragmentary structure following three days and three
nights in Los Angeles' sexual underground. Through a series of 'voice overs',
the book conjures up a vivid picture of the cruising grounds and sex scenes
of metropolitan America in the mid-1970s and it is this very potent, urban
milieu peopled by macho hypersexualised gay men that not only provides
a model for the setting (implied or otherwise) for bareback porn but also
the idea of 'documentary' realism that is so prominent in the marketing
pitch and claims for seriousness of intent made by Morris. I would argue
that in Treasure Island films, something rather fantastical and heightened
takes place. The disruptive and unruly nature of hypermasculine gay sexual
drives are situated in the context of the banal, the corporate, the urban and
the everyday. So hotel chains are used as the venue for multi-participant
orgies, 'regular guys' who write to Morris in order to have their fantasies
realised and captured on screen are used sexually by hypermasculine (and
hypersexualised) bareback performers. Consequently, it can be argued that
the 'real' settings of the apartment/sex club/hotel chain operate as liminal
spaces due to their banality and anonymity and that the realist rhetoric of
the films does not capture, as Williams describes it, the 'truth of sex' but
instead describes the extraordinary, the extreme and the excessive aspects
of sexual play enacted by hypermasculine gay men who define their identities by their sexual desires. These films are then as much about sexual tran-
scendence and abandon, often through the enactment of outré or abject
sexual practices, as they are about capturing the 'real sex' that 'real' gay
men have in the privacy of their homes. This extends to the iconography
of bareback porn, which frequently draws on the visual repertoire of kink/
BDSM, but this is often much less refined in its deployment and execution and less systematic in terms of mise-en-scène. So whilst the key purveyors of pareback porn (and this subgenre extends beyond the work of
Morris and Treasure Island alone, as I will note at the end of this chapter)

draw on the elements of the rhetoric and styling of kink, the theatricality of the mise-en-scène of kink is replaced with the hotel room and the apartment, settings that oscillate deliberately between banality and sleaze and work to disrupt the generic same-ness of the 'non places' of corporate America. Bareback porn is about 'messy' abandon, about uncontrolled and 'unlimited' excess rather than refinement, control and the 'aristocratic' values of kink.

I see Treasure Island films as useful for considering the operations of porn as a mode of expression more generally. As Garcia notes, they provide a locus to call into question the fantasy/reality binarism because they act as 'a discursive site for the recitation of the fact and fiction binarism, while at same time being an important site for testing and complicating the viability of any such opposition. It is a site where the taxonomy of objective/subjective representation collapses in on itself' (ibid.). A rather dramatic example here is offered by a scene in *Bad Influence* (dir. Liam Cole, 2008), in which Tommy Haine (a slim young teenager) undergoes hypnotism and is then fucked bareback by two hypermasculine performers. The scene is described on the Treasure Island website:

> So LIAM decided to take the boy to a serious hypnotherapist. He instructed the hypnotist to plant slutty ideas in TOMMY's suggestible young mind: namely to give him an uncontrollable compulsion to take loads on camera from any cock anytime.
>
> The result? Little TOMMY submits totally to hairy muscle man CRISTIAN TORRENT and German pornstar FELIX. Both tops are twice the size of little TOMMY. The bottom is truly lost in a fuck-focussed trance while his tight hole and mindless mouth are relentlessly pounded. CRISTIAN and FELIX feed both ends of TOMMY with their throbbing cocks, finishing by squirting into his fucked-out teen ass a double-helping of daddy dick-juice.[52]

Haine's supposed 'fantasy' of being 'used' by the paradigms of gay hypermasculinity that Cristian Torrent and Felix represent, is complicated here by his autosuggestive state. In short, Haine becomes a liminal presence, both present and absent at the moment of the realisation of his fantasy. Whilst the mise-en-scène, the rhetoric and the performance style of this scene might be realised by drawing on the visual language of realism, the scene itself is presented as a hyperbolic fantasy of coercion and sexual domination. Morris has frequently demonstrated that he can provide critically engaged accounts of his practice, and in 'No Limits: Necessary Danger in Male Porn', a paper written as early as 1998, he makes a powerful case for his film making and the kinds of controversial representations that the *Bad Influence* scene, directed by his UK protégé Liam Cole, exemplifies, by arguing that they are reflective of inherent aspects of (American) masculinity and that they are an antidote to what he sees as the arid and sterile fantasies of mainstream porn that he describes as 'disconnected fantasy'.[53] It is ironic, then, that the mainstream has now assimilated bareback practice into its repertoire as well as, at least some of, the elements of the stylisation and mise-enscène of bareback porn of the variety that Morris is known for. Morris could scarcely have imagined that mainstream producers of the type that he poured so much ire upon in 1998 would adopt bareback and that the genre would grow exponentially through this kind of assimilation of outré practice into the repertoire of mainstream representation. So, for example, Michael Lucas of Lucas Entertainment, a longtime and vocal supporter of safer-sex initiatives and condom use in porn, attracted controversy when he diversified into bareback production, under the Lucas Raunch imprimatur, eschewing some of the more cinematic elements of their productions to reference the rhetoric of Treasure Island output, albeit in rather more glamorous settings, as in *Bareback Sex Fest* (dir. Adam Killian and Chris Crisco, 2014).[54] A consequence of these developments is that as bareback has become mainstreamed as a practice (though still sold as daringly novel), performers now traverse between mainstream studio work with condoms and mainstream and marginal work without condoms. In many respects this means that bareback has become a performative act that is not discernibly different to a model sporting leather drag in the manner that I described in the previous section. Indeed, it is often performers such as Adam Killian who do exactly this: *adopting* the accoutrements of kink for fetish play in one scene and then *removing* the prophylactic for 'authentic' hardcore play in another.

In conclusion, then, whilst the limited field of view of this study, focusing on the construction of masculinity in gay porn, does not allow for the kind of detailed expansion and discussion of the aesthetic patterns of bareback porn that Tim Dean and others have already started, it is important to note here that discussion of the subgenre has been dominated by a discussion of Paul Morris and Treasure Island and this has tended to imply that Treasure Island exemplifies the entirety of bareback output. I am conscious that I have been complicit in this distortion in this chapter too. This is in large part a consequence of expediency and also due to Morris' reputation and public profile as well as his rather elevated accounts of his ambitions, which suggest a seriousness of intent and vision that is less evident in the work of his contemporaries. However, producers such as Hot Desert Knights, Factory Videos and Dick Wadd, as well as new online sites such as Bareback My Hole and Fucker Mate, all position the hypermasculine gay male at the heart of their output and construct an equally compelling vision of bareback culture. The work of Dick Wadd is especially significant as the studio has consistently foregrounded the eroticisation of race and racial difference, sometimes with controversial results, as in the notorious *Nigga's Revenge* (dir. Dick Wadd, 2001) that Dean discusses in detail in *Unlimited Intimacy*. It's also notable that black masculinities are often marginalised in gay porn, represented as 'othered' through their deployment in kink porn, or indeed that racial difference itself is represented as a 'kink'. Race and ethnicity (and national identity), then, is another one of the organising axes around which masculinity is articulated in contemporary gay porn and is the subject of the next chapter.

# 5

## A World of Men: Race, Ethnicity and National Identity

*Whiteness permeates all aspects of porn as white bodies medi-*
*ate pornoscapes or, in the absence of white bodies, an assumed*
*white male viewer is often centrally positioned and catered to by*
*the producers [...]. Thus, race in porn coalesces into kink, fetish,*
*and fantasy. It is equally problematic that 'race' itself is defined by*
*anything nonwhite. This merely serves to centralize and reinforce*
*'whiteness' as a legitimate and indispensable category within por-*
*nographic mediums.*

Zeb J. Tortorici, *Queering Pornography: Desiring Youth, Race,*
*and Fantasy in Gay Porn* (2008:208)

In 1996, in what now seems like an act of some prescience, the porn pro-
ducer/director/auteur Kristen Bjorn released *A World of Men*. Filmed in five
countries, taking in the Americas, Europe and the vestiges of the Eastern
Bloc, the video produced what seemed at the time a rather idiosyncratic
vision of global gay culture that perhaps reflected the history and experiences of the director more than anything else. In this regard, *A World of*
*Men* can be regarded as akin to a contemporary psycho-geographic act,
mapping the world that Bjorn had tended to extract his distinctively handsome and athletically proportioned performers from. Consequently, rather
than a more routine focus on the recognisable 'gay capitals' of New York,

San Francisco, Paris, London, Amsterdam and Berlin, the film uses a disparate set of locations ranging from Miami (relatively predictably) but also Brazil, Puerto Rico, Hungary and Russia. The film, unsurprisingly, reproduces a set of stereotyped notions about the lifestyles and sexual predilections in each of these locales: beach volleyball in Puerto Rico; spa luxury in Miami, tropical exoticism in Recife, Brazil; smoky biker bars and pool tables in St Petersburg; and rundown industrial locations that hide lavishly appointed sex clubs in Budapest. Claire Westcott (2004) argues, in an early short essay on Kristen Bjorn, that nation and ethnicity are invoked as states of alterity in his films, which were made, at the time at least, with a largely north American (and presumably Caucasian) market in mind. Westcott, however, refers to a set of videos and to a context of production and consumption that has changed almost beyond recognition since her essay was published, and whilst her observations about the 'othering' of race and ethnicity are perhaps true of some of Bjorn's early output, I think what is most notable about A World of Men is the high degree of homogeneity in terms of the models, the scenarios and the sex that takes place in each of the far-flung locations. Retrospectively, this video might be regarded as prophetic on more than one count. For example, in a scene set in Recife, one of the largest cities in Brazil (but here represented as the location of a tropical plantation), Jose Gonzales sits in his study using a video game to construct his ideal man from a combination of faces, bodies and of course sex organs. As promotional material for the scene on the Kristen Bjorn website describes it:

> When he puts together his ideal combination, massive membered Joao Pauzao pops out of the computer screen. Jose manages to accommodate Joao's massive meat in both his mouth and his tight ass until both studs have shot many loads.[1]

Not only is A World of Men set in locations that have become rather more prominent both culturally and geopolitically in the intervening years, it also presages the technological developments that have taken place and that result in, what I see in this chapter as, a globalised gay pornography and, in turn, what I have already described in this book as an 'international style' of gay erotic representation where cultural specificity is replaced by a largely transnational model of male sexual desirability. In addition, A World of Men has provided a title that was to inspire Colin O'Neal's award-winning 'World of Men' series of DVDs (and latterly a website of the same title)[2] that also emphasised an internationalist vision of a global gay scene that was not confined to the metropolitan centres of the USA but extended to locations that ranged from the national to more specific locales, including; *Argentina* (dir. Colin O'Neal, 2008), *Australia* (dir. Colin O'Neal, 2010), *Cuba* (dir. Colin O'Neal, 2011), *Colombia* (dir. Colin O'Neal, 2009), *Lebanon* (dir. Colin O'Neal, 2006), *Serbia* (dir. Colin O'Neal, 2008), *Spain* (dir. Colin O'Neal, 2007), *Turkey* (dir. Colin O'Neal, 2009), *London* (dir. Colin O'Neal, 2006), *Miami* (dir. Colin O'Neal, 2007), *Sao Paulo* (dir. Colin O'Neal, 2006), *Edinburgh* (dir. Colin O'Neal, 2007), *Santo Domingo* (dir. Colin O'Neal, 2007) and *East Berlin* (dir. Colin O'Neal, 2007).

In this chapter, then, I consider the relationship between race, ethnicity and masculinity and the ways in which a 'national identity' is constructed in gay porn. I also return to the idea of an 'international style' introduced in Chapter 3 as another marker of saturated masculinity that transcends national, social and cultural boundaries and becomes part of a global culture of sexualised masculinity that has been facilitated by the internet.

## The Fact of Whiteness

The saturated masculinity we find in mainstream gay porn needs to be understood in terms of not just the bodies, types and identities that have been assimilated into the demotic idiom of gay porn, but also by those masculinities that are either marginalised or even excluded from mainstream representation. When we think about sexual representation, what is included and excluded, what is placed at the centre (and at the margins) maps onto wider social and cultural determinations and normative models, but nonetheless tells us a great deal about contemporary ideals of gay sexual desirability and, by inference, their obverse. The commercial gay porn that is the focus of this research clearly has an international audience, which can be evidenced through even the most basic web analytics. However, porn that is largely made in the US and Europe (or produced as a result of US and European finance) is ostensibly Anglophone, and assumes an audience that also speaks English primarily and, I would argue, is presumed for the most part to be Caucasian. The seemingly inevitable consequence of this is that the mainstream representations of gay porn and the saturated masculinities that

emerge from these representations are overwhelmingly white and furthermore ostensibly an American version of whiteness. There are both pragmatic
as well as ideological significances at play here. As I noted in Chapter 2, in
the early days of what was to become the gay pornography industry (during
the 1970s and into the 1980s), California (and San Francisco in particular)
was the principle locus of production, and as film-making practice gave way
to video production and a commercial gay porn industry started to emerge,
so the iconography, setting and themes that I have described as a demotic
idiom were formalised. During the industry's period of exponential growth,
during the mid to late 1980s, the major studios – HIS Video, Catalina and
most importantly Falcon – dominated both production and distribution of
gay pornography and the genre became axiomatically associated with selling
the ideal of the Californian, blond beach boy. This mode of representation
became the standard measurement of gay desirability (in gay porn at least)
and whilst, as I have noted, this ideal has been challenged, supplanted and
augmented by an array of types and physicalities, the commercial ideal of an
athletic, youthful and white masculinity remains dominant. Although there
have been exceptions to this rule for many years, as evidenced in the work
of Cadinot in France, Kristen Bjorn and latterly DuRoy's Bel Ami, some of
which will be discussed in this chapter, the iconography of the American gay
porn industry has remained pervasive both in its influence and reach.

This means that the saturated masculinity that I am arguing is a distinctive feature of contemporary popular culture and is manifested in the
representations of gay porn, is a phenomenon linked to the cultural and
social construction of whiteness. Richard Dyer suggests that recognising
the ubiquity and also the apparent invisibility of whiteness across culture is crucially important and I would argue that it is especially significant when looking at gendered and sexualised representations because, as
Dyer notes:

> Whites are everywhere in representation. Yet precisely because
> of this and their placing as norm they seem not to be repre-
> sented to themselves as whites [...]. At the level of racial repre-
> sentation in other words whites are not of a certain race, they're
> just the human race.
>
> (1997:3)

The privileging of whiteness, then, in gay porn as elsewhere, is systemic, institutional and articulated in representation through the 'specific techniques of exnomination, naturalization and universalization' (Gabriel, 2000:67). In the particular case of mainstream gay porn, this is clearly linked to the cultural and economic dominance of America, which Dyer regarded, writing in the late 1990s, as contributing to 'the homogenization of world culture' (ibid.) that has proceeded apace in the intervening years. The latest manifestation of this is what I will describe later on as the 'international style', where ethnic/cultural/national diversity is replaced by a hybrid transnational gay sexual identity and mode of representation.

However, whilst whiteness permeates the iconography and masculinities that gay porn produces, race and ethnicity, even as they are marginalised, are consistently eroticised. Frantz Fanon argues in the seminal *Black Skin, White Masks* that 'not only must the black man be black; he must be black in relation to the white man' (1967:110) in a chapter contentiously translated from the French, *L'expérience vécue du Noir* as 'The Fact of Blackness'. Inevitably then this chapter must engage with the ways in which men of colour, and black masculinities in particular, are incorporated into the vernacular of gay porn. This is a subject that continues to occupy something of a lacuna in scholarship in the field. Notwithstanding the important early interventions of Kobena Mercer (1991, 1993), as well as isolated examples such as a useful essay on black masculinity by Patricia Hill Collins (2006) and the comments of Zeb Tortorici (2008) that prefaced this chapter, the work of Dwight McBride (2005), who devotes a chapter to the topic, and Tim Dean, who provides an extended discussion in *Unlimited Intimacy* (2009) which also includes a pretty robust critique of McBride and that I will subsequently refer to, it seems something of an oddity that black masculinities in porn (gay or otherwise) have not been given the focused attention that they deserve.[3] In this specific setting, my intention is to lay out the issues that are at stake, conscious that this is a particular case where there is an urgent need for more sustained critical engagement, but one that I note, ironically, again falls to the margins of the scope of this study too.

# Ethnicity and the 'Black Man' in Gay Porn

I want to argue that whiteness is not just presented as a fact, as Dyer describes it as 'non-raced' (1997:2) and as an ideal, but is demonstrably positioned as the default or 'exnominated' reading position from which masculinity is to be understood in gay porn. Consequently, non-Caucasian ethnicities are represented as either what might be described as 'generic states' of alterity (as I will discuss later in this chapter) or, in particular instances, as relatively marginalised kink or niche 'interests'. This is not a surprising revelation in and of itself, as porn foregrounds and exaggerates difference in order to exploit its erotic potential. Inevitably, even taking into account the lack of critical attention given to black masculinity more broadly, there is a body of literature that explores the often problematic representations of race and ethnicity that gay porn produces and their relationships to the experiences of people of colour and wider attitudes in gay culture (and beyond) regarding race (Mercer, 1993; Nguyen, 2014; Ortiz, 1994; Tsang, 1999). Richard Fung, for example, expressed concern about the ways in which commercial gay pornography in the 1980s and 1990s prescribed a preferred viewing position and the ways in which this affects the positions and self-image of non-white viewers. He asserts that:

> Porn can be an active agent in representing *and* reproducing a sex-race status quo.
>
> (1991:159/160)

Although Fung's comments relate primarily to the representation of Asian men in gay porn, an ethnic group that has all but disappeared completely from mainstream gay porn since the 1990s, his observations have wider applicability. They are perhaps drawn into the sharpest of reliefs by the ways in which black masculinities are represented and eroticised in both mainstream gay porn and materials that might be regarded as niche. I think, then, that the construction of the fantasy figure of the 'Black Man', perhaps one of the most potent of the sexual prototypes of gay porn (and as I have noted here, a conspicuous blind spot for porn scholarship), deserves particular attention because of what this hyperbolic summoning up of black masculinity can reveal about the racialisation of gender in the pornosphere.

In the first instance, we should note the relatively low numbers of men of colour who are employed by mainstream gay porn producers. Based on a very unscientific method of scrolling through the model profiles at a sample of popular mainstream sites, out of 252 models listed at Sean Cody, only four appear to be black. For Corbin Fisher (with its comparable roster of 'college jocks'), the ratios are 10 out of 493, and even with a major company such as Men.com, which produces a diversity of output, out of 608 models listed, only 17 appear to be black.[4] This is not the same as saying that representations of black men are uncommon in gay porn at all, as whilst mainstream producers like Sean Cody and Men.com infrequently cast black performers, even the most perfunctory of surveys of the many tube sites and porn aggregators that are so ubiquitous, reveal a mass of content that is uploaded by producers and fans alike that features black models. However, even whilst these representations are far from uncommon, as Dwight McBride notes in *Why I Hate Abercrombie & Fitch* in a rare chapter on black men in gay porn, black masculinities are often confined to specialist subgenres and this is the content that tends to be uploaded to sites such as Tube8, Redtube and Xtube, which more often than not categorizes black men as a discrete, niche 'interest'. McBride identifies subgenres such as 'the all-black genre (self-explanatory), the blatino genre (films featuring black and Latino performers), and the interracial genre (films that feature black and white performers together)' (2005:102). Writing before 2005 and the expansion of the genre, McBride fails to note that bareback porn is a further subgenre in which black men tend to appear with a degree of regularity, and on websites with names such as Rawebonybreeders, Nextdoorebony, Gayblackbangers, Gaygangsta and Traphouseboys ('trap house' is urban slang for a crack den), we can see men of colour as manifestly ghettoised in every imaginable sense.[5] The critical mass of gay porn represented by this sample of titles summons up what McBride describes as 'the fetishistic world of racial blackness' that draws on 'many of the most readily imaginable stereotypes about black masculinity, these films do not disappoint viewers who bring to them a desire for a variety of black manhood closely associated with the brutish, the socially and economically disempowered (though never physically or sexually), the violent, and a fantastic insatiable animal sexuality that will fuck you tirelessly and still be ready for more' (ibid.). Tim Dean, who, as noted in the previous chapter, provides a detailed analysis of the Dick Wadd video *Nigga's Revenge* (dir. Dick Wadd, 2001) in *Unlimited Intimacy*, takes issue not only with McBride's reading of race in gay porn, but also with the premise on which his argument is based:

> The complaint that pornography traffics in stereotypes and that, in so doing, it fetishizes virtually every physical attribute or social marker seems to me entirely accurate but wholly misplaced [...] because it objects to the defining structures of pornographic representation. In asking porn to be more responsibly realistic, we forget that it functions primarily as fantasy and that something akin to stereotypes may be indispensable to fantasy's effective operation. Trying to make fantasy conform to political dictates, no matter how progressive the political principles involved, is misguided and dangerous – misguided because the unconscious remains definitively uneducable and dangerous because such an Orwellian project smacks of thought control and censorship.
>
> (2009:159–60)

Conscious of Dean's useful reminder that the function of porn is to deal in fantasy and that at least some of the sexual fantasy of porn is based on a conflation of stereotype, repetition and hyperbole, we can see, for example, how the website Flavaworks, which has attracted a degree of controversy in recent years,[6] and its subsidiaries, Cocodorm (college age 'amateurs'), Mixitupboy (interracial), Rawrodz (exclusively bareback) and Thugboy (urban black men), eroticise black masculinities in terms of their hyper-masculinity, urban and class-bound associations. McBride acutely notes that there is 'no place for the articulate, educated black gay man in the porno market' and that the black man instead is 'relegated to the margins of commerce in the gay marketplace of desire' (p. 103). It's hard to argue with McBride's diagnosis of the problem; however, his prescription for a solution is rather more debate, and Dean contests McBride's formulation fairly roundly by emphasising that porn is not in the business of producing 'positive representations', arguing that 'McBride's account of the contemporary "gay marketplace of desire" keeps stumbling over the distressing realisation that gay men's erotic desire tends to be organised around types and that the distinguishing feature of any particular type tends to be fetishized' (p. 162).

Whilst black men remain rare in mainstream commercial gay porn (and I can think of no mainstream example where two black performers are paired together, for example), this is not to say that they are completely absent. Interracial fantasies are not an uncommon feature of the mainstream's repertoire of scenarios and it is in this context that the fantasy 'Black Man' is summoned up for mass market consumption and his deployment is often, notwithstanding Dean's comments, at the very least problematic. In such cases, the interracial sex depicted almost exclusively involves a white performer (and whiteness is often emphasised physically in the most hyperbolic of terms in contrast to the dark skins of the black models) who is situated as an insatiable bottom on the receiving end of the brutish attentions of the hypermasculine black fucking machine. A particularly popular and long-lived example of this is offered by the *Black Balled* series of films that have been released over two decades, originally made by All Worlds Video (a studio that aimed to provide a diversity of ethnic representation in gay porn) and now released through Channel 1 Releasing. In the first film of the series, *Black Balled* (dir. T. J. Paris, 1995), the sports car of blond 'surfer dude' Sean Diamond breaks down in a black neighborhood. His car is taken to a mechanic's yard where Diamond sexually services ten 'hung, hot and horny' black performers in situ. The film makes much of the casting of Bam, whose status as the 'Black Man' par excellence is assured by his 13-inch endowment. The film reduces narrative and motivation to a minimum and the black performers have little in the way of agency. Instead they exist to provide an air of macho menace in the first instance and then to reveal their muscular physiques and large penises in order to give pleasure to the insatiable white power bottom.[7] This format has been repeated across all of the eight *Black Balled* films and whilst the setting may change – a limo driver taking a wrong turn in *Black Balled 2* (dir. Chi Chi LaRue, 1998), a 'tea room' cottaging scenario in *Black Balled 3: 12 Man Gangbang* (dir. Peter Goesinya, 2000), a gambling den in *Black Balled 4* (dir. Doug Jeffries, 2005), a soap opera set with an all-black crew in *Black Balled 5: Starfucker* (dir. Chi Chi LaRue, 2006), the mechanic's yard again in *Black Balled 6: Under the Hood* (dir. Chi Chi LaRue, 2008), the prison scenario in *Black Balled 7: Jail Slammed* (dir. Chi Chi LaRue, 2009) and a pool bar in *Black Balled 8: Behind the Eight Ball* (dir. Chi Chi LaRue, 2011) – the scenario remains remarkably consistent. In all of the films, with the possible exception of the rather more rarified film-set scenario of *Black Balled 5: Starfucker*, a white man strays into unfamiliar territory and arenas that are stereotypically the domain of the urban black male. This traversing of a geographic or social divide results in a (supposed) reversal of power relations: the privileged gay white male is physically and sexually overpowered by the potency of black masculinity. This overturning of social relations, however, is complicated. The black performers are almost never positioned as points of identification for the audience. Instead I think when black men are cast in these scenarios, we are ostensibly presented with the white fantasy of a sexual encounter that may be coercive, or even violent, with a 'black man' who is positioned as the axiom of hypermasculinity.[8] Dean notes, for example, in his discussion of bareback porn that the 'musculature of the African American performers, [suggests] that their whole bodies have been phallicised, engorged through weight training and what appears to be steroid use' (p. 156). This is, however, a hypermasculinity inflected by an ambiguous sexual identity that I believe is qualitatively different in many regards to the gay hypermasculinity discussed in the previous chapter, even though the 'black man' and the hypermasculine gay male are often found in the same types of porn. It is almost as if blackness itself is so over-determined in representational terms that it overshadows, perhaps even negates, any sense that there might be a simultaneously black *and* gay sexual identity. Instead performers, like Cutler X, who work for European studios such as Cazzo, the website Tim Tales and bareback studios such as Treasure Island, Raw Fuck Club and Bareback That Hole, represent the fantasy 'black man' of gay porn who is hyperpotent, hypermasculine and pansexual (or omnisexual); he *is* sex itself.[9] It is not an insignificant detail that Rocco Steele, the performer identified in the previous chapter as the epitome of gay hypermasculinity, works for the same group of producers who routinely cast Cutler X. The performances demanded from both Steele and Cutler X are about acting out a resolutely dominant and sexually predatory sexuality and in every case taking on the determinedly active 'top' role in an encounter, often paired with a younger and physically slighter man. Unlike Cutler X, Steele has been fêted by media outlets, with numerous interviews and much publicity surrounding his personal 'charisma', and he has made the transition to working with all of the major mainstream studios and establishing his own production company. Steele, then, as a white man, is positioned as having an agency that provides him with status and access in the professionalised mainstream of the pornodphere, whereas Cutler X (whose Twitter account reveals him to be an engaging and intelligent man) does not and is consequently relegated, like so many performers of colour, to the margins of bareback and kink porn, or to the arena of 'amateur' porn that I will discuss in the final chapter.

## The National and the International

Race and ethnicity inevitably intersect with questions of nationality and therefore it's important to make some mention of what I would describe as the national/regional characteristics of gay porn. As already noted, the porn industry generally and the gay porn industry specifically has often been dominated, for pragmatic as well as cultural reasons, by the ubiquity and volume of material made in the USA and distributed by American producers. The consequence of this has been that, until relatively recently, the iconography of gay porn has constructed an overwhelmingly American vision of gay life, sexuality and desirability. As Alan McKee noted in an early essay about national identity and gay porn, 'the "America" of American gay porn videos is often exnominated. The national origin of these products is so predominant and familiar that it most often vanishes, leaving only "gay porn videos"' (1999:179).

I would argue that one of the further consequences of the advent of the internet and the attendant ease of access and bifurcation of the market for gay porn has been that conditions have increasingly emerged whereby access to regionally specific porn materials (what I am describing here for the sake of simplicity as 'national' and 'international' gay porn) can flourish. This manifests itself in distinct ways, I think: first, gay porn becomes more readily available when it has a regional or national specificity and was perhaps made to speak to regional tastes and patterns of consumption, such as the significant body of material produced in the relatively established gay porn industries in Brazil and Japan, for example. Second, gay porn is produced that draws on, plays with and eroticises ethnic, racial and national stereotypes for consumption by a broader, international audience. The work of Jean Daniel Cadinot in France, for example, illustrates porn production that was expressly conceived as 'a departure from [...] the American scenarios and their too perfect models' (Martel, 2000:166) and made with an export market in mind. The distinction I am drawing here then is (an albeit heuristic one) between gay porn that is made for (and speaks to) a national market/audience and gay porn that eroticises ideas of nation and ethnicity more broadly for an assumed international market. In the rest of this chapter, I will compare 'national' gay porn and the intersections of notions of class, ethnicity and masculinity contained therein, and that are relatively parochial in nature (meaning here culturally specific), and the production of a generic idealised 'international style' of gay porn where ethnicity is hybridised for its erotic potential.

## 'National' Porn: 'Britishness', Class and Race in Europe

Gay porn made in Britain provides some interesting examples, not least because the legislative and regulatory context that prevailed in the UK until the 1990s[10] has meant that an 'indigenous' gay porn industry could not emerge in the same way that it had in comparable nations in mainland Europe, such as France or Germany. I would argue that the result of this is that even in the contemporary moment, as production in the UK continues to be largely artisanal rather than industrial, so there is a relatively unified set of themes and aesthetics that have been well established and have a lengthy cultural provenance that constitute a British gay porn aesthetic and style.

Alan McKee, for instance, writing in the late 1990s (and referring to now rather antique examples) notes that:

> much of their Britishness seems to rely on an obsession with class, and the lure of the bovver boy [...] it seems clear to me that this is a particularly *English* archetype rather than being 'British'. In these tapes I see Europeanness, and I see Englishness. I see little Britishness.
>
> (1999:179–80)

Whilst McKee's essay is old and whilst I don't agree with everything that he has to say (even based on the evidence of his source materials), he makes some especially important observations: in the first instance, that what he describes as 'despised cultural objects', may reveal something rather profound about notions of national identity in the context of globalisation and, more usefully for us here, that 'Britishness' is cast and constructed in very specific terms in gay porn that necessarily map onto wider, perennial cultural preoccupations about nation and identity that continue to this day. Drawing on McKee's remarks, then, we can see that, over 15 years later, it is still the case that gay porn made in the UK largely posits 'Britishness' as Englishness and is organised around the eroticisation of notions of social class, social role and whiteness.

Gay porn made in the UK routinely plays with the erotic charge of working-class masculinities, but in recent years this has coalesced around a very particular iteration of contemporary, urban, white, working-class masculinity: the so-called 'chav', a figure who – as Paul Johnson notes in an essay about the ways this fairly parochial social type has been eroticised by gay culture – is represented 'as a particular type of person (potentially or actually criminal, unintelligent, tasteless in every way) and as a social group (a violent, threatening rabble)' (2008:66). Though Johnson argues that the idea of 'rough trade' is a longstanding feature of gay porn more widely, the chav (initially at least) is an especially distinctive culturally and nationally specific manifestation of the 'fetishization of classed masculinity' (p. 70) that, as Brewis and Jack (2010) have noted, has become complicated as it has been appropriated as a stylistic trope by gay men in recent years. Furthermore, in the context of the phenomenon that I have described as saturated masculinity, the clear hierarchical distinctions implicit in the cultural constructions of class that the idea of rough trade, embodied by the chav, suggests, have to be problematised.

# Triga

The most prominent and longstanding purveyors of what might be described as 'chav porn' is Triga.[11] The studio started making videos that unambiguously eroticised British working-class culture and masculinities in the late 1990s with a specific focus on urban types such as the skinhead, manual labourers, the unemployed and socially excluded (so-called scallys) and in more recent years the chav figure.

In contrast to the view expressed by Paul Johnson, I think Triga's chav porn is doing something more complex than merely eroticising the chav as an alterity object for the desiring gaze of gay men who are in turn constructed as middle-class consumers. Instead, I would argue that what is interesting here is how a version of white working-class masculinity is produced as an object of erotic investment for viewers that is culturally very specific (and would be read as such by a British audience) *irrespective* of their class origin. My argument here is, in fact, that material like that produced by Triga is not just created for middle-class 'slumming' or for the fantasy of rough trade. On the contrary, I argue that Triga is making what I see as an 'indigenous' gay porn with a mode of address that illustrates that it is intended first for a local market, and that is, in part at least, intended to appeal to an audience who recognises (and perhaps belongs to) the same social and class origin as the masculinities that are represented. Furthermore, I see the sexualisation of the chav – the 'White Van Man', the football player and the skinhead that Triga trades in – as a further indicator of the condition of saturated masculinity, where ostensibly banal and everyday white working-class masculinities can become a site of erotic investment. The cultural specificity of Triga's mode of address and the masculinities that they present for erotic consumption is evidenced both through their online marketing strategies and in the content of their films.

The Triga website for example articulates a very particular, class-bound notion of Englishness. This is effectively realised through a set of formal, stylistic and aesthetic decisions that have been made in the design of the web pages that promote Triga and their products. The site deploys a visual design that self-consciously references the aesthetics of a British tabloid newspaper and in particular the online versions of both the *Sun* and the *Daily Mirror*. The Union Jack is recurrently used as a background design motif and the site's palette is largely red, white and blue. Hypocorrected and vernacular English are consistently used in promotional copy to conjure up a stridently white working-class masculine 'voice'. For example, a revolving banner advertising the latest downloadable video releases instructs consumers to 'get ur swag out ur bags lads' in order to download the release *Theivin' Robbin' Bastards* (dir. James Carlyle, 2014)[12] or that 'any hole's a goal' for the release *Saturday Nite Special* (dir. Anon, 2014),[13] which we are

**158**

advised is a 'A Fuckin' Dirty Northern Cunt Production.' This particular film epitomises the themes, aesthetic patterns and discourses of masculinity at stake in the entirety of Triga's output. Located in an unspecified urban domestic setting, which is the living-room of what most British viewers would assume to be a council flat, a group of men in their mid to late 20s congregate for an evening's recreational drinking and straight-porn viewing. An inflatable sex doll 'named' Angela is produced in part to signal the putative heterosexuality of the participants, and perhaps more importantly, as the pretext for the sexual play to move from the screen to the living-room. The sexual shenanigans (which are presented as largely a breaking down of sexual inhibitions as a result of copious alcohol consumption) escalate from rowdy horseplay to oral and anal sex, spanking and watersports. The video's location and impromptu quality are designed to ensure that the resultant staged orgy looks instead like the kind of amateur material available on tube sites that I will discuss in the final chapter. The performers are cast on the basis that they conform to the social and class types that Triga specialises in, dressing and looking as if they belong to this working-class milieu. The performers do not possess the kinds of gym-trained and sculpted bodies that have become the gay porn standard. Instead they have pale, loose, untoned and recognisably 'average' physicalities. They are not handsome nor studiously groomed in their appearance. In fact, they are not idealised physical examplars in any sense. In no respect is this a hyperbolic summoning up of the over-determined hypermasculinity discussed in the previous chapter. Instead, this is porn concerned with what I would describe as a banal commonplace physicality and an everyday working-class English masculinity. Similarly, the sexual performances are notably absent of the exaggerated and excessive register of bareback porn, or the sexual gymnastics that are typical of mainstream US productions. By contrast the sex is performed in a manner that seems matter of fact, in a manner that suggests a degree of detachment that approaches boredom in some instances, and certainly aims to be 'realistic' in its lack of finesse and performative polish. I will subsequently discuss the relatively complex category of amateur gay porn, but at this stage I would describe Triga's output in terms of aesthetics, themes and performances as 'amateur style' porn, or as an example of the phenomenon that Chapter 6 will identify as 'symbolic amateurism'. The popularity of Triga, and a wider context in which the iconography of working-class masculinities has become assimilated into the stylistic vocabulary of gay men, has provided the conditions under which a plethora of websites can emerge that trade in the erotic charge of white, working-class Englishness, ranging from sites such as Hardbritlads,[14] which focus on younger models and in many respects are nothing more than British versions of the ubiquitous US sites such as Nextdoormale, to UKnakedmen, which, with much higher production values and by casting porn professionals, has also drawn on similar class-based notions of Englishness.[15] I am of course conscious here that whilst I am suggesting that Triga films represent an indigenous, 'national' gay porn, the sexualised white working-class milieu that the studio produces is not unique to either this particular studio or to the UK. For example, so called 'trailer trash' have routinely been presented as figures of desire in American porn. In Germany, Kallamacka[16] and to a lesser degree in France Eric Videos[17] and Jalif Studio in Spain,[18] draw on a similar vernacular to produce equally nationally distinctive, class-bound notions of culturally specific and largely urban masculinities.

Although the 'national' gay porn of the UK constructs Englishness as almost entirely white, and (to a greater or lesser degree) this is also true in the output of similar indigenous producers in Germany, the French case is productively (perhaps surprisingly) different. For example, in what I would see as the 'national' porn of France, in particular, a range of ethnicities is presented by JNRC for consumption,[19] and the residents of the deprived *banlieues* of Paris, and comparable locations often associated with urban social issues, are eroticised by Citébeur.[20] In the context of this material, which also has a very distinctively French flavour, the question of race/ethnicity, which is complicated (as the designation *'beur'* is a French colloquialism that describes French-born men of Arabic and African origin), looms as large as class. In his book on French queer cinema, Nick Rees-Roberts sees Citébeur as reproducing negative stereotypes of the 'garçon Arabe':

> The Citébeur performers parody all the trappings of lower-class masculinity (particularly sports such as kick-boxing – unlike affluent gym queens, these boys cannot pay through the nose for a fit body) and channel them into a package of sexual fantasies by developing their bodies as merchandise.
>
> (2008:19)

Whilst Rees-Roberts regards Citébeur's construction of a sexualised *'beur'* identity as ostensibly racist, Evangelos Tziallas (2015) in an essay on Middle Eastern masculinity in gay porn sees the kinds of representations that the studio offers as challenging and confounding the simplistic production of stereotypes that McBride and others tend to see in gay porn. In his essay, Tziallas points, in particular, to the success of the French porn star François Sagat and his adoption (as a Caucasian, French, gay male) of the *'beur'* iconography:

> Sagat embodies the critical potential of racial performativity, sporting a crescent moon and star tattoo on the very same back upon which he power bottoms [...]. Sagat made his video debut in *Wesh Cousin 5: Relax Man!* and crystallises Citébeur's attempts to break down stereotypes by playing a burglar who bottoms for his partner in crime. His muscular frame, masculine stature, tanned skin, beard and tattoos dissolve the threshold between 'French' and 'other,' active and passive and performing and passing. It was precisely this unique personae and physicality that landed him an invitation to California where his breakout role in *Arabesque* shot him to stardom.
>
> (2015:97)

Notwithstanding the reservations I might have about the rather overstated claim that Citébeur's articulations of urban French ethnicity provide a radical challenge to stereotyping, Tziallas points to an important development that matters outside of the context of what I see as distinctively 'national' gay porn, and that is the idea of the dissolving of thresholds that extends itself far beyond categories such as class and race. In fact, this dissolving of thresholds, characteristic of saturated masculinity, is an indicator of a wider trend across gay porn towards the production of a hybridised 'international style' of gay porn.

## An International Style

In the early 1930s, the architectural historian Alfred Barr Hitchcock and the architect Philip Johnson coined the term 'International Style' to refer to a lean, minimal, modernist architecture that transcended national and parochial stylistic idiosyncrasies. In the book *The International Style* that was to follow, they advise readers that 'this contemporary style, which exists throughout the world, is unified and inclusive, not fragmentary and contradictory like so much of the production of the first generation of Modern arhcitects' (1932:35/36). Nathan Glazer, in his work on modernism and America, observes the rigour and rationality of the International Style and notes that 'its practitioners and proponents saw the international style not as a style, to be succeeded by others, but indeed as the end of style in architecture, the conclusion of the history of architecture as style' (2007:14).

I am using the International Style of architecture with its rationality and transnational reach as a metaphor here for a variety of gay porn that has emerged since the early 2000s, and that can be described as epitomising a similarly international style. Gay porn that is typical of this now established international style is largely (but not exclusively) made outside of the US and includes the output of Bel Ami (producing idealised visions of Central and Eastern European beautiful boys), Kristen Bjorn (as the purveyor of Hispanic and Mediterranean ideals) and also Lucas Kazan, who operates in a similar territory (a focus on Italian men),[21] and to a lesser degree the work of Michael Lucas, which is made in the US, and also falls into this category.[22] I am also thinking here about the British producers Men at Play, who have marketed themselves as catering to a niche interest in tailoring and uniform fetish and who have, over the past decade, produced an International Style gay porn that can be regarded as 'corporate' at several levels.

Unlike 'national' porn, which produces a distinctively regional aesthetic and set of themes and concerns, instead this is gay porn that is ostensibly concerned with the erasure of cultural and national specificity and replacing these qualities with a hybridised transnational vision of an international gay 'culture' and just as importantly a 'standard' of masculine desirability that largely transcends (or dispenses altogether with) geography, class and ethnicity. I regard this as a variety of gay porn that constitutes an (albeit unconscious) attempt to flatten out cultural, social and ethnic difference and to create a homogeneous utopian vision of gay culture and gay desire. Whilst, as I have noted elsewhere in this book, so much of the workings of porn (gay and otherwise) hinge on the eroticisation of binarisms, contrasts and differences, it is not true to say that this is a universal feature of porn. Indeed there is also an equally large body of porn that deals in the fantasy of, as Martin Barker (2014:155) notes, a journey to a 'utopian' realm populated by exemplars of a physical perfection that is uniform, idealised and 'perfected'. This drive to produce homogenous idealised visions of sexualised masculinity has surfaced throughout the short history of industrialised gay porn. I have argued, for example, that the distinctive look of mid-1980s US gay porn, and in particular the so-called Falcon 'cookie cutter' look, was motivated by precisely this utopian vision. What I think is different in this case is that what I describe as the International Style is collectively the production of a relatively unified vision (though there are differences of course) of sexualised masculinities that are non-American and that eroticise and also conflate Mediterranean, Latin American and Eastern European exemplars. I would connect the phenomenon described here to a wider set of debates and a body of literature about sex and geography in which scholars indicate, as Lynda Johnston and Robyn Longhurst point out, that 'sex is a global commodity' (2010:76) and in particular the implications of globalisation on sexuality most notably explored in John Binnie's *The Globalization of Sexuality* (2004).[23]

Nicholas Radel, for instance, writing about both cinema and porn emerging from Eastern Europe in during the 1990s, in his essay 'The Transnational Ga(y)ze', identifies issues with the circumstances that have provided the conditions for this International Style to emerge. Talking about gay porn that predates this phenomenon, he argues, somewhat prophetically, that 'the fantasy of homoerotic universalism as revealed in their international or transnational settings is directed more strongly toward an imperialistic project because, in creating gayness as a desire that transcends nationality, these movies maintain older, hierarchical discourses of gendered penetration and the imperialistic discourses of Western liberation'. And furthermore that 'seen uncritically, they may help us to evade the increasingly disturbing sense that within an affluent, global community, sex and gayness itself can be and is being commercialised by the West on an international scale' (2001:56). Radel points to something fundamental here, and whilst I would share Alan McKee's note of caution (1999) about the often reductive arguments that assume that globalisation is by definition always a problem and always results in banality and the generic in place of the 'authenticity' of the culturally specific, there is inevitably also an ambivalence that I feel about the emergence of the International Style in gay porn and the implicit production of transnational 'global' masculine ideals.

International Style gay porn is a development that has taken a relatively long time to become fully established. In the first instance, a fairly developed international market for gay porn and systems of production and distribution had to be in place before this generic variant could find an audience. Secondly, and paradoxically, I would argue that most of the producers associated with what I am describing as the International Style were in fact the very same producers who initially established their reputations and markets on the basis that they were in the business of providing a diversity of representation that was missing in mainstream (which in this case we can read as American) gay porn during the 1990s for the most part. So an international market opened up with the advent of the internet, and a concomitant market demand for a variety of gay porn results in material that is, in part, a response to the homogeneity of US commercial gay porn during the 1980s and 1990s that, ironically, has itself over time transformed into a new vernacular and produced a new set of homogenous, non-American sexualised masculinities.

This International Style has then emerged due to a quite complex range of factors that are not reducible to the vagaries of the gay porn industry alone and include the increased mobility of gay men, the wider accessibility of gay culture and its exponential growth perhaps as a result of travel and tourism. I also think that a not insignificant factor is the emergence during the 1990s of so-called 'circuit party' culture which resulted in the circulation of a specific aesthetic that in some respects is antithetical to the Northern European, or WASP, model of American masculinity and instead privileges a 'European' (and that often means a Mediterranean) physicality and sexuality: sultry, dark, hirsute. Clearly this is not the entirety of what constitutes the International Style in gay porn, as one of the most pervasive influences has been the so-called 'Europorn' phenomenon and the legion of beautiful boys discussed in Chapter 3.

## Bel Ami, Kristen Bjorn and Men at Play

The emergence of 'Europorn', which I regard as the precursor to and progenitor of the International Style, can largely be attributed to the porn director and producer William Higgins, perhaps best known for his 'discovery' of Jeff Stryker, who relocated from the USA to the Czech Republic in the early 1990s. Based in Prague, Higgins was to begin producing videos using both his own name and the pseudonym Wim Hoff, such as the wrestling video *European Military Alliance 2* (1997), *Czech is in the Male* (1998) and by forming his own production company. A combination of financial hardship for an indigenous population resulting from the collapse of the Eastern Bloc, the hard upbringing and an ostensibly rural labour force in the Czech Republic had resulted in a ready source of young men prepared to enter into either prostitution or pornography as a way of capitalising on the sudden influx of wealthy European and North American visitors to Prague. The same gene pool that was to produce a generation of successful fashion models also seemed to provide a steady succession of handsome, well-built, fresh-faced young men for porn producers. Though Higgins was to be the first gay porn producer to relocate to Prague, it was George Duroy who was to most fully capitalise on this new pool of ready-made talent with his production company Bel Ami. The early Bel Ami productions constructed a pastoral idyll of an idealised Eastern Europe, inspired by the colours and bright lighting of Western TV advertising, full of playfulness, romance and the 'naturalness' of the performers. This construction of an idyllic Eastern European Ruritania has largely disappeared now and has, instead, been replaced with a panoply of holiday resorts and luxury villas in productions such as *Rhys Jagger Is our Romantic Hero* (dir. Luke Hammill, Mart Stephens, 2015) and *Gino's Summer Adventure* (dir. Lukas Ridgeston, 2015). For instance, in *The One & Only Jerome Exupery* (dir. Luke Hammill, 2015), filmed on the Greek island of Mykonos – famed for its nude beaches and gay bars – the film's eponymous star is interviewed and asked about his views of his invented porn star name. He notes with approval that 'It sounds French […] and it's sexy.' Here the beautiful Czech boy with an invented, French-sounding stage name – who looks like any number of similarly beautiful, blond, Californian beach boys from 1970s porn loops – illustrates the extent to which ethnic and national/regional differences fold in on themselves in the construction of the gay porn performers associated with the International Style. This Bel Ami 'look', which is a determining feature of the studio's casting policy, is a clear example of the homogenous International Style, the distinctive beauty of 'unspoilt' and 'natural' Eastern European boys instead becoming a corporate style that speaks directly to values of the Bel Ami brand.

Kristen Bjorn is another of the other major exponents of International Style gay porn. Like Duroy's Bel Ami, his work has changed over time, moving from producing, as Clare Westcott observes (2004), porn that offers a diversity of ethnicities and a vision of ethnic difference figured as exotic and 'othered', as an antidote to the sameness of American porn of the late 1980s, to his contemporary output, which epitomises the International Style in its focus on the production of a sense of generic and stylistic consistency. Bjorn began his career as a porn producer by working as a layout photographer for gay magazines such as *In Touch* and *Men Magazine* whilst he was based in Brazil. In a profile in the anniversary edition of *Men Magazine* he notes that his photographs of men of colour were often rejected, as 'there was some resistance to the fact that not all of the models were white' and that furthermore, 'he was even told not to send photo sets of black models to several different magazines' (Anon., 1999:80) Frustrated by the restrictions of working with art directors in print publishing, Bjorn started to produce self-funded porn videos over which he had complete artistic control. Since the first Kristen Bjorn video release, *Tropical Heatwave*, in 1988, his work has been consistently commercially successful and has resulted in the emergence of a lavish, visual style. Bjorn has also pretty scrupulously cast performers who, to some extent, challenge the dominance of what was during the 1980s the white, blond, Californian ideal and this strategy has continued throughout his career. Over 25 years, though, the diversity of models that Bjorn was initially recognised for, has been replaced by the establishment of a standardised model of masculinity that is pervasive across his output. Just as the exotic locations that provided the backdrop for stylised sexual performances between statuesque Adonises in films like *Paradise Plantation* (dir. Kristen Bjorn, 1994), *Carnival in Rio* (dir. Kristen Bjorn, 1989) and *Island Fever* (dir. Kristen Bjorn, 1989) have given way to European cities (especially Barcelona and Madrid), in *Men in the City* (dir. Strongboli, 2015) and the *Bare to the Bone*[24] online series, so the diversity of performers has coalesced into a homogeneity that epitomises the International Style. For example, according to the Kristen Bjorn website, his most popular models of 2015 are Milos Zambo, Marco Rubi, Julio Rey, Jalil Jafar, Jared, Manuel Olveyra, James Castle and John

Rodriguez. Whilst these names speak of ethnic and national diversity, the models are extraordinarily similar in terms of looks, physique, hair colouring and endowment. Each of them is comparably handsome, similarly muscular and sculpted, alike in sultry appeal. The International Style I am describing here appears to erase the culturally specific in the production of what Radel describes as a 'homoerotic universalism' (ibid.).

The British production company Men at Play is perhaps the most appropriate point at which to conclude not just this discussion of the International Style of gay porn, but also this chapter, as in many ways their focus and their aesthetic vision is its logical conclusion.[25] Initially conceived by Andy Thomas and Adrian Wilkie as a specialist fetish site for consumers interested in men in suits and uniforms, the corporate world continues to be the primary location for the sexual scenarios that Men at Play stage.[26] The models who are cast in Men at Play scenes are clearly chosen for their ability to carry off tailoring and for their conventionally handsome good looks, with, once again, a particular focus on performers with Mediterranean looks. This fetishisation of the corporate world, populated in the sexual fantasies of Men at Play by exceptionally (and uniformly) handsome 'European' men, results in an especially meticulously realised corporate vision for the brand, which extends itself beyond the careful marketing to an equally selective choice of scenarios, settings and of course models. Performers, ranging from longstanding porn professionals such as Edu Boxer[27] and Adam Champ[28] to recent acquisitions such as the Argentinian *Big Brother* contestant Emir Boscatto,[29] are representatives of an International Style of gay porn that works at more than one level: as a flattening out of ethnic and social difference and a 'transnationalisation' of gay desire and also as representatives of a 'corporitisation' of sexualised masculinity; a saturated masculinity that not only exceeds national, social and cultural boundaries but in fact erases them.

What I have described here as the International Style of gay porn might be regarded as providing visible textual evidence that, after the expansion of the gay porn industry that has taken place over the past 20 years or so and the diversity of output and new markets that have been opened up as a result of the internet, like all industries reaching maturity, the gay porn business is now developing 'corporate' styles. It's consequently possible to argue of course that the tendency of all forms of cultural production under capitalism is towards management and control of markets and the maintenance of market share through increased homogeneity and a reduction of diversity and choice, by a process of conglomeration and concentration of ownership and also by the professionalisation and institutionalisation of industrial practices. Why then should the gay porn 'industry' be any different?

However, the (albeit short) history of gay porn has shown us that aesthetic patterns, stylistic tropes and models of masculinity are dynamic and have a cyclical development in the gay pornosphere, and as I will argue in the final chapter of this book, the emergence and blossoming of the category of the 'amateur' contributes to and complicates this dynamic in dramatic ways.

# 6

# The Celebrity, the Amateur and the Self

> With few exceptions, the public doesn't want ordinary; they
> want beautiful, handsome, etc. To quote Joan Crawford: If you
> want the girl next door, go next door! [...] Of course, men now
> have the ability to film themselves having sex – replete with
> hair on their back, a micro-penis and 'moobs' – but this doesn't
> mean the 'average person' will want to watch them.
>
> Todd Morrison, *Sexercising our Opinion on Porn* (2014:122).

It would be quite possible, in this final chapter, to argue that gay pornography is in terminal decline, in the manner of Jeffrey Escoffier, in his rather
elegiac epilogue to *Bigger Than Life* in which he informs us of 'the end of
gay hardcore films' (2009:345). Similarly Michael Stabile's nostalgic recol-
lections of a 'golden age' of porn, when large budgets and high production
values yielded huge profits, are contrasted with the 'monumental crisis'
that he believes the industry now faces.[1] Indeed, in the years following the
global recession of late 2007, there have been numerous reports that the
porn industry is struggling to remain profitable in the face of a constellation of factors.[2] In the especially apocalyptically entitled 'The Last Days
of Gay Porn', Benjamin Scuglia also claims that the gay porn industry is
at an end:

Take a good look around. The gay adult industry – or 'all-male
porn' if you prefer – as we know it, is in its last days […]. Today,
explicit pornography is background noise. A few clicks of a
computer mouse brings you absolutely anything you could possibly want for free – there is a porn movie or website or forum
for every sexual fetish under the sun. All you need is internet
access; there is no middleman, no arbiter of taste, no gatekeeper
[…]. The point and purpose of gay adult entertainment has
been irrevocably altered. Its specialised thrills are now commonplace and readily available to virtually anyone.

(2015:111–16)

Under the rubric of this kind of analysis, the professionalism of the gay
porn 'industry' is threatened by a set of issues that tend to coalesce around
'amateur' porn production. Scuglia's assessment of the industry extends far
beyond the specifics of gay porn and is such that he arrives at the rather
surprising (and dramatic) conclusion that 'we appear to have reached a
tipping point in modern culture when a pornography industry is simply
no longer needed or necessary' (p. 113). Whilst I do not accept Scuglia's
doom-laden evaluation, he (along with Escoffier, Stabile and the many
other commentators who bewail the plight of the porn industry) raises a
set of important issues that I discussed at the start of this book (usually
framed as problems in the type of commentary that these authors provide)
relating to industrial, technological, social and cultural changes that have
impacted on the status and function of porn more generally, and gay porn
specifically, in the 21st century. Whilst I acknowledge and accept the factors that these commentators point to, I would want to frame the consequences rather differently. The masculinities that gay porn produces have
a cultural influence that reach beyond the narrow confines of the gay porn
text alone and have been assimilated to a greater or lesser degree into the
wider culture. This extends to the practices of self-representation that many
men now engage in, and that involve the production of the self as an erotic
object and representations of the sexualised masculine body operating in
a contemporary economy of sexual desire. Laura Mulvey (1975) famously
talked about voyeurism and narcissism (narcissistic scopophilia, to be pre-
cise) to describe the operations of the cinematic apparatus. However, in
the contemporary pornosphere, these psychoanalytical concepts need to

be augmented by (or perhaps more meaningfully replaced with) surveil-lance and exhibitionism as frames through which to understand the ways in which the figure of the amateur and erotic representations of the self function. David Bell, for example, argues in the essay 'Surveillance is Sexy' that the eroticisation of surveillance technologies and the appropriation of a 'surveillance aesthetic' (2009:203) can be regarded as a form of resist-ance to wider controls on behaviour and freedoms. He argues that this is a productive and overtly political turn that points to a 'reflexive engage-ment with looking and being looked at (p. 211). I see the ways in which porn has increasingly become imbricated into everyday life as a result of a complex set of determinants. One consequence of this is that the porn of the everyday has risen in prominence through the emergence of the rather amorphous category of amateur porn. Amateur porn and the figure of the amateur are then positioned at the nexus of a constellation of interactions, and furthermore, who the amateur *is* and what amateur *means* is far from straightforward.

In this final chapter, I want to think about amateur gay porn and the figure of the 'amateur' and the various articulations of masculinity that this especially broadly cast terrain entails. I intend to do this by interrogating the professional/amateur distinction in gay porn. Rather than establish-ing an artificial binarism, I will note the degree of porosity between these superficially discrete categories. I focus in the first instance on the gay porn star/celebrity as the paradigmatic example of the 'professional' performer and then look at amateur porn as a paradoxical arena in which a distinc-tion between professional and amateur becomes progressively blurred and where the highly personal and the anonymous collide. In the conclusion I will look at the ways in which the masculinities that gay porn trades in have a wider resonance, through a consideration of the relations between gay porn representation, masculinity and the self.

## The Gay Porn 'Star' as 'Celebrity'

In order to discuss the meanings of the amateur in gay porn, I think it is useful to situate the amateur performer in relation to a putative opposite; the professional and the apogee of the professional gay porn performer must surely be the figure of the gay porn 'star'. This is a category that

I intend to problematise here, not least because the distinctions between the professional and the amateur in porn (as elsewhere in popular culture) have become increasingly porous.

In 2006, I wrote an essay for Sean Redmond and Su Holmes' collection *Framing Celebrity* (Mercer, 2006), in which I described the formal and aesthetic characteristics of the gay porn star. Even as I was writing the essay, the gay porn industry was in flux, and the status of the gay porn star, at the centre of an industrial firmament constructed in order to market feature-length DVD releases, was losing the purchase that it had retained ten years earlier. Indeed the stars that were my object of study in 'Seeing is Believing' were largely figures who had been in the ascendant during the previous decade (in the case of Ken Ryker) or, as in the case of Ryan Idol and Jeff Stryker respectively, had been major figures in the mid to late 1980s. I had chosen these specific performers as exemplars of gay porn stardom, conscious that the term 'gay porn star' had become an overused one, attached to any number of performers who had yet to gain what might conventionally be understood as star status. I argued that it was possible to draw a parallel between the workings of Hollywood stardom (albeit during the classical period) and the ways in which gay porn stars were constructed. Implicit in this argument is the assertion that stardom is the product of a specific set of industrial determinations and is a mechanism that is deployed in order to manage markets; that stars can be used to differentiate between competing studios, to demarcate the style and tone of a film, are used as a mechanism to ensure brand loyalty, to develop audiences and also that they provide the conditions in which a system of contract players as well as an ancillary industry of agents, casting directors, talent scouts and bookers can flourish. Furthermore, I argued that gay porn stars typified a very specific iteration of gay masculinity and worked as axioms for the values of the industry at that moment with an emphasis on youth, health and athleticism. I noted that the constructed nature of gay porn stardom was not shrouded in discourses of 'charisma and 'authenticity'; on the contrary I argued that 'the processes by which the star is constructed appear transparent' (p. 150) and that this was fundamentally different to Hollywood stardom. My core assertion was that, as the gay porn star had to embody a set of artificial and unrealistic ideals of masculinity, in fact the less 'authentic' and the less 'charismatic' they were, the better. This seemed like an idea that worked at the time to describe the porn stars of the 1980s and 1990s (Jeff Stryker, Rex Chandler, Ryan Idol, Ken Ryker and their imitators and followers) as well as the remaining vestiges of the industry and star system in the early 2000s. However, I want to now suggest that some years later, this model is no longer especially useful to discuss the status and function of the so-called 'gay porn star' in a contemporary context.[3] The term 'gay porn star' is now ubiquitous and, like so many of the words that circulate in the pornosphere, is used loosely, and it is this very ubiquity and fluidity that alters the term's meaning and utility, referring, as it is, to a different (and very much broader) category of performer than it did for example in the 1980s. In the contemporary moment, 'gay porn star' tends to denote any performer who chooses to adopt the nomination as an indicator of their profession in the first place, as well as referring to those performers who are positioned as celebrities as a result of media coverage and fan commentary. Repositioning gay porn stardom as a form of celebrity is a productive way into thinking about the proliferation of masculinities that the gay porn star can now embody, and just as importantly the shift in the framing of the gay porn star away from discourses of exceptionality (uniqueness, 'star quality', 'talent') that I always regarded as problematic, towards accessibility, the ordinary and the 'authentic'. The gay porn star of the 1980s and 1990s, for instance, was almost inevitably an athletically built and exceptionally endowed model of hegemonic masculinity, not least because the term was attributed to individual performers on the basis of their ability to embody these values. Now a range of performers fit the celebrity bill, and furthermore the gay porn 'star' is enmeshed within celebrity culture.[4] The gamine Brent Corrigan, Pierre Fitch or Jake Bass; the muscular and conventionally handsome Paddy O'Brien or Darius Ferdinand; the idiosyncratic Colby Keller and François Sagat and even the bald, tattooed and pierced FTM performer Buck Angel (the so-called 'man with a pussy') are all regarded as prominent gay porn stars/celebrities. Just as the condition that I describe as saturated masculinity means that masculinity is freighted with multiple significances, so gay porn stardom, conflating celebrity, professionalism and presentation/reinvention of the self is saturated with meaning within popular culture.

**173**

# The Discourses of Gay Porn Celebrity

A range of discourses that circulates through a panoply of paratextual materials – including interviews, articles, Twitter feeds and blogs, discussion
fora as well as documentary films – frames the gay porn star as a celebrity
who will be all too familiar to readers as the ways in which celebrity discourse is articulated more generally: professionalism, ordinariness, damage and celebrity as a means of self-expression/actualisation. Paradoxically,
as we will note in the second half of this chapter, many of these are either
the same (or comparable) framing devices as those that can be used to
account for, and make sense of, amateurism in gay (or indeed straight)
porn. My intention here is to identify these recurrent discursive formations
to illustrate their ambivalent and contradictory nature, which once again
maps onto the complicated ways in which masculinity is constructed and
deployed in gay porn and to illustrate that the relationship and distinction
between the professional (embodied in the gay porn star) and the non-
professional (embodied in the amateur) is mutable and porous.

# Manly Work: Professionalising Gay Porn

First, in a wealth of the commentary available online, the workaday nature
of being a porn performer is insistently emphasised: the everydayness
of the porn industry and that, first and foremost, gay porn is a form of
employment. The Chaosmen 'exclusive' Gavin Sevin, in an interview for
*Pink News*, notes:

> It's a job [...]. I mean, if there's a pay check involved you've got
> to earn it somehow, right? So it's definitely work. But I suppose
> I do enjoy it. Plus I get to travel and spend time in different cit-
> ies too, so that's good.[5]

In some settings, performers who self-identify as stars foreground the
labour involved in porn performance. Some emphasise the attendant perks
and attractions of the porn industry and just as many accounts draw attention to the shifting nature of the industry and that working as a porn actor,
even one identified as successful, is now a form of precarious labour not
attracting the same pay and opportunities that were possible prior to the

expansion in content and competition for markets brought about by the internet.[6] The documentary *I'm a Porn Star* (dir. Charlie David, 2013), originally distributed in instalments via the social media and dating platform Guyspy, establishes working in the gay porn industry as, simultaneously, a combination of mundane labour and the 'fun' of realising sexual fantasies onscreen. Organised around a series of interviews with celebrity performers, a rather contradictory set of discussions emerge around personal and professional motivations, the sexual orientations of models and attitudes to porn consumers and fans. We discover that the semi-pro rugby player Colby Jansen regards most of his fans as 'weird'. The petite Johnny Rapid likes 'rough sex' with his girlfriends and fantasises about fast cars to maintain an erection. Rapid's stereotypically heterosexual fantasies are then further complicated by the revelation that his favourite sexual partner is the muscular and extremely well-endowed Rafael Alencar, who, we discover, is not only a considerate lover but also a professional dentist. The 'stars' of *I'm a Porn Star* (Colby Jansen, Rocco Reed, Johnny Rapid and Brent Everett) illustrate that the term is now used in an altogether more fluid way than it was in previous periods. This collection of well-known industry figures does not constitute the pantheon of godlike examplars of the 1980s and 1990s, but instead is a group of familiar faces demonstrating the possibility of the democratisation of fame that celebrity offers to audiences. Gay porn performance is a job, but one with professional standards and expectations that have their own reward. In an interview for Vice, Darius Ferdynand for example notes that porn is:

> just a part of the entertainment industry, like theatre, movies, music or dance. You have to perform. It's good to have fun at work, but this is my job. I consider it a real profession. I just wanted to do my best from the first time I was approached to work in porn [...]. Some people may think it's just simply fucking, but at the end of the day there's a whole production team there working to create something that's entertaining, satisfying, impressive and meaningful to the audience.[7]

Gay porn is also repeatedly positioned as a stepping stone or even a direct route to another career, usually in the 'legitimate' entertainment industry. Consequently, many interviews and accounts emphasise that, far from a desperate attempt to achieve fame and fortune that will, inevitably, be fore-closed by an involvement in sex work, gay porn does indeed 'open doors' to the persistent, the ambitious and the professional. For example, the docu-mentary *Naked Fame* (dir. Christopher Long, 2004) follows Colton Ford (a successful performer of the late 1990s and early 2000s) as he pursues his 'true' ambition to have a singing career. Similarly, a great deal of media attention has been paid to the career of Sean Paul Lockhart, who, using the name Brent Corrigan, had an especially notable (and scandal-laden) career and was latterly to diversify into mainstream acting.[8] Similarly, Johnny Hazzard's retirement from gay porn resulted in an emergent act-ing career.[9] Perhaps one of the most surprising examples here is the case of Fredrik Eklund, profiled by the *New York Times* due to his success in Manhattan real estate, who makes no secret of his former career, working as Tag Errikson, in gay porn.[10]

## 'Real People'

Just as porn performance is positioned as a job in much media commen-tary, so the ordinariness of gay porn celebrities is also, fairly consistently, foregrounded. In an interview for Nightcharm, Colby Jansen is, once again, pictured in snapshots playing Rugby, showing off his tattoos and lounging in his garden. He is revealed, as in his interview for *I'm a Porn Star*, as a 'regular guy' who is married, plays sports, drinks and dislikes having to pay too much attention to his physical appearance or adhere to a fitness regime; in short, he is constructed in the interview as a 'real' person and also by inference a 'real man' recognisable to and accessible by his audience.[11] This picture of the gay porn celebrity as an individual with a recognisably ordi-nary life outside of the porn industry is a discourse that is repeated almost ad infinitum.[12]

The rise of social media, and the fact that many porn performers main-tain personal websites, Twitter feeds, Facebook pages, alongside profiles on escort or dating websites, mean that accessibility is a core feature of the gay porn celebrity persona and becomes part of the professional responsibility that goes along with this status. As an interviewer at Queerty notes, 'Porn stars used to be unattainable. Now fans can poke you [...] on Facebook.' The subject of the interview, Chris Porter observes:

It definitely helps build a brand and create a following. People want personality from the performers. Some viewers don't give a shit what we think or what we do, but a lot do. For some performers, though, it can be bad because it just lets everyone see how much of a mess they really are. I love connecting with my fans, the people that spend their hard-earned money on videos of me. The very least I can do is thank them and hear what they have to say. I've even become friends with some of my fans.[13]

Porter's remarks are paradoxical, of course, as he correlates ideas of authenticity and 'realness' with professionalism and the construction of a celebrity self through branding. This kind of commentary tellingly reveals the ambiguous relations between celebrity status, authenticity and self-dom. The proliferation of social media has inevitably had profound consequences for the ways in which consumers can gain access to, and make meaning out of, celebrities, and gay porn performers are no different in this regard. Social media has consequences that mean that the kind of public image management associated with stardom in the classical sense can easily be bypassed by consumers (and also by performers), resulting in a rich paratext that surrounds the gay porn celebrity in which for example romantic entanglements, on-set spats or arguments between performers can become public property and inform the ways in which individual celebrities are made sense of.[14] Indeed, so-called 'Twitter wars' have become a core strategy for many aspiring gay porn celebrities, ranging from the vaguely comic name-calling that Brent Corrigan has long been associated with[15] or the inexplicable feud between Jake Bass and Tommy Defendi over Bass' career aspirations as a DJ.[16] Corrigan, in particular, has attracted a singular level of invective from fans, with discussion fora devoted to the most personal of criticism.[17] The ire directed at Corrigan is, in no small part, due to the rather more sensational aspects of his porn career that have formed the basis of James Franco's film *King Cobra* (dir. Justin Kelly, 2016) about the murder of Bryan Kocis, the founder of Cobra Video who hired Corrigan as an underage performer at the start of his career. The sordid details of the Kocis case lead quite neatly onto another altogether different discourse that frames the gay porn celebrity.

## Celebrity Damage

The cliché that fame costs is frequently drawn on in discussion of celebrity more generally and in gay porn celebrity in particular, and the vicissitudes of living a celebrity life are marshalled fairly consistently in commentary and reportage. The orthodoxy that fame is damaging and that it also exacts a cost from those who seek it is consequently a discourse that is summoned up repetitively. In marked contrast to the rather more sunny image of the happy gay porn professional doing an 'ordinary' job of work that much media commentary constructs around the porn celebrity, narratives of shame, abuse, mental illness, drug addiction, criminality and even tragic death are still prevalent. According to the logic of this discourse, gay porn is positioned as an especially fertile site of celebrity damage: drawing already vulnerable or damaged individuals into a vortex of drug taking and risky sex and exacting a high personal and professional cost in later years from those who became involved in gay porn for whatever reasons. As Nayar notes, 'fame damage comes from the inability to understand one's celebrity status, the constant surveillance and the lack of fit between a natural tendency and one's expected role' (2009:139–40). For example, revelations of a parallel gay porn career have resulted in the dancer Jeppe Hansen's alleged removal from a prestigious Canadian dance school,[18] in the Sean Cody model Noel being expelled from high school[19] and Shawn Loftis (who performed as Colin O'Neal) being suspended and then sacked from his teaching post, only to later be reinstated after a legal appeal.[20]

The anguished revelations of the 'reformed' sex worker or realisations of the perils of porn are also recurrent tropes, as in MMA fighter Dakota Cochrane's confession that 'every time I was down there I hated it', referring to the reputed $80,000 he made performing under the name of Danny for Sean Cody.[21] Jake Genesis' surprising retirement, following a renewed commitment to his Roman Catholic faith, was an incident that provoked some degree of controversy and motivated fellow porn professional, John Magnum, to challenge what he regards as clichés concerning the exploitative nature of the porn industry.[22] This same exploitative gay porn industry is exposed in its most wretched form in the documentary *All Boys* (dir. Markku Heikkenen, 2009).

Amongst the most extreme instances of celebrity damage are those illustrated by the recurrent stories of premature deaths as a result of a range of factors not limited to drug taking and depression that came to particular prominence with the tragic suicides of Wilfried Knight and his partner Arpad Miklos.[23] Another especially dark example is provided by the tragedy, played out in large part online, of James Elliot Naughtin, the one-time Falcon exclusive 'Erik Rhodes', who struggled with mental health problems and drug abuse and kept a blog, tellingly entitled 'A Romance with Misery' (still available to view) that charted his career as a sex worker, his emotional turmoil and self-loathing.[24]

However, the discourse of fame damage also has within it the hope, for the celebrity protagonists and the audience alike, of the redemptive ending and offers the possibility for personal transformation. In an article for the Huffington Post, for example, Johnny Hazzard, now preferring his real name of Frankie Valenti, discusses the pitfalls and perils of gay porn, noting that emotional stability and making prudent choices have allowed him to have a successful longterm career as a gay porn performer. He notes that 'there are no porn stars anymore' and that hard work and groundedness (the discourses of professionalism and ordinariness) are the qualities that matter.[25]

## Performance, Transformation and Self-expression

As a corollary to the previous category, then, the final discourse of celebrity that is drawn upon in gay porn reportage and paratexts is one that revolves around porn performance as a route to (and a means of) self-expression and transformation. Since the early days of avant garde and experimental cinema there has been a relationship between homoerotic film, gay porn and art performance,[26] and these connections persist, evidenced in the ways in which the public image of a group of a diverse group of porn celebrities is constructed. For instance, the one-time Titan Exclusive François Sagat, now largely retired from commercial gay porn, has incrementally reinvented himself through a succession of acting and modelling jobs, including the lead role in *L.A. Zombie* (dir. Bruce la Bruce, 2010) as a performance artist, fashion designer and muse. His enigmatic persona, distinctive iconography and reputation as an idiosyncratic porn celebrity is such that he was the subject of a 'documentary', *Sagat* (dir. Jerome Oliviera and Pascal Roche 2011), that was screened as part of a retrospective devoted to him at New York's Museum of Art and Design in 2011.[27] There are precedents here, naturally enough, and one of the progenitors of this exotic persona, poised at the brink between the worlds of art and porn, must surely be Peter Berlin.[28]

In a rather different vein, both Colby Keller (who is also an artist) and Dale Cooper have been associated with contemporary 'hipster' aesthetics and attitudes.[29] Both performers have talked, at length and with some degree of eloquence, about how gay porn performance connects to their creative work (in the case of Keller and his popular blog, Big Shoe Diaries)[30] and to perhaps more personal projects relating to reinvention of, or playing with, identity. Dale Cooper, for instance, talks about the performative qualities of gay porn in a very intelligent and reflective manner and connects it to an idea of 'celebrity' that he sees as inherently illusory:

> I think intrinsic to the idea of being a porn performer and having an online persona is there is a lot of performance acting and performing going on even if I'm away from the camera [...]. With Dale Cooper, and again, that's part of the performance aspect, I have this opportunity to be this weird pseudo-celebrity – even using the word celebrity is ridiculous![31]

Cooper notes that in his onscreen performances and online interactions with audiences, the distinctions between the celebrity and the audience (or indeed the amateur) are in fact mutable and indeterminate and essentially performative. The contemporary gay porn star/celebrity is, then, distinguished by a breaking through or rupturing of the industrial processes that were, in previous years, used to market and manage access to gay porn stars. Their celebrity status is now conferred instead by their facility to present themselves as having agency, a degree of self-determination and a defiant selfhood.

## The Amateur

I have left discussion of the amateur and amateurism until the end of this book for several reasons but primarily because, surprisingly, given the entirely unambiguous mode of address that is implied by the term, it is perhaps the most amorphous and ill defined of categories of gay porn. Porn more widely, and gay porn in particular, is an especially rich seam of cultural production to mine in order to think through some of the debates that have emerged around the domain of amateurism studied in the field of cultural studies in recent years (Stebbins, 1979, 2004, 2006; Leadbeater and Miller, 2004, 2010). 'Amateur' is relentlessly used as a marketing tool across gay porn to variously describe specific types of models, types of settings, modes of production, distribution and consumption and it is in its ubiquity that its problem lies: what do we mean when we refer to amateur porn and how useful is the term 'amateur' beyond the semantics of a marketing keyword phrase? As Maria Pini notes, the issues at stake are considerable:

> The notion of 'amateurism' therefore operates at several different levels within the production of porn. Professionally produced 'amateur' porn is generally produced by the commercial porn industry, which has access to a range of marketing and distribution channels. It is also possible to identify *independent* porn, which is produced outside of this system and is generally available only by mail order through a catalogue or website, and *alternative* porn, which typically caters to specialised tastes (including those of female consumers) that are poorly served by the mainstream industry [...]. Truly 'amateur' porn would then be material produced not for profit, by individuals working on their own behalf; and if it is circulated at all, this happens within networks of friends or acquaintances. Yet despite these labels, distinct differences are very difficult to identify. Many producers of such material themselves disagree on definitions, motivations, sexual or political agendas, and so forth. In this context, 'amateurism' is a flexible and ambiguous quality, whose significance is open to a considerable degree of negotiation.
>
> (2009:175–6)

Federico Zecca, in an especially useful essay, also indicates the heterogeneous nature of amateur porn and similarly argues that reducing discussion of the category to artisanal conditions of production and non-professional performers is 'too restrictive to account for the wide variety of materials that are labelled as amateur pornography'; furthermore, and importantly, he notes that amateur is a catch-all term that 'gathers together practices and

texts that are very different to each other and to a certain extent mutu-
ally contradictory' (2014:321–2).[32] Zecca constructs a typology of amateur porn encompassing 'home movies' (the conventional domain of the
amateur) and, drawing on Leadbeater and Miller (2004), 'pro-am' productions. In particular, Zecca identifies, referencing Esch and Mayer (2007),
the category of 'corporate amateur porn', a ubiquitous and yet largely overlooked category in discussion of amateur porn production that he defines
as '(pseudo) amateur porn directly produced by porn companies through
industrial processes' (p. 331). By way of an illustration, a very large proportion of the material that has been the subject of discussion in this book
is explicitly marketed as 'amateur porn' or featuring 'amateur guys' (often
'amateur straight guys'); however, it would be hard to argue that Sean
Cody, for instance, a site that has from its inception made the claim to
work with amateur models, and now owned by the same porn conglomer-
ate, Mindgeek, that also owns the avowedly corporate, commercial, 'professional' producer Men.com, is a purveyor of 'amateur' gay porn. Likewise,
it is hard to make a persuasive case that the Corbin Fisher network that
includes Amateur College Men and Amateur College Sex with their glossy
styling and co-production agreement with Bel Ami, can be seen in any
meaningful sense as 'amateur' studios, employing 'amateur' performers,
drawing in any sustained way on an amateur aesthetic or providing an
alternative to commercial production. Rather these are instances of the
type of production that Zecca sees as 'corporate amateur porn' and can
also been seen as examples of what Caroline Hamilton has very usefully
defined as symbolic amateurism:

> one of the increasingly common phenomena in the present
> media landscape [...] *symbolic* amateurism [...] is adopting
> the pose of the amateur even while inhabiting the sphere of the
> professional.
>
> (2013:182)

The exponential proliferation of 'amateur' porn sites, the emergence of
symbolic amateurism in the porn industry and the strategic marketing
deployment of 'amateur' as a keyword perhaps maps onto the wider popularity of 'reality' broadcasting formats and a fetishisation of the 'real' across
the media. In porn, the promise that amateurism extends to audiences lies

in what Paasonen describes as 'complex and yet dualistic notions' (2011:85) that are positioned in relation and as an alternative to a supposedly inferior commercialism. The real vs the faked, the natural vs the artificial, the impromptu vs the staged and the attainable (the recognisable, ordinary body) vs the unattainable (the idealised, fantasy 'pornified' body) – these dualities are played out in gay porn that hails itself as 'amateur', as are the variously mutable distinctions between the home made, the pro-am and the symbolic amateurism of commercial gay porn, and this is reflected in the aesthetics and rhetoric, the tropes of 'amateur' porn and the masculinities and performances of masculinity that these texts produce. I will use these three regimes (aesthetics, rhetoric and performance) to organise my discussion of amateur gay porn in this chapter. Inevitably, given the sheer volume of material at my disposal, once again my field of view for this final section will out of necessity be narrow and selective, indicative of recurrent themes and trends and the way in which they situate and construct the figure of authentic 'real' masculinities that subsequent scholars may well choose to expand and develop. Readers will, naturally enough, be able to connect this discussion to much of the material that I have used to frame my analysis of the contemporary condition of saturated masculinity elsewhere in the previous chapters of this book.

## Amateur Aesthetics, Amateur Tropes, Amateur Rhetoric

Lurid Digs,[33] conceived as a comedy supplement by the publisher of the gay website Nightcharm, has attracted a devoted following, including such luminaries as John Waters (unsurprisingly) and David Sedaris, by providing a camply acerbic analysis of nude photographs, found on the web, made presumably for the purpose of online dating. On the site, a team of 'design experts' critique the mise-en-scène of the photographs, focusing less on the usually failed attempts at sexual magnetism of the principle subjects (i.e. the nude 'models') but instead on the composition of the images and the interior design of the domestic spaces that act as the setting for these often comic (and sometimes wretched) displays of compromised masculine virility. The humour that is derived from these images is located not just in the matter-of-fact acknowledgement that a naked man is exhibiting his tumescence in a faux rococo bedroom setting or amidst a pile of storage crates, but also that we collectively understand the generic and stylistic conventions of amateur porn imagery and that amateurism and the mise-en-scène of the amateur is located in the domestic sphere, is technically and stylistically inept: in short, that amateur porn is both domestic and provincial and that its purveyors and practitioners have appalling taste. This is a simplification, of course, for comedy purposes; however, as I have argued throughout this book, porn is a form of culture concerned with hyperbole and with stereotyping, and consequently this amateur aesthetic is one that can easily be appropriated and extends beyond the realm of the artisanal and the home made to manifest itself in pro-am and commercial amateur porn in varying ways. The specifics of the mise-en-scène of amateurism also incorporates the technicalities by which the moving image porn (that is my focus here) is captured, composed and edited, and amateur porn often exhibits a specific filmic rhetoric that speaks of non-professional levels of technical competency, impromptu capturing of the moment, extreme subjectivity in terms of point of view and narration. The rhetorical and generic tropes that amateur porn draws on, in its various manifestations, are largely familiar elsewhere across gay porn: so, the audition, solo masturbation scenes or street pick-ups that have been discussed elsewhere in this book. However, amateur porn is also positioned as the locus of some quite particular scenarios, sexual acts and types of performer. My intention here is not to provide an exhaustive list but to identify a prevalent amateur aesthetic and rhetoric and provide a few brief examples of prominent practices and scenarios most often associated with the category.

Bareback porn, for example, as distinct from the mainstreaming of representations of bareback practice that I discussed in chapter 4, continues to be closely associated with amateur performers, and the rhetoric of amateurism lies at the heart of the representational strategies that studios like Treasure Island, Hot Desert Knights, Dark Alley or Wurst Film deploy. Indeed, the principle mode of address that this kind of porn (which to a greater or lesser degree is illustrative of the category of symbolic amateurism) is concerned with is promoting the idea, in hyperbolic terms, of the representation of unmediated, 'raw' and 'real' sex acts. Treasure Island in particular position themselves as a studio that both represents amateur performers and 'real' sex acts but additionally as a facilitator for 'real' men to live out a specific fantasy. For instance, the now notorious *Dawson's 50 Load Weekend* (dir. Max Sohl, 2011) and *What I Can't See* (dir. Paul Morris, 2009) were promoted on the basis that the personal fantasies of their amateur performers were both the inspiration for the films and the reason for the intensity of the performances. Notably, the term 'amateur' is not one that the studio uses, preferring instead to insistently refer to 'real men' and 'real sex'.

Scenarios featuring 'straight' men, either merely masturbating or engaging in some level of homosexual contact, as we have already discussed at some length in this book, are also a common amateur trope. This ranges from the symbolic amateurism of Broke Straight Boys and the many equivalent sites that were the subject of chapter 4, to the popularity of sites such as Active Duty and All American Heroes in which the conceit is that American military men, usually supposedly recently returned from active duty and therefore mentally and physically hardened by the privations of military life, are prepared to earn money through filmed gay sexual encounters.[34] The site My Straight Buddy is perhaps the most vividly realised example of this variety of amateur porn, as I will subsequently illustrate. Once again military men who, through a mixture of boredom, inaction and (it seems) the encouragement of copious amounts of alcohol, are filmed using a mixture of impromptu, non-professional devices, in various states of undress and sexual contact.[35] In terms of aesthetics, rhetoric and performance, My Straight Buddy content is manifestly presented as amateur porn. The unkempt 'bachelor pad' setting of these videos and the voyeuristic rhetoric captures a domestic 'visual landscape' that is both 'mundane and cluttered' (Paasonen, 2011:98). The site features a disparate range of content, from videos that include nudity but little or no sexual content at all, to filmed sex scenes. So scenes such as 'Naked Surfers'[36] involve performers undressing and a final short masturbation scene, and 'Four Horny Marines Pt.1'[37] records nude exhibitionism and sexual horseplay using an amateurish, documentary style, whereas 'Blowjob Buddies' (dir. Anon, 2012) imitates the rhetoric and styling of pro-am sites such as Active Duty. However, 'Porch Fuck' (dir. Anon, 2013), filmed almost entirely using night vision, and consequently in grainy, unfocused monochrome for extended periods, conforms to almost none of the conventions

of the demotic idiom of commercial gay porn. At almost an hour in duration, the video has lengthy sequences of a drunk marine stumbling around
whilst being filmed in conversation. The drinking, smoking, distracted
porn viewing and conversation continues throughout a succession of lazy
attempts at oral and then anal sex with a second 'marine'. In fact, the scene
pays almost no regard to the principles of maximum visibility that Williams
sees as a precondition of porn representation. The sexual frisson (or to
use Paasonen's expression, the 'carnal resonance') of the scene emerges not
from what *can* be seen in terms of conventionally 'pornographic' visibility
but instead from the voyeuristic charge that emerges from glimpsing intimate (and not necessarily sexual) exchanges of what can only *just about* be
seen, or what we thought *we might* have seen. This then is gay porn that
relies, more than usually, on the imaginative work of the viewer.

Material that eroticises the sex trade, sex tourism and a variety of sexual
'transactions' is also manifestly the domain of the amateur and amateurism, as in the case of Czech Hunter and innumerable other amateur sites
that purport to present, largely straight, men who are prepared to perform
gay sex acts for financial reward. Jiri and Honza, the names attributed to
the owners of Czech Hunter, foreground and emphasise their own amateur
credentials and those of their models:

> We are the Czech Hunter. Pursuing boys is our hobby.
> We are tired of websites offering staged bullshit.
> We know the strategy. Czech boys do it for money!
> It's true: the difficult social situation in the Czech Republic sup-
> ports our hobby.
> We are your special Prague-guides.[38]

What might be described as 'specialist interests' are also often the domain
of the amateur and range from the exotic (sex play featuring specialist sex
toys, or extreme forms of fetish play) to the relatively prosaic and either
draw on the rhetoric of amateurism or are made and distributed under
quasi-amateur conditions of production. An example here is offered by ex
gay porn star Ray Dragon's website that promotes and sells material under
the Dragon Media imprimatur, as well as Joe Gage's back catalogue and
current work, and that distributes the Old Reliable label and their extensive
catalogue of videos. The site sells a combination of material ranging from

the symbolic amateurism of Gage's *Lunchtime Milking Club* series, appealing to an audience who enjoys watching men being masturbated without any kind of reciprocal activity, to the appeals of the retro styling of the solo 'street trade' tapes of anonymous men masturbating that were filmed during the 1970s and 1980s.[39]

## Amateur Performance and Amateur Bodies

In terms of performance and the range of masculine physicalities on display, amateur porn is especially interesting in part due to its amorphous nature and to the promise of difference that 'amateur' as a category seems to extend. Corporate amateur porn (the symbolic amateurism of Sean Cody for instance) out of commercial necessity and ambition, as well, presumably, as consumer demand, deploys a set of performance strategies elicited from their models that belong to the demotic idiom of gay porn discussed previously in this book: a sexual script and physicality that conforms to the generic 'types' that commercial porn tends to trade in. However, much of the 'home-made' amateur porn circulated on sites such as Xtube and Xvideos, often unconstrained by commercial imperatives, produces a diverse and complex range of performative registers that often elude easy categorisation. Similarly, home-made amateur porn offers the possibility of, indeed representations of, bodies and physicalities that do not conform neatly to the marketing categories and organising axes that have been discussed in this book. In this way, the figure of the amateur (in home-made porn and to a lesser degree in pro-am porn) acts as a reminder that contemporary saturated masculinity is a complex and contested site and a phenomenon that is not solely reducible to the logic of the marketplace. Amateur porn opens up further vistas of masculinities that resist easy categorisation and becomes a flexible generic container for all of those masculinities that are 'left over' or perhaps 'left out' of the commercial mainstream of gay porn. This necessarily includes the untoned or out-of-condition body, the 'ordinary' physique, physicalities that are not muscular, not sculpted, not scrupulously groomed, not hypertrophic and not excessively endowed. Likewise, the performance styles, especially in home-made amateur porn, suggest a sphere in which masculine sexuality is not of the always hard, always ready, not always acrobatic and gymnastic, culminating with a cum shot on demand variety, that we associate with professional porn performers. Instead sex can be clumsy, messy, funny, disappointing, even boring. Amateur performers can appear to imagine themselves as sexual adventurers, sharing their exploits, and they can also be self-absorbed and preoccupied with documenting the specifics of their own, sometimes narrow, sexual interests. This is what, I think, home-made amateur porn offers that is distinctive from commercial variants; it provides evidence that just as masculinities are various, so the ways in which men perform sex are diverse. Xtube, probably the most extensive resource for home-made amateur porn, provides an apparently limitless supply of examples of amateur performance that I will draw on as examples, alongside instances of corporate and pro-am gay here. As elsewhere in this book, I reiterate that the examples I have chosen are not identified because of their exceptionality, as my concern is typicality. However, I should qualify this in this final section as, ironically, in the case of amateur porn, given the heterogeneous nature of this material, the typical quite often *is* exceptional.

So amateur porn, in its all of its variants, produces and deploys a range of performative registers. In the first instance, narcissistic and exhibitionist display is an integral feature of online sexual play through the use of webcams and broadcasting sites such as Cam4. These performances result in a wealth of material in which men display their naked bodies and masturbate via webcams that can then be recorded and uploaded to sites such as Xtube. Narcissistic display ranges from video recordings of broadcasters on Cam4 and comparable sites, trying to entice viewers to tip them (a form of digital payment) in order for them to reveal more of their body or perform sexual acts[40] (these individuals are often disparagingly described as 'token whores' by viewers), to exhibitionists who choose to film themselves sexually exposed outdoors and in public spaces.[41]

What might be described as sexual 'spectacle', of one description or another, is another performance strategy that is a particularity of amateur porn. I am referring here to what is usually a very specific sex act executed with close attention to the details and specifics of that practice. An example here is an Xtube user, prosaically named as Btcellnet, whose interest is in capturing his own explosive ejaculations. This interest in the spectacular nature of sexual climax is articulated in terms of capturing the 'best', the 'ultimate' and the 'insane' cum shot, even going so far as providing a video tutorial on the preparations for, and execution of this act.[42] Whilst the cum shot is indeed a standard component of the demotic idiom of commercial gay porn, what is distinctive here is that this hyperbolic eruption of ejaculate becomes the exclusive focus of these videos. The performer has an 'average' body and equally an 'average' penis and he covers his face to ensure his anonymity in these videos as his intention is not to specifically eroticise his own 'average' corporeality but instead to show the spectacular cum shot that can issue from such an everyday physique.

Whilst commercial gay porn encourages us to think of sex as inherently exciting, amateur porn of all descriptions provides examples of sex being performed in less than optimal conditions or by performers who, for any number of reasons, cannot (or do not) commit to their performances. This results in a register that for the sake of brevity I am concatenating here as sex performance that is 'failing' in one way or another, and that includes disengagement, detachment, distraction, reticence, nervousness and boredom. This incorporates the sense of nervous discomfort and detachment from sexual play that is displayed by the 'straight' amateurs on sites such as Active Duty, New York Straight Men and Broke Straight Boys.[43] I would also include here instances where poor videography, or a lack of technical virtuosity or consideration of the basics of camera positioning and framing or a lack of enthusiasm or performative brio on the part of the participants, means that a filmed sex scene 'fails'.[44]

Whilst some amateurs may not choose to immerse themselves in the heat of the moment, at the other end of the scale altogether, others perhaps overinvest in the idea of what might be described as 'acting like a pornstar'.[45] This means that some of those who make and distribute home-made amateur porn are inspired by, and choose to act out, the stylistic and performative register of professional performers, aspire to produce materials with 'professional' productions values or indeed see the videos that they make as a route to either a quasi or fully professional porn career. So for example Xtube user Barcelonamorbo, in a video called 'Blowjob at the gym', uses his mobile phone to record a sexual encounter in which he assumes a posture, with one hand placed on his hip, that apes the gay porn conventions for oral sex performance.[46] Domagbbtop deploys similar performance techniques in his own videos, accompanied with vocalisations encouraging his sexual partners that are drawn from the clichéd vocabulary of gay porn professionals in similar scenarios. He preludes his videos with a title card that announces them as 'Domagbbtop Productions'.[47] Bbcumluvnpig sets up shots for his sexual encounters and performs anal sex on all fours using compositions and arrangements that are designed for maximum visibility.[48] However, both he and Fsissy524 augment this attention to the details of the demotic idiom of gay porn with repeated glances to the camera, consequently compromising the illusion and, in an unintentionally humorous fashion, reminding the viewer that they are not acting like 'real' porn stars after all.

The final performative register I would draw attention to is probably the one that it's reasonable to assume most viewers might hope to see enacted in gay porn: enthusiasm and enjoyment. I would argue that the range of materials that constitute amateur porn are particularly important in their facility to represent gay sexual desire in terms of pleasure that, as I have already noted, is not confined necessarily to the exigencies of the commercial gay porn industry. However, it is important remind ourselves, as I indicated at the start of this chapter, that the distinctions between the professional and the amateur are not at all clear cut in contemporary gay porn. A useful final example is offered here by what might be described as the 'crossover' success of Maverick Men, who have made the transition from home-made to pro-am to corporate amateur porn on the basis of the popularity of their enthusiastic sexual performances.[49] Cole and Hunter of Maverick Men began their career as porn producers and performers gaining a following on Xtube and consequently were amongst the first Xtube 'stars'. They still maintain an Xtube profile, largely in order to promote their commercial operation.[50] Cole and Hunter were able to turn their personal and intimate interests in exhibitionism and sex with younger men as well as their distinctively abandoned enjoyment of sexual performances with their various pick-ups into a lucrative career that has resulted in a wealth of media coverage, a book contract and the acquisition of the Maverick Men 'label' by Manhunt.[51] The example of Maverick Men indicates that amateurism is a mutable rather than a static category. Furthermore, access to and command of recording technology means that amateur porn as a category is constantly evolving. As technology changes, software and hardware becomes more accessible and more affordable, 'professional' production standards become a possibility for the amateur producer and this inevitably means that the aesthetics, form and textures of amateur porn also evolve and change.[52] Amateur porn, then, can provide the opportunity for individuals to put their leisure time and their sexual pleasure 'to work' and thereby potentially transform leisure into a form of both labour and commerce. The return for this is the chance for self-invention and self-expression and the manifold rewards of celebrity status.

## Conclusion: The Self

The intention of this book has been to explore the ways in which masculinities are constructed and eroticised in gay porn. I have argued that porn (and in this case gay porn) is no longer a marginal, taboo form of entertainment and has, instead, expanded its reach, increasingly imbricating itself into the mainstream of popular culture. Furthermore, my goal has been to simultaneously observe the extent to which masculinities appear to proliferate in contemporary culture, that masculinity is progressively sexualised and that this has resulted in conditions in which masculinity carries the burden of various and sometimes competing meanings. I describe this condition as saturated masculinity. This saturated masculinity has emerged under conditions that Feona Attwood describes:

> In contemporary societies, new kinds of sexual experience are emerging and sex is taking on new forms and meanings. Online sexual activities are perhaps the most visible manifestation of this. Today people access porn, buy sex toys and seek advice about sex online, and as O'Brien and Shapiro argue, 'sex-related activities can be seen as a major variable in the technological and economic growth and development of the internet' [...]. It is also increasingly common for people to connect and interact sexually with each other online.
>
> (2009:279)[53]

In concluding, then, I want to makes some final observations about the ways in which the network of fantasies, representations, ideals, desires and models of masculinities that I have discussed in this book might connect to a 'real' world, a lived experience and selfdom, mindful, as Catriona Mackenzie usefully reminds us, that 'the term "self" does not refer to any single, unified entity. Rather, what we call "the self" refers rather messily to a cluster of different aspects of selfhood' (2008:127). The 'self', then, is always contingent and an assemblage of disparate elements and this is especially apposite in relation to the presentations of the self (especially representations of the sexual self) that appear online in the context of a contemporary saturated masculinity. My concluding observations therefore are, out of necessity, quite provisional and point to the direction that future research into sexualised and saturated modern masculinity might take.

The exponential growth of social media, online dating and hook-up apps means that the iconography and elements of what I've described in this book as the demotic idiom of gay porn has found its way in a more or less attenuated fashion into the vocabulary that many men used to construct their sexualised bodies for consumption online. This means that porn and masculinity, both sites of a complicated mixture of fear, anxiety and desire, coalesce in the representations of male sexual desirability that can be found everywhere from Tinder to Grindr and at all points in between. At one level, this can be regarded as a shift in attitudes towards sexuality and the body that are indicative of nothing more than a move from 'the "passion for privacy" "empowering exhibitionism" of the internet' (Nikunen, 2015:1). However, Katrin Tiidenberg argues that something more expansive and potentially more progressive may be taking place:

> pointing the camera at oneself can be an emerging personal
> media genre [...] which may offer new forms 'for self-narration
> and representation' [...] self-shooting can be a constitutive,
> self-exploratory practice, and thus much more than merely
> something vain.
>
> (2015:2)

As Ori Schwarz suggests, these practices have some quite profound consequences that are only now starting to be realised in any substantive manner:

> The camera both answers desires formerly produced by this
> increased visual sensitivity and encourages further develop-
> ment of these sensitivities in new directions, re-moulding sex-
> ual scripts and kinds of sexual knowledge. Photographed sex
> is still very much a space of experimentation: unlike pornog-
> raphy consumption (which strongly influenced it), it is not yet

organized by collective patterns, not yet homogenized by mass-
media representation or public discourse.

(2010:641)

Schwarz, writing in 2010, perhaps fails to note the very clear representational patterns that *have* emerged in the ways in which individuals represent
their sexuality and themselves as sexual beings. These are rhetorical patterns that are manifestly structured by both the limitations and specifics
of a chosen medium (a mobile phone or a webcam) but also reference the
iconography and language of porn. I would argue that what we can see in
these sexual representations of masculinity that proliferate across the web
on any number of apps and websites is a paradoxical production of the self
as fantasy object and simultaneously evidence of the documentary impulse
that Tim Dean suggests in *Unlimited Intimacy* (2009) was the dominant
discourse that informs and motivates the production of bareback porn.

A final example to illustrate this is offered by a user of the free porn
website Xvideos that, like Xtube, hosts a range of material including clips of
commercial porn releases, trailers and a substantial amount of home-made
amateur porn. According to his profile page, Morenos1972 is a 43-year-old
Brazilian who travels around the country for work, and to meet men for
sex.[54] He uses the site as a venue to both document and share his sexual
encounters with various (often anonymous) men that he has met online.
The videos (404 of them as of November 2015) are in no way especially
remarkable in style, tone or content. The videos appear to have been captured on a mobile phone or webcam, and the shaky camera work, tightly
cropped shot compositions and peculiar angles all speak of an interest in
recording and documenting a moment in time rather than a performance
for the benefit of an audience. In one rather more considered short entitled 'Calção branco x shortinho vermelho' (white shorts and red shorts) it
appears that Morenos1972 is, in a rather postmodern fashion, referencing the style and rhetoric of the website MENPOV discussed in Chapter 3,
which might illustrate the extent to which the language of gay porn (even
when it imitates amateur porn) has informed, in a curious feedback loop,
the production of at least some of these videos.[55] In these short clips, collected on Xvideos, Morenos1972 uses the site to both document his sexual conquests and, in a similar fashion to Maverick Men, by drawing on

elements of the demotic idiom of gay porn, to represent a fantasy sex life (for some) of endless hook-ups in hotel rooms and carefree sexual encounters with strangers.[56]

Jean Burgess has coined the term 'vernacular creativity' to talk about the connections between acts of everyday creative practice via new media, and this is a useful term to situate the textual strategies at work not just on Xvideos, Xtube, Cam4 and so on, but also across dating apps and websites and other places where men engage in the eroticisation of their own masculinity:

> 'Vernacular creativity', then, does not imply the reinvigoration of some notion of a preexisting 'pure' or authentic folk culture placed in opposition to the mass media; rather, it includes as part of the contemporary vernacular the experience of commercial popular culture [...]. Above all, the term signifies what Chris Atton calls 'the capacity to reduce cultural distance' between the conditions of cultural production and the everyday experiences from which they are derived and to which they return.
>
> (2006:206)

Finally, it's important to re-emphasise that these representational codes and strategies are not the exclusive preserve of gay men. Rather, the rhetoric and iconography of gay porn can be clearly seen to be informing the ways in which heterosexual men produce their bodies for erotic consumption. As Lasén and García note in their work on Spanish men who post nude selfies on dating websites, heterosexual men feel compelled to sexualise their own bodies in order to engage in an online sexual market place but sometimes also feel, what the authors describe as 'disquiet' (2015:714–30) about the erotic vocabulary available to them to do so. Whilst contemporary saturated masculinity may be overburdened with meaning, the implications of some of those meanings may be difficult for some men to negotiate and the ways in which straight-identified males make sense of the ways in which their own bodies and sexualities are eroticised, not just in gay porn but across popular culture, is certainly a topic that requires further investigation.

So the materials that I have discussed in this book and the masculinities that gay porn produces and trades in, do not in operate in a marginalised ghetto speaking to an exclusively gay (or indeed even a gay-friendly) audience but, instead, in an increasingly complex social and cultural network that results in a sexualised and saturated masculinity that is constantly rearticulated, reinvented and in flux. What this book has tried to reveal is that, beneath the surface of gay porn representation, behind the cliché, the hyperbole and the generic representations of masculinity that gay porn offers, is a degree of complexity and ambiguity. Saturated masculinity as illustrated in gay porn is a complex contemporary phenomenon and its complexity is a consequence of the equally complex social world in which we live.

# Notes

## Introduction: Coming to Terms (Again)

1   I would like to extend my warmest thanks to the artist Bruce Cegur whose help in dating and offering background information on the painting *Shop by Male 1-Make Me a Man* has been greatly appreciated.

2   Though as I will note in Chapter 2, these qualitative differences are not eternal and in recent years there has been a wider transformation in the visibility of sexualised representations of masculinity and gay porn is one element in a matrix of mechanisms through which such erotic representations circulate.

3   This of course is not to deny or disregard the considerable and diverse alternative audiences that there may well be for this material, which include heterosexual women for example (see Guy Ramsay, 2016/17). An illuminating presentation of traffic statistics for 2014 from the porn aggregator Pornhub adds traction to the detail of Ramsay's article as it transpires that the second most searched-for category by women viewers of the site (second only to search requests for 'lesbian') was gay (male) (http://www.pornhub.com/insights/2014-year-in-review/).

4   See T. E. Perkins (1979), 'Rethinking Stereotypes' in M. Barrett, P. Corrigan, A. Kuhn and J. Wolff, *Ideology and Cultural Reproduction*. London: Croom Helm.

5   See J. Mercer (2003), 'Prototypes: Repetition and the Construction of the Generic in Gay Pornography' in *Paragraph* special edition. In J. Still (ed.), *Men's Bodies*. London: University of Edinburgh Press.

6   It should be noted though that the orthodoxy that Williams defined the field, tends to overlook the contributions of others, whom she notes in her essay are also important writers on the subject, including (but not limited to) Stephen Marcus' historical study *The Other Victorians* (1964), Susan Sontag's essay on literary pornography, *The Pornographic Imagination* (1967), and Walter Kendrick's *The Secret Museum* (1987).

7   Though this correlation is a tenuous one, as in both the cases of Tom Waugh and Richard Dyer the research that resulted in the published work predates the AIDS crisis.

8   In a special edition of *Porn Studies, Gay Porn Now!* (forthcoming) Waugh revisits the essay and the cultural and political context in which he wrote it.

**196**

9 See also Casey McKittrick's essay 'Brother's Milk: The Erotic and the Lethal in Gay Pornography' in D. Monroe (ed.) (2010) *Porn: Philosophy for Everyone* and Paul Morris' own considerations of the social significance of bareback porn in his essay 'No Limits: Necessary Danger in Male Porn,' http://www.managingdesire.org/nolimits.html.

10 Champagne's intervention in an essay published in 1997 ' "Stop Reading Films!": Film Studies, Close Analysis, and Gay Pornography' in *Cinema Journal*, vol. 36, no. 4 (Summer, 1997), pp. 76–97 has been referred to frequently by subsequent scholars largely because of its self-consciously polemic tone. Cante and Restivo, for example, do sterling work in unpacking and questioning the wisdom of his call, in 'The Voice of Pornography' in Tinkcom and Villarejo (eds), *Keyframes: Popular Cinema and Cultural Studies* (2001).

11 This approach in part also addresses Champagne's aforementioned critique of text-based porn analysis that disregards conditions of consumption.

12 I note that José B. Capino also uses the term 'triangulation' to describe what he sees as a thoroughgoing analysis of porn, in 'Seizing Moving Image Pornography', *Cinema Journal*, vol. 46, no. 4 (Summer, 2007), pp. 121–6.

13 Examples of what I am describing here as web-based para-scholarship (which itself is a term that carries unintentionally dismissive connotations that I am not comfortable with) are considerable and range from the polished professionalism and rigor of The Rialto Report http://www.therialtoreport.com to the more artisanal (but no less informed) Bjland http://bjland.ws/bjland1a.html.

# 1 Saturated Masculinity

1 This body of work has in turn informed and emerged alongside scholarship across disciplines, including film, media and cultural studies, that explore the social and cultural construction of masculinities. See for example Steve Neale's seminal essay 'Masculinity as Spectacle' (1983) as well as the important work of Peter Lehman, who has been writing about the sexual representation of the male body in film since the 1980s (see *Running Scared* (1993, 2007) and Lehman (ed.) (2001)), the work of Joan Mellen (1977), Cohan (1993, 1997), Penley and Willis eds. (1993), Nixon (1996), Tasker (1993), Holmlund (2002) and Kirkham and Thumin (eds) (1993).

2 Much of the productive work in this area has been conducted by scholars interested in masculinity and sport. See also Nick Trujillo's essay 'Hegemonic Masculinity on the Mound' (1991, 290–308) in *Critical Studies in Mass Communication*, vol. 8. Trujillo provides a summary of the five characteristics of hegemonic masculinity based on the work of previous scholars (p. 290) and these are: physical force and control, occupational achievement, familial patriarchy, frontiersmanship and heterosexuality.

3 Global hegemonic masculinity is an idea that is also contested. See the excellent essay by Christine Beasley and Juanita Elias, 'Hegemonic Masculinity and Globalization: "Transnational Business Masculinities" and Beyond, *Globalizations*, vol. 6, no. 2, pp. 281–96.

4 See Rhonda K. Garelick's excellent cultural history of the late 19th century, *Rising Star: Dandyism, Gender and Performance in the Fin de Siecle* (1999).

5 See Michael Kimmel's *Manhood in America: A Cultural History* (1996) and James Gilbert's *Men in the Middle* (2005).

6 It is important to note here the influence of the journalist Mark Simpson, whose opinion pieces for the gay and mainstream press as well as essays that constitute what I describe as 'para-scholarship' have made major interventions in the debates around contemporary masculinity and popular culture since the 1990s. He is famously attributed with coining the term 'metrosexual'. See: http://www.marksimpson.com/here-come-the-mirror-men/.

7 See: http://www.theguardian.com/commentisfree/2014/nov/14/lumbersexual-beard-plaid-male-fashion and http://www.telegraph.co.uk/men/fashion-and-style/11412161/Why-the-lumbersexual-has-a-lot-to-answer-for.html and also http://time.com/3603216/confessions-of-a-lumbersexual/.

8 See: http://www.esquire.co.uk/culture/features/7588/the-rise-and-rise-of-the-spornosexual/ and http://www.telegraph.co.uk/men/fashion-and-style/10881682/The-metrosexual-is-dead.-Long-live-the-spornosexual.html and also http://www.washingtonpost.com/blogs/style-blog/wp/2014/06/10/step-aside-metrosexuals-and-make-way-for-the-spornosexual-man/.

9 Whilst I appear to cite Sinfield here as one of the key figures in this debate, the term *Postgay* was probably first used by Edmund White to describe writers who whilst open about their sexuality did not choose to make it the sole (or even a significant) focus of their writing. See White quoted in Fritz Lanham, 'Beginnings of liberation', *Houston Chronicle*, 27 November, 1994.

10 For example, an interesting discussion is offered in an article on the German artist Lukas Duwenhogger. In his essay, Roger Cook asks, drawing on the work of Ranciere, how useful the term homosexual is in the context of contemporary art and culture. See Roger Cook 'Lukas Duwenhögger: Homosexual Signs' in *Afterall: A Journal of Art, Context, and Enquiry*, Issue 31 (Autumn/Winter 2012), 58–70

11 See also W. C. Harris, *Queer Externalities: Hazardous Encounters in American Culture* (2009), which develops and updates much of what Warner had to say ten years earlier.

12 See also Alison Phipps' interesting chapter, 'The Commodified Politics of the Sex Industry' in *The Politics of the Body: Gender in a Neoliberal and Neoconservative Age* (2014). Phipps argues that sex positive and sex radical politics are in fact equivalent to and therefore complicit in shoring up right-wing neo-liberal values.

13 I make this distinction here because it is ostensibly in Anglophone scholarship and media where we can find the most heated debates around the so-called 'sexualization of culture'.

14 See Sheila Jeffreys' very clear outlining of the sexualisation debate in the preface to the second edition of *Beauty and Misogyny: Harmful Cultural Practices in the West* (2015).

15 For an extremely intelligent and thoughtfully considered investigation of young people's relationship to sexualised media, including porn consumption, see Monique Mulholland, *Young People and Pornography: Negotiating Pornification* (2013) and Danielle Egan's thoroughgoing critique, *Becoming Sexual: A Critical Appraisal of the Sexualization of Girls* (2013).

16 A YouGov survey conducted in August 2015 suggests that as many as 49 per cent of British 18- to 24-year-olds self-describe as other than 100 per cent heterosexual. See https://yougov.co.uk/news/2015/08/16/half-young-not-heterosexual/ and the full survey results at: https://d25d2506sfb94s.cloudfront.net/cumulus_uploads/document/7zv13z8mfn/YG-Archive-150813-%20Sexuality.pdf.

17 Arthur Schlesinger Jr. opines in an essay written for *Esquire* magazine entitled *The Crisis of American Masculinity* published in 1958, 'What has happened to the American male? [...] Today men are more and more conscious of maleness not as a fact but as a problem' (2008:292).

18 As the proponents of the 'precarious manhood' thesis note, it is an argument that is open to critique. In a very useful overview essay 'Hard Won and Easily Lost: A Review and Synthesis of Theory and Research on Precarious Manhood' in *Psychology of Men & Masculinity* 2013, 14(2), 101–13, the authors Joseph Vandello and Jennifer Bosson note that a 'criticism of the idea that manhood is precarious is that this represents an overly stereotypical and caricatured view of manhood, and one that many men do not personally endorse.'

# 2 History, Industry and Technological Change

1 This observation was made in an earlier chapter. See 'Gay for Pay: The Internet and the Economics of Homosexual Desire' (2011) in Karen Ross (ed.), *The Handbook of Gender, Sex, and Media*, Oxford: Blackwell.

2 See J. Mercer (2003), 'Prototypes: Repetition and the Construction of the Generic in Gay Pornography.' Collected in *Paragraph* special issue; J. Still (ed.), *Men's Bodies*, London: University of Edinburgh Press; and J. Mercer (2006), 'Seeing is Believing: Constructions of Stardom and The Gay Porn Star in U.S. Gay Video Pornography' in S. Holmes and S. Redmond (eds), *Framing Celebrity*, London: Routledge.

3 For a very much more abstract discussion of this idea, see the work of the French philosopher Bernard Steigler, who in *Technics and Time 1* notes that the

very human condition is one marked by an 'originary' lack that is fulfilled or at least substituted by what he describes as a 'technical prosthesis' (1998:188).

4 In 'Smut, Novelty, Indecency: Reworking a History of the Early-Twentieth-Century American Stag Film' (2014), Russell Scheaffer notes the problems associated with the study of the 'stag' film, one of which is the extended time frame that is indicated here, which for Scheaffer at least means 'it seems curious to group them together under a single unifying term' (p. 347).

5 See also Waugh's essay 'Homosociality in the Stag Film' in L. Williams (ed.) (2004), *Porn Studies*, Durham, NC: Duke University Press.

6 A search of the complete print run of *Physique Pictorial* suggests that AMG started distributing short film in 1957.

7 See Benshoff and Griffin's passages on this material in 'Physique Films: The First Gay Male Erotic Cinema' in *Queer Images: A History of Gay and Lesbian Film in America* (2006), Lanham: Rowman & Littlefield.

8 Dallesandro also performed in a hardcore loop (probably made by Bob Mizer) during the late 1960s in which he has oral and anal sex with an anonymous male performer. This loop makes an appearance in Jack Deveau's *Hot House* (1977), used as the 'mood making' prelude to a threeway between Gary Hunt, Roger and David Hunter. The loop is also presented in its own right in the film.

9 See volume 3 of *The Complete Reprint of Physique Pictorial* (1997), Cologne: Taschen.

10 Jeffrey Escoffier provides a much more complete historical account than it is my intention to offer here, replete with detail and anecdote. Alongside Waugh's work and that of writers such as Eric Schaefer and Kevin Heffernan amongst others – including a much earlier essay from 1997 by Jack Stevenson, 'From the Bedroom to the Bijou: A Secret History of American Gay Sex Cinema' – his important work points to a rich history of adult film production, distribution and consumption that has emerged as an object of study across film, media and cultural studies since the 1990s.

11 See also Jose Capino's 'Seminal Fantasies: Wakefield Poole, Independent Cinema & The American Avant-Garde' in C. Holmlund and J. Wyatt (eds) (2004), *Contemporary American Independent Film: From the Margins to the Mainstream*, Cologne: Routledge; Edward Miller (2013), 'Clean Feet and Dirty Dancing: The Erotic Pas de Deux and *Boys in the Sand*', in H. Maes (ed.), *Pornographic Art and the Aesthetics of Pornograph*, London: Palgrave Macmillan; Roger Edmonson (1998), *Boy in the Sand: Casey Donovan, All-American Sex Star*, New York: Alyson and the Rialto Report podcast with Wakefield Poole at http://www.therialtoreport.com/2013/06/16/wakefield-poole-theater-dance-and-pornpodcast-14/.

12 I would further note that a rather more pragmatic attraction of these films for porn scholars is that such foregrounded authorship facilitates attribution and therefore the possibilities for close- and cross-textual analysis.

13 The narrative that I am presenting here is truncated out of necessity and I am all too conscious that it's a convenient (though not altogether uncommon) myth to reduce the entirety of gay porn production during the 1980s to Falcon Studios, and this is not my purpose. Instead I would re-emphasise that my intention here for the sake of clarity is to use the studio as an exemplar of the ways in which a change in technology and commercial context was to result in a change in style and content.

14 Escoffier usefully notes in *Bigger Than Life* how the politics surrounding condom use were played out during the mid to late 1980s. (2009:196–7) He observes that it was not until the early 1990s that condom use was routinely and explicitly represented in videos.

15 http://atkol.com/replies.asp?Forum=3&Topic=2163&ScrollAction=Page+2

16 See Falcon CEO John Rutherford's comments in 1998 about this new technology: http://atkol.com/replies.asp?Forum=11&Topic=74&ScrollAction=Page+4.

17 See a 2004 interview with Keith Webb at: http://gaydvdreview.com/keith_webb.asp.

18 This is in the context of a wider discussion about the declining commercial viability of the porn industry. See: http://www.cnbc.com/id/45989346 and http://www.advocate.com/news/2009/04/06/porn-panic?page=0,0 and http://www.salon.com/2012/03/03/life_after_the_golden_age_of_porn/.

19 Director and producer Michael Lucas (a vocal campaigner for condom use in gay porn) reversed his policy in 2014 and began filming bareback scenes, with a resulting controversy. See: http://www.queerty.com/michael-lucas-explains-his-controversial-decision-to-make-condom-free-adult-films-20140331/.

20 See also J. Mercer (2003) and Sarah Schaschek's *Pornography and Seriality* (2014).

21 It would have been equally possible to pull together a list of studios from which to draw examples based on statistics of online sales or through reference to variously unreliable metrics of web traffic. (The website Alexa, for example, reveals some interesting information about web traffic.)

22 See: http://www.xbiz.com/articles/187726.

23 See: http://business.avn.com/articles/video/VOD-Giant-AEBN-Acquires-Falcon-Studios-Merges-with-Raging-Stallion-419756.html.

24 See: http://thesword.com/exclusive-sean-cody-acquired-by-mindgeekmanwin-a-k-a-the-same-company-that-owns-men-com.html.

25 See: http://www.cnbc.com/id/45989405 and http://www.slate.com/articles/technology/technology/2014/10/mindgeek_porn_monopoly_its_dominance_is_a_cautionary_tale_for_other_industries.html.

26 Robert Kirsch's comments on the conventions of gay pornographic representation are available in the article 'Visual AIDS: Gay Male Porn and Safer Sex Pedagogy' at http://hivinsite.ucsf.edu/insite.jsp?doc=2098.4218.

27 This, however, is not a universally held view. Nguyen Tan Hoang in *A View From the Bottom* insists that what he describes as a 'polarization of sexual positions' (2015:11) is a relatively recent but prevalent feature of contemporary porn, going on to cite a range of sources (tellingly all from the 1990s). Needless to say, I don't subscribe to this view, which doesn't correspond with the evidence of the research that I have conducted.

28 See the YouTube channels devoted to examples of bad porn acting, affectionately named after and apparently hosted by the two especially gifted purveyors of porn 'acting' from the early 1990s, Steve Rambo: https://www.youtube.com/channel/UCP5OXzrzlftUEwc5gt7he3Q and Ray Harley: https://www.youtube.com/channel/UCZI2jjwyM-K2y4c1qQpYBzQ.

29 See also Heather Berg's essay 'Sex, Work, Queerly: Identity, Authenticity and Laboured Performance' in M. Laing, K. Pilcher and N. Smith (eds) (2015), *Queer Sex Work*, Abingdon: Routledge.

30 See this rather dramatic storyline that indicates a professional background that emphasises my point: http://www.villagevoice.com/news/theres-drama-on-both-sides-of-the-camera-at-nyc-porn-powerhouse-cockyboys-6440187.

31 http://www.men.com/scene/18131/gay-of-thrones-part-6/.

32 http://kristenbjorn.com/web/model/video/detail-1527-Bare-To-The-Bone-sc-4-Letterio-Amadeo-Raul-Korso-Toffic.

33 http://menpov.com/video/running-hard.

# 3 Generation: The Boy-Next-Door, the Twink and the Daddy

1 In an even more downbeat essay, 'The Last Days of Gay Porn' (2015), Scuglia's assessment is that the gay porn industry is now largely at an end, arguing (somewhat contentiously) that the social function that gay pornography used to perform for a marginalised group has largely now been supplanted by developments in media technology, in particular social media and dating apps. The essay, written for a special edition of *Sex and Psychology*, has nothing to say about the function of pornography in the imaginative lives of its users and sees porn as little more than a delivery mechanism for sexually explicit images.

2 See Adolphe Thiers and Frederic Schoberl, *The History of the French Revolution*, vol. 4 (1846:57), and *The Gilded Youth of Thermidor* (1993) by François Gendron.

3 Escoffier notes that the star of *The Boys of Venice* (dir. William Higgins, 1979) 'Kip Noll [...] was the first major "twink" porn star. In fact he personified the twink – an attractive young gay man with a slender build and little or no body hair' (2009:162).

4 The sometimes imprecise nature of subcultural terms and slang can cause problems that extend beyond the issues posed for scholarship, such as in a case in 2015 where a gay man was falsely accused of making and storing child pornography, because the police force did not understand what the term *twink* referred to: http://www.pinknews.co.uk/2015/05/08/man-arrested-for-having-twink-images-on-computer/ and http://www.mirror.co.uk/news/uk-news/police-need-gay-lingo-lessons-5654737. In an altogether less serious story, a US television executive had to apologise for using the 'derogatory' term to describe the boy band One Direction: http://www.towleroad.com/2012/11/andy-cohen-forced-to-apologize-for-calling-one-direction-twinks/. The term also presents problems for members of the gay community as it has become so freighted with 'negative' connotations related to effeminacy, a lack of judgement or intelligence: https://www.vice.com/en_uk/read/its-hard-out-here-for-a-twink-456 and http://themoderngay.com/2015/05/03/the-twink-is-dead/, and an especially considered online piece by Thomas Rogers for The Awl in which he observes, 'Somewhere along the way "twink" has stopped being just a cutesy, mildly negative stereotype and become something more malignant: An easy shorthand for a lot of vicious stereotypes about gay people, a way to covertly make fun not just of someone's mild gender variance but really their "gayness" as well', http://www.theawl.com/2013/07/what-comes-after-the-twink.

5 http://www.menatplay.com/movie/papi-rules and http://www.menatplay.com/movie/boylust.

6 http://www.nextdoormale.com/en/Ivan-James/film/77484.

7 http://www.nextdoormale.com/en/Wes-James/film/76469.

8 http://www.nextdoormale.com/en/Ken-Riley/film/71324.

9 The list of broadly equivalent performers is lengthy and includes examples such as Jake Bass, Jett Black, Mason Starr, Kevin Warhol, Jesse Santana, Brent Everett, Pierre Fitch, Benjamin Bradley. However, in each of these cases there are nuances and differences.

10 http://www.nextdoormale.com/en/Justin-Owen/film/49134.

11 Almost as famous for his expressions of surprise, shock and/or alarm in the stills that promote his many bottoming scenes across the web, his 100th scene with Paul Wagner, *House Boy Part 1*, http://www.men.com/scene/7421/houseboy-part-1/?nats=MTQ1NzEuMTEuMS4xLjAuMC4wLjAuMA, was heavily promoted and provoked bloggers to review his prolific career: http://str8upgayporn.com/johnny-rapid-gay-porn-star-men/.

12 http://www.dylanlucas.com/en/film/53411/Justin-Owen-At-The-Beach.

13 http://www.randyblue.com/video/18-year-old-twink-billy-taylor-has-a-first-time-fuck-with-justin-owen/2790.

14 See: http://www.salon.com/2013/09/01/the_walt_whitman_of_gay_porn/; http://www.cybersocket.com/gay-porn-magazine/issue-157/the-original-cocky-boy-an-interview-with-jake-jaxson; http://gay.fleshbot.com/6004477/meet-jake-jaxson-the-jake-jaxson-of-gay-porn.

15 http://www.cosmopolitan.com/sex-love/advice/g3705/porn-for-women/?slide=13.

16 See the Cockyboys 'manifesto' at http://cockyboys.com/movietour/.

17 http://www.queermenow.net/blog/cockyboys-and-bel-ami-kick-off-their-model-exchange-program/.

18 An example here being the quasi-rural idyll that is the setting for the exchange between Ty Roderick and lithe and boyish Max Ryder (http://cockyboys.com/movietour/trailer.php?id=925) and the metropolitan ideal set-up in a scene where Hayden Lourd goes on a date with Levi Karter before engaging in a 'flip fuck': http://cockyboys.com/movietour/trailer.php?id=861.

19 http://cockyboys.com/movietour/trailer.php?id=1279.

20 This is probably the most vividly realised in Jaxon's magnum opus, *A Thing of Beauty* (2013). See: http://cockyboys.com/featureFilms/thing-of-beauty/.

21 http://tour.boycrush.com/boy-crush-watch-gay-movies/bc776_maxandrews_interview/Self-Confessed+Sex+Addict?nats=Mi43LjEuMS4yLjAuMC4wLjA#BoyCrush.

22 For example see: http://www.nextdoormale.com/en/John-Stone/film/72044.

23 See: https://www.helixstudios.net/video/3259/introducing-logan-cross.html.

24 http://www.randyblue.com/video/welcome-to-la-venice/2685.

25 http://www.randyblue.com/video/welcome-to-la-burbank/2669

26 http://www.randyblue.com/video/justin-owen/2656.

27 For example see: http://kristenbjorn.com/web/model/video/detail-1526-Bare-to-the-Bone-sc-3-Jared-Patryk-Jankowski.

28 http://www.czechhunter.com/.

29 http://vip.citiboyz.com/tour/.

30 http://www.citiboyz.com/videos/volume77/index.php.

31 For example see: http://www.euroboyxxx.com/tour/showgal.php?g=groups/30429/35_1&s=201.

32 http://tour.boycrush.com/boy-crush-about?nats=Mi43LjEuMS4yLjAuMC4wLjA.

33 http://www.alexa.com/siteinfo/cockyboys.com http://www.alexa.com/siteinfo/helixstudios.net http://www.alexa.com/siteinfo/boycrush.com.

34 See George Duroy's comments on casting choices and strategy: http://www.towleroad.com/2010/07/an-interview-with-bel-amis-george-duroy/.

35 http://tour.belamionline.com/tour.aspx?Page=3&ModelID=2394&Previous=2361&Next=2356.

36 http://www.salon.com/2010/05/21/twincest/ and http://menofporn.typepad.com/menofporn/2009/10/interview-with-the-peters-twins-we-like-to-have-sex-together.html.

37  http://www.daddymugs.com/?page=Daddy.
38  http://www.daddymugs.com/?page=Models.
39  See: http://atkol.com/replies.asp?Forum=3&Topic=10272&DaysOld=2&Sort=ASC.
40  http://jakecruise.com/general/about.php.
41  http://jakecruise.com/tour/index.php?talent_grouping=Brad Kalvo.
42  http://jakecruise.com/tour/index.php?talent_grouping=Bo Dean.
43  http://jakecruise.com/tour/description/Brady_Jensen_Serviced/.
44  https://www.helixstudios.net/video/2670/man-on-twink-the-art-gallery.html.
45  https://www.helixstudios.net/video/2666/man-on-twink-the-photographer.html.
46  https://www.helixstudios.net/video/2700/man-on-twink-the-waiting-room.html.
47  https://www.helixstudios.net/video/2688/anything-to-pass.html.
48  https://www.helixstudios.net/video/2689/man-on-twink-the-lunch-date.html.
49  http://www.hotoldermale.com/video/detail/82/.
50  http://www.hotoldermale.com/video/detail/79/.
51  http://www.hotoldermale.com/video/detail/179/.

# 4  Straight Acting? Heterosexuality, Hypermasculinity and the Gay Outlaw

1  http://www.towleroad.com/2010/07/an-interview-with-bel-amis-george-duroy/.
2  See Chris Beasley, Heather Brook and Mary Holmes' essay 'Heterodoxy: Challenging Orthodoxies about Heterosexuality', *Sexualities*, September 2015, vol. 18, no. 5–6, pp. 681–97, in which the authors suggest alternative ways to conceptualise heterosexuality as a 'terrain' (690) rather than as a monolith.
3  An opinion piece on the Advocate website typifies the tone of discussion: http://www.advocate.com/commentary/2013/01/04/op-ed-what-straight-acting-really-means.
4  http://www.straightacting.com/phpbb3/index.php?sid=fd8acbd37ee8399b0ef3e82911615e7b.
5  Seidman, for instance, says that 'Heterosexuality has meaning only in relation to "homosexuality"; the coherence of the former is built on the exclusion, repression, and repudiation of the latter [...] gay identity constructions reinforce the dominant hetero/homo sexual code with its heteronormativity' (1993:130).
6  I have consciously avoided describing this phenomenon as 'queering' straightness. The reasons for this decision are eloquently described by Susanna Paasonen in *Carnal Resonance* (2011). See pp. 150–3.
7  See Jane Ward's *Not Gay: Sex Between Straight White Men* (2015).

8  John Stadler's essay 'Dire Straights: The Indeterminacy of Sexual Identity in Gay-For-Pay Pornography' explores this territory also and be found at: http://www.ejumpcut.org/archive/jc55.2013/StadlerGayForPay/text.html.

9  http://www.randyblue.com/video/the-coach/1013 http://www.randyblue.com/video/the-coach-2/1552 and http://www.randyblue.com/video/the-coach-3-post-game-fucking/2720.

10 http://business.avn.com/company-news/Corbin-Fisher-CEO-Recognized-for-Commitment-to-LGBT-Equality-507371.html and http://business.avn.com/articles/Corbin-Fisher-Provides-Models-with-Benefits-54752.html.

11 http://www.seancody.com/?frame=model.

12 See Curtis and Tate discussing their enjoyment of anal sex: http://www.seancody.com/?frame=movie&movie=1925.

13 For instance, see the scene 'Chris and Mitch': http://www.seancody.com/?frame=movie&movie=719.

14 See Randy and Matt exercising in a park: http://www.seancody.com/?frame=movie&movie=1777.

15 I provide here some examples of the exhaustive fan appreciation (and criticisms) of Brandon: http://givemegayporn.com/10-of-the-best-seancody-guys-tanner-brandon-billy-trey-more/; https://www.datalounge.com/thread/13266994-brandon-from-sean-cody-2; http://thesword.com/sean-cody-still-has-stars-brandon-comes-back-to-fuck-porter.html; http://marcdylan.com/2015/06/15/brandon-bottoming-debut-at-sean-cody-when-will-it-happen/; http://www.queerclick.com/qc/2015/07/qc-open-forum-is-sean-cody-brandon-trying-to-get-out-of-the-porn-industry.php; http://thesword.com/brandon-returns-to-sean-cody-to-make-ginger-top-david-bottom-again.html; http://str8upgayporn.com/brandon-sean-cody-gay-porn-bareback-dicks/ and http://str8upgayporn.com/hunter-page-sean-cody-brandon-twitter/.

16 See Brandon and Brodie talking about the range of sports that they engage in: http://www.seancody.com/?frame=movie&movie=1471.

17 http://www.seancody.com/?frame=movie&movie=1855.

18 http://www.seancody.com/?frame=movie&movie=1777.

19 http://www.seancody.com/?frame=movie&movie=1487.

20 For example, see porn performer Devon Hunter's remarks about his experiences working for Sean Cody: http://www.devonhunter.info/archives/1625/, and the responses to these revelations on discussions fora: http://atkol.com/replies.asp?Forum=3&Topic=11042&DaysOld=2&Sort=ASC. Also see reportage (and posters comments) about Sean Cody models and their ambivalent relationship to their porn careers: http://thesword.com/sean-cody-model-hates-it-when-gay-guys-hit-on-him.html and http://www.towleroad.com/2012/02/ultimate-fighter-contestant-says-gay-for-pay-past-was-mistake/.

21 http://www.baitbus.com/t9/.

22 http://www.ungloryhole.com/t7/?nats=ODM3LjEuOC45MjEuMC4wLjAuM
C4w.

23 http://thecastingroom.nl/index1.php?nats=MDowOjU&step=2.

24 http://www.fraternityx.com/about.php.

25 http://www.breederfuckers.com/index02.php?nats=MDowOjE4.

26 See http://www.breederfuckers.com/men2015.php.

27 The 'join our fraternity' tab on the site directs to: http://www.ultimatema-
lemodels.com/.

28 The short film *Hypermasculinity on the Dance Floor* (dir. Selin Davasse and Emre
Busse, 2015), which can be found here: https://vimeo.com/134999123, features
young German gay men talking about the ways in which a hypermasculine
aesthetic reflects their sexual desires and attitudes towards their sense of themselves as men. The film is reviewed here: https://broadly.vice.com/en_us/article/
dicks-on-the-dancefloor-ber-manly-gay-germans-talk-about-masculinity and
here: http://m-maenner.de/2015/07/hypermasculinity-on-the-dancefloor/.

29 The iconography of the hypermasculine gay male has been significantly shaped
and constructed for mainstream consumption through the activities of the
photographic studio Colt. Emerging as a consequence of the proliferation of
physique photography during the 1960s and 1970s, Colt were to specialise in
producing material that featured body builders and rugged 'natural' men. Their
popularity was based on both the extremely high production standards of their
work and their choice of models that epitomises over-determined macho masculinity that conflates the iconography of the body builder, the clone and the
leatherman. Models such as Steve Kelso illustrate the Colt look well. Muscled,
hirsute, ruggedly handsome, referring back to the history of physique photography as well as to the gay clone, models such as Kelso exemplify the Colt 'look'.
During the 1980s, Colt began to diversify into moving image with the *Minute
Men* series, featuring their most successful models in either solo, posing and
masturbation sequences, or in short sex sequences with celebrity Colt models
such as Rick Wolfmeier and Mike Betts.

30 http://www.butchdixon.com/tour/showgal.php?g=content/BD/videos/hardcore/
john_ted/20896/33_1&s=125&uvar=MC4yLjQwLjEyNy4wLjAuMC4wLjA.

31 http://atkol.com/replies.asp?Forum=3&Topic=11822&DaysOld=2&Sort=
ASC.

32 As well as Fred Fele and Ted Colunga, he has also appeared as Attila Ferescsi,
Ferenc, Giovanni Floretti, Giovanni Floretto, Attila Fereczi, Mick Houston,
Norbert Somlay. See the interview at: http://www.queermenow.net/blog/ted-
colungafred-felegiovanni-floretto-new-video-interview/.

33 http://www.butchdixon.com/tour/showgal.php?g=groups/21290/20_1&s=125
&uvar=MC4yLjQwLjEyNy4wLjAuMC4wLjA.

34 http://www.lucasentertainment.com/scenes/play/hairy-dudes-alessio-
romero-and-dirk-caber-flip-fuck.

35 http://www.vice.com/read/the-worlds-best-male-escort-is-more-than-his-10-inch-penis-100.

36 http://store.treasureislandmedia.com/FLOODED.html.

37 http://www.barebackthathole.com/tour/models/RoccoSteele.html.

38 http://www.men.com/scene/17551/eat-prey-fuck-part-4/.

39 http://www.luciosaints.com/modelos/detalle/allen-king.

40 http://www.breedmeraw.com/tour/trailers/rocco-steele-and-nick-tiano.html.

41 http://www.roccosteelestudio.com/. Steele has garnered a great deal of media and fan attention and some of his many interviews can be found at: http://www.manhattandigest.com/2014/07/27/get-know-smart-sexy-rocco-steele/; http://thesword.com/rocco-steele.html; http://str8upgayporn.com/rocco-steele-bareback-gay-porn/; http://twistedmalemag.com/rocco-steele-interview/; http://manhuntdaily.com/2014/10/an-interview-with-rocco-steele-the-man-behind-the-massive-10-x-7-inch-cock/; http://bearworldmagazine.com/?p=3612; http://blog.treasureislandmedia.com/2014/08/iamroccosteele/.

42 http://www.bearfilms.com/index.php.

43 Given the ephemeral nature of this marginal area of porn distribution and production, I have chosen not to cite specific examples as I am conscious that the links that I would provide would be out of date by the time the reader has chance to access them. The same basic web browser search with the same search parameters that I have used in 2015 will no doubt produce equivalent and more relevant results for the reader.

44 http://pantheonproductions.com/aboutus.html.

45 http://butchdixon.com/tour/show.php?a=186_1.

46 http://www.butchdixon.com/tour/showgal.php?g=content/BD/videos/hardcore/BD_jose-quevedo_felipe-ferro_HK15/33974/33_1&s=179&uvar=MC4yLjQwLjEyNy4wLjAuMC4wLjA.

47 Butch Bear DVDs are now distributed by *BEAR Magazine*, which also produced and released gay porn under the Brush Creek Media label from the late 1980s onwards with titles such as the solo tape *Live Bear One: Original Bear 1* (dir. Anon, 1989) and *Bear Fuck Party: Original Bear 2* (dir. Richard Bulger, 1989). The development of the company is rather complex and can be found at http://www.bearmagazine.com/winter/about.html.

48 Though of course this quasi-unkempt, quasi-rural persona is a contrivance with Radcliffe, revealing in his interview that he spends five to six days a week training in the gym and that his 'real' job is a computer programmer (Wright, 2001:174–81).

49 For contemporary online examples, see *Batter Up* (http://www.hotoldermale.com/video/detail/552) and also *Brief Encounters: A Ripping Good Time* (http://www.hotoldermale.com/video/detail/246).

50 See Gregory Storm's very useful overview and intervention in the barebacking debate in Comella and Tarrant (eds) (2015) *New Views on Pornography: Sexuality,*

*Politics, and the Law* and Oliver Davis's special edition of *Sexualities* (2015), 'Bareback Sex and Queer Theory Across Three National Contexts'.

51 See: http://www.kink.com/.

52 http://store.treasureislandmedia.com/BAD-INFLUENCE-DIRECTOR-S-CUT.html.

53 http://www.queerrhetoric.com/?p=350.

54 See: http://www.aumag.org/2014/09/23/michael-lucas/; http://www.edgemedia network.com/entertainment/celebrities/news//167566/michael_lucas:_the_polarizing_prince_of_porn; http://www.pinknews.co.uk/2014/04/02/michael-lucas-gay-bareback-porn-is-hotter-and-i-dont-use-condoms-with-my-hiv-positive-partner/ and http://www.queerty.com/michael-lucas-explains-his-controversial-decision-to-make-condom-free-adult-films-20140331 and http://www.queerty.com/michael -lucas-breaks-vow-releases-first-bareback-sex-scene-20130917.

# 5 A World of Men: Race, Ethnicity and National Identity

1 http://kristenbjorn.com/web/model/video/detail-377-A-World-of-Men-Scene-3.

2 http://www.worldofmen.com/tour/?nats=MC4yLjEzLjEzLjAuMC4wLjAuMA.

3 At the time of writing, there is no equivalent for example to Nguyen Tan Hoang's study of Asian-American masculinity, *A View from the Bottom* (2014), or to Mirielle Miller Young's *A Taste for Brown Sugar: Black Women in Pornography* (2014).

4 See: http://www.seancody.com/tour/models/ https://www.corbinfisher.com/ #theguys/viewall and http://www.men.com/models/by-name/asc/.

5 Rawebonybreeders is now defunct but examples of their material are freely available via tube sites. See also: http://www.nextdoorebony.com/en# http://www. gayblackbangers.com/site/network.html and http://www.gaygangsta.com/ http:// traphouseboys.com/tour/.

6 Flavaworks has been criticised for the lack of care shown to models often regarded as deprived and vulnerable, who have been drawn into risky sex out of economic necessity. See: http://www.bejata.com/wp/2006/04/29/porn-hiv-and-the-lives-of-young-gay-men-of-color/ and http://www.jasmyneacan-nick.com/blog/gay-porn-king-sues-black-lgbt-bloggers-for-exposing-truth/. Flavaworks' white owner has attracted further criticism for taking legal action against piracy. See: http://www.forbes.com/sites/kashmirhill/2012/11/02/gay-porn-website-gets-3-million-in-damages-from-bittorrent-uploaders/.

7 This point is rather vividly underscored (if any further emphasis was needed) through the marketing of a 12-inch *Black Balled* dildo. http://c1r.com/prod-ucts/rt1042-black-balled-dildo.

8 A rather more extreme example is provided by the series Black Dick Terror made by Macho Fucker, who describe themselves as the 'award winning no. 1 website for amateur interracial bareback porn': http://www.machofucker.com/freepreview/movie.php?movie=xq222hnc.

9 See: http://www.cazzofilm.com/scene/adam-russo-cutler-x https://www.timtales.com/model-videos/cutlerx/; http://store.treasureislandmedia.com/HARDCUTS1.html; http://www.rawfuckclub.com/vod/RFC/browse.php?by_actor=5201 and http://www.barebackthathole.com/tour/models/CutlerX.html.

10 See Simon Watney's eminently clear and cogent analysis of the context of policing and legislation around pornography in the UK in *Policing Desire: Pornography, Aids and the Media* (1987).

11 http://www.trigafilms.com/sart.asp?paid=1.

12 http://www.trigafilms.com/shops/info_p.asp?prid=786.

13 http://www.trigafilms.com/shops/info_p.asp?prid=1086.

14 http://www.hardbritlads.com/tour/category.php?id=185&s=d&nats=MC4yLjQ2LjE1Ny4wLjAuMC4wLjA.

15 http://www.uknakedmen.com/tour/?nats=MC4yLjM5LjEyNi4wLjAuMC4wLjA.

16 http://www.kallamacka.com/#/en/videos/.

17 http://www.ericvideos.com/EN/homepage/1.

18 http://www.jalifstudio.com/.

19 http://jnrc.fr/en/accueil/.

20 http://citebeur.com/.

21 http://www.lucaskazan.com/.

22 http://www.lucasentertainment.com/.

23 See also Browne, Lim and Brown (eds) (2007), *Geographies of Sexualities Theory, Practices and Politics*, London: Routledge.

24 http://kristenbjorn.com/web/model/video/detail-1517-Bare-to-the-Bone-sc-1-Letterio-Amadeo-Patryk-Jankowski.

25 http://www.menatplay.com/.

26 See: http://www.gaylesbiantimes.com/?id=9598 and http://www.qxmagazine.com/feature/ten-at-play/.

27 http://www.menatplay.com/model/edu-boxer.

28 http://www.menatplay.com/model/adam-champ.

29 http://www.menatplay.com/model/emir-boscatto-0.

# 6 The Celebrity, the Amateur and the Self

1 http://www.salon.com/2012/03/03/life_after_the_golden_age_of_porn/.

2 See: http://www.advocate.com/news/2009/04/06/porn-panic?page=0,0 and http://www.cnbc.com/id/45989346.

3  I would not wish to suggest here that there is a fixed pantheon of gay porn stars. On his blog, the journalist and author Matthew Rettenmund lists 125 porn stars: http://www.boyculture.com/boy_culture/2013/01/125-hottest-gay-porn-stars.html. He includes an eclectic mix of performers, some of whom would be recognised as gay porn stars according to the analysis in my own essay and some who would not. His list amounts to a recollection of names (sometimes forgotten) from gay porn's past rather than an indicator of success or renown. So he identifies Casey Donovan, Al Parker, Jack Wrangler and Jon King, who were all popular performers during the 1970s and early 1980s, a period in which the industrial infrastructure did not exist for them to be marketed as stars in the same manner as Ryan Idol and Jeff Stryker, who are also on the list. In fact what Rettenmund compiles is a list that illustrates that gay porn has consistently produced celebrities, some of whom have then been constructed as stars but many others who have not.

4  Producer, director and performer Michael Lucas has an especially high public profile as a socialite in Manhattan (see article in *Butt Magazine*: http://www.buttmagazine.com/magazine/interviews/michael-lucas/), warranting a profile in *New York Magazine* in 2007: http://nymag.com/movies/features/23146/ and *Vice* in 2014: http://www.vice.com/read/body-of-an-american-0000320-v21n5. Fashion designer Calvin Klein attracted some degree of media attention for dating Nick Gruber (a model over 40 years his junior), who had appeared in gay porn: http://gawker.com/5626955/calvin-kleins-underwear-model-boyfriend-also-did-some-gay-porn?tag=nickgruber, http://www.advocate.com/news/daily-news/2010/09/01/calvin-kleins-porn-star-boyfriend, http://www.villagevoice.com/blogs/more-photos-from-calvin-kleins-porn-party-6374595 and http://www.nydailynews.com/entertainment/gossip/confidential/calvin-nick-gruber-joins-dire-straights-article-1.1431268. Mark Jacobs has regularly been romantically linked to a succession of gay porn stars (http://gawker.com/390102/marc-jacobs-goes-upmarket), most recently the Brazilian Harry Louis: http://www.papermag.com/marc-jacobs-on-louis-vuitton-porn-stars-and-going-on-grindr-1427427464.html and http://www.queerty.com/marc-jacobs-and-porn-star-boyfriend-harry-louis-call-it-quits-20131007.

5  http://www.pinknews.co.uk/2012/10/26/interview-chaosmens-gavin-sevin-talks-gay-for-pay-in-the-adult-entertainment-industry/.

6  See Milan Gamiani's reflections on the state of the gay porn industry and a discussion urging hopefuls to think carefully about their aspirations prior to embarking on a porn career: http://milangamiani.blogspot.co.uk/2013/04/milan-etrevistado-para-una-revista.html?zx=b5758619a266858c.

7  http://www.vice.com/en_uk/read/darius-ferdynand-britains-best-bottom-394.

8  http://www.queerty.com/photos-adult-film-star-brent-corrigan-tries-his-hand-at-hollywood-acting-20140110.

9  See: http://www.out.com/michael-musto/2015/6/29/johnny-hazzard-being-dramatic-actor-tour-guide-and-single and http://www.gaystarnews.com/article/leaving-johnny-hazzard-behind-we-meet-frankie-valenti-%E2%80%93%C2%A0actor030615/#gs. KTiMWwI and http://www.slate.com/blogs/outward/2015/07/31/frankie_valenti_aka_johnny_hazzard_shines_in_tiger_orange.html.

10  http://www.nytimes.com/2010/11/14/fashion/14eklund.html?pagewanted=all&_r=0.

11  http://www.nightcharm.com/2014/06/03/tackling-the-mans-man-of-gay-porn-the-nightcharm-interview-with-colby-jansen/.

12  See the interview with Tim Kruger here: http://www.kaltblut-magazine.com/tim-kruger/ and the mass of interviews with porn celebrities produced for Queer Pig here: https://vimeo.com/132328512.

13  http://www.queerty.com/dont-call-porn-star-turned-twitteractive-rapper-chris-porter-a-twink-20110509.

14  http://str8upgayporn.com/best-gay-porn-star-twitter-fights-2014/.

15  http://thesword.com/fight-brent-corrigan-calls-chris-crocker-a-bitchy-queen-but-says-his-hole-isnt-that-bad.html and http://str8upgayporn.com/fight-brent-corrigan-and-trevor-knight-threaten-each-other-on-twitter/.

16  http://thesword.com/tag/jake-bass and https://twitter.com/FuckingJakeBass/status/612047990832951296.

17  http://www.bitchless.net/index.php?s=865ee4de6ef3335111249eed1cfc3ff2&showforum=1030.

18  http://www.cbc.ca/news/canada/manitoba/ballet-school-accused-of-kicking-out-dancer-for-doing-porn-1.1329099.

19  http://www.queerty.com/high-school-principal-suspends-sean-cody-model-for-porn-work-wont-let-him-graduate-20140118/.

20  http://www.huffingtonpost.com/2012/03/11/shawn-loftis-gay-porn-star-teaching_n_1337528.html and http://www.miaminewtimes.com/news/miami-dade-teacher-shawn-loftis-fired-over-gay-porn-career-6383471 and http://gawker.com/5892203/teacher-fired-over-gay-porn-career-has-been-reinstated.

21  http://www.mmafighting.com/ufc/2012/2/28/2831727/dakota-cochrane-discusses-controversial-past-as-he-prepares-to-chase.

22  http://queerpig.com/exclusive-jake-genesis-is-done-with-porn-read-his-shocking-statement/ and http://www.queerty.com/gay-porn-star-jake-genesis-apologizes-20130503 and http://www.christianpost.com/news/ex-gay-porn-star-jake-floyd-genesis-returns-to-catholic-church-96920/ and http://johnmagnumxxx.tumblr.com/post/49494855584/there-is-no-truth-out-there.

23  See: http://www.out.com/news-opinion/2013/05/09/porn-problem-star-death-arpad-miklos and http://www.advocate.com/politics/marriage-equality/2013/03/12/porn-star-wilfried-knight-commits-suicide-after-long-battle and http://www.nydailynews.com/new-york/gay-porn-star-found-dead-nyc-apt-article-1.1257645. This spate of deaths provoked wider concerns about welfare in the

gay porn industry. See: http://www.villagevoice.com/blogs/so-many-gay-porn-stars-have-died-lately-why-6367840.

24  http://gawker.com/5918779/gay-porns-erik-rhodes-is-dead-after-slowly-dying-in-public-for-years and http://www.towleroad.com/2012/06/gay-adult-film-star-erik-rhodes-dead-at-30/ and https://www.frontiersmedia.com/frontiers-blog/2012/06/15/did-erik-rhodes-commit-suicide/ Erik Rhodes blog can be found here: http://erikrhodes.tumblr.com/archive

25  http://www.huffingtonpost.com/frankie-valenti/gay-porn-why-did-i-survive_b_3405589.html.

26  See Richard Dyer (1990) *Now You See It*, London: Routledge.

27  See: http://madmuseum.org/series/fran%C3%A7ois-sagat and http://www.out.com/entertainment/popnography/2011/11/16/gay-porn-star-francois-sagat-gets-us-museum-retrospective and http://www.huffingtonpost.com/2011/11/17/franois-sagat-gay-porn-star-master-class-museum_n_1099528.html.

28  See *Butt* magazine interview: http://www.buttmagazine.com/magazine/interviews/peter-berlin/ and http://www.sfgate.com/entertainment/article/Peter-Berlin-made-a-work-of-art-out-of-his-sex-2504598.php.

29  http://www.papermag.com/a-guide-to-hipster-pornstars-1426849375.html.

30  See: http://bigshoediaries.blogspot.co.uk/?zx=b36d7517b9a9cf78 and http://www.vice.com/en_uk/read/colby-keller-is-the-marina-abramovic-of-gay-porn.

31  See: http://www.theawl.com/2013/08/bodies-commerce-complicity-porn-star-dale-cooper and http://slutever.com/dale-cooper-porn-interview. Cooper's critique of the models of masculinity that gay porn produces is interesting: http://www.huffingtonpost.com/dale-cooper/hulking-macho-fantasy_b_1640508.html.

32  See also Paasonen (2011), Dery (2007) and Jacobs (2004).

33  http://www.luriddigs.com/.

34  http://all-americanheroes.net/tour212/ and http://www.activeduty.com/en.

35  http://mystraightbuddy.com/?CA=938661-0000&PA=2489988.

36  http://mystraightbuddy.com/videos/lockdown_preview.php?id=203&size=800k?ip=1.

37  http://mystraightbuddy.com/videos/lockdown_preview.php?id=164&size=800k?ip=1.

38  http://www.czechhunter.com/.

39  http://www.raydragon.com/index2.php.

40  The Xtube user Honeybeee123 has amassed a collection of recordings of webcam broadcasters: http://www.xtube.com/community/profile.php?user=honeybeee123.

41  The Xtube user Taglionnonno collects exhibitionist videos: http://www.xtube.com/user_videos.php?u=TAGLIANONNO.

42  http://www.xtube.com/user_videos.php?u=btcellnet.

43 See Nolan and Korbin at active duty: http://www.activeduty.com/en/movie-show/Korbin--Nolan/70204; see Derrick the ditch digger at New York Straight Men: http://www.straightmaletube.com/Straight-Guys/Newyorkstraightmen/138927/Derick-The-Ditchdigger.html and Diesel and Jimmy at Broke Straight Boys: http://www.straightmaletube.com/Straight-Guys/Brokestraightboys/21805/Diesel-And-Jimmy-Part-3.html.

44 In this fairly typical example, the camera is positioned so that the viewer sees little more than the back of Latinoanaheim's head and backside through the duration of the sex scene: http://www.xtube.com/watch.php?v=KlmDz-G507-.

45 See Nightcharm's hilarious critique of gay porn vocalisations: http://www.nightcharm.com/2015/02/26/top-10-worst-gay-porn-lines/.

46 http://www.xtube.com/watch.php?v=tUqgS-G698-.

47 http://www.xtube.com/amateur_channels/play.php?v=kqbUUPxE9jp&type=p review.

48 http://www.xtube.com/amateur_channels/play.php?v=36WJZ4qdWhK&type= preview.

49 http://www.maverickmen.com/mmwp/

50 http://www.xtube.com/amateur_channels/amateur.php?u=maverickman222.

51 See: http://www.edgeboston.com/index.php?ch=style&sc=life&sc3=&id=1118 46&pg=1 and http://www.gaydemon.com/blogs/interview_cole_and_hunter_ maverick_men.html and http://manhuntdaily.com/2010/06/exclusive-interview-with-cole-maverick/ and http://thesword.com/the-maverick-men-open-up.html and http://dismagazine.com/blog/40558/maverick-men-1-amateur-couple-on-xtube/.

52 In a similar trajectory to Maverick Men, see the work of Eric from Paris. Eric originally recorded his sexual encounters for distribution online and released several of these via a subsequent co-production with Treasure Island. See: http://store.treasureislandmedia.com/ERIC-S-RAW-FUCK-TAPES-5.html. Eric now runs his own website and production company and his output has been transformed from the clearly homemade to work that draws on the rhetoric of amateurism but is highly elaborate and cinematic in its realisation. See: http://ericvideos.com/EN/homepage/1.

53 See also Brickell's 'Sexuality Power and the Sociology of the internet' (2012), Ross' 'Typing Doing and Being' (2005) and Briggle's 'Love on the internet' (2008).

54 http://www.xvideos.com/profiles/morenos1972#_tabAboutMe.

55 http://www.xvideos.com/video15879717/calcao_branco_x_shortinho_vermelho#_tabComments.

56 A further fascinating, though altogether more self-consciously arch example is offered by the Xvideo user Tiery B, a visual artist and photographer who uses

the site as a venue to exhibit highly performative sexual displays of the self and sexual encounters with partners that often make use of mirrors and a mode of address that acknowledges the gaze of an voyeuristic, unseen viewer. See: http://www.xvideos.com/profiles/tiery-b#_tabAboutMe http://www.tiery-b.com/ and http://tieryb-pornographer.tumblr.com/.

# Bibliography

Aboim, S. (2010) *Plural Masculinities: The Remaking of the Self in Private Life*. Farnham: Ashgate.

Acker, J. (2004) 'Gender, Capitalism and Globalization', *Critical Sociology* vol. 30, no.1, p. 1741.

Alexander, B. K. (2011) 'Queer(y)ing Masculinities' in Jackson, R. L. and Balaji, M. (eds), *Global Masculinities and Manhood*. Champaign: University of Illinois Press.

Anderson, E. (2014) *Twenty-first Century Jocks: Sporting Men and Contemporary Masculinity*. London: Palgrave.

_____ (2012) *The Monogamy Gap: Men, Love, and the Reality of Cheating*. New York: Oxford University Press.

_____ (2010) *Sport, Society and Social Problems: A Critical Introduction*. New York: Routledge.

_____ (2009) *Inclusive Masculinity: The Changing Face of Masculinities*. New York: Routledge.

Anon. (1999) 'Kristen Bjorn', *15 Years of Men: Special Anniversary Edition*, pp. 80–1.

Arvidson, A. (2006) 'Quality Singles: Internet Dating and the Work of Fantasy', *New Media & Society* vol. 8, issue 4, pp. 671–90.

Attwood, F. (2014) 'Immersion: "Extreme" Texts, Animated Bodies and the Media', *Media, Culture & Society* vol. 36, issue 8, pp. 1186–95.

_____ (2009) 'Deepthroatfucker and Discerning Adonis: Men and Cybersex', *International Journal of Cultural Studies* vol. 12, no. 3 pp. 279–94.

_____ (2007) 'No Money Shot? Commerce, Pornography and New Sex Taste Cultures', *Sexualities* vol. 10, no. 4, pp. 441–56.

_____ (2006) 'Sexed Up: Theorizing the Sexualization of Culture', *Sexualities* vol. 9, no.1, pp. 77–94.

Bad Object Choices (eds) (1991) *How Do I Look? Queer Film and Video*. Seattle: Bay Press.

Baird, R. and Rosenbaum, S. (eds) (1991) *Pornography, Private Right or Public Menace?* New York: Prometheus.

Barcan, R. (2002) 'In the Raw: Home-Made Porn and Reality Genres', *Journal of Mundane Behavior* vol. 3, no. 1.

Barker, M. (2014) 'The "Problem" of Sexual Fantasies', *Porn Studies* vol. 1, no. 1–2, pp. 143–60.

Barker, M. J. (2013) 'Gender and BDSM Revisited: Reflections on a Decade of Researching Kink Communities', *Psychology of Women Section Review* vol. 15, no. 2.

Baudrillard, J. (1998) *Consumer Society: Myths and Structures*. London: Sage.

_____ (1994) *Simulacra and Simulation*. Ann Arbor: University of Michigan Press.

_____ (1993) *Symbolic Exchange and Death*. London: Sage.

_____ (1981) *For a Critique of the Political Economy of the Sign*. London: Telos Press.

_____ (1975) *The Mirror of Production*. London: Telos Press.

Bauman, Z. (2006) *Liquid Times: Living in an Age of Uncertainity*. Cambridge: Polity.

_____ (2005a) *Liquid Fear*. Cambridge: Polity.

_____ (2005b) *Liquid Life*. Cambridge: Polity.

_____ (2003) *Liquid Love*. Cambridge: Polity.

_____ (2001) *The Individualized Society*. Cambridge: Polity.

_____ (2000) *Liquid Modernity*. Cambridge: Polity.

Beasley, C., Brook, H. and Holmes, M. (2015) 'Heterodoxy: Challenging Orthodoxies about Heterosexuality', *Sexualities* vol. 18, no. 5–6, pp. 681–97.

Beasley, C. and Elias, J. (2009) 'Hegemonic Masculinity and Globalization: Transnational Business Masculinities and Beyond', *Globalizations* vol. 6, no. 2, pp. 281–96.

Becker, R. (2009) *Gay TV and Straight America*. New Brunswick: Rutgers University Press.

Beckmann, A. (2009) *The Social Construction of Sexuality and Perversion: Deconstructing Sadomasochism*. London: Palgrave.

Bell, D. (2009) 'Surveillance is Sexy', *Surveillance & Society* vol. 6, no. 3, pp. 203–12.

Benshoff, H. and Griffin, S. (2006) *Queer Images: A History of Gay and Lesbian Film in America*. Oxford: Rowman and Littlefield.

Benwell, B. (2002) 'Is there Anything "New" about these Lads?: The Textual and Visual Construction of Masculinity in Men's Magazines' in Litosseliti, L. and Sunderland, J. (eds), *Gender Identity and Discourse Analysis: Discourse Approaches to Politics, Society and Culture*. Amsterdam: John Benjamins, pp. 149–74.

Berg, H. (2015) 'Sex, Work, Queerly: Identity, Authenticity and Laboured Performance' in Laing, M., Pilcher, K. and Smith, N. (eds), *Queer Sex Work*. London: Routledge.

Bersani, L. (1995) *Homos*. Cambridge, MA: Harvard University Press.

Best, A. L. (2007) *Representing Youth: Methodological Issues in Critical Youth Studies*. New York: NYU Press.

Binnie, J. (2004) *The Globalization of Sexuality*. London: Sage.

Blachford, G. (1979) 'Looking at Pornography', *Screen Education*, no. 29, pp. 21–8.

_____ (1978) 'Looking at Pornography: Erotica and the Socialist Morality', *Gay Left*, no. 6, Summer, pp. 16–20.

Boyle, K. (ed.) (2010) *Everyday Pornography*. London: Routledge.

_____ (2005) *Media and Violence: Gendering the Debate*. London: Sage.

Brewis, J. and Jack, G. (2010) 'Consuming Chavs: The Ambiguous Politics of Gay Chavinism', *Sociology* vol. 44, April, pp. 251–68.

Brickell, C. (2012) 'Sexuality, Power and the Sociology of the Internet', *Current Sociology* vol. 60, no. 1, pp. 28–44.

Briggle, A. (2008) 'Love on the Internet: A Framework for Understanding Eros Online', *Journal of Information, Communication and Ethics in Society* vol. 6, no. 3, pp. 215–32.

Brod, H. (1987) *The Making of Masculinities: The New Men's Studies*. London: Allen & Unwin.

Brod, H. and Kaufman, M. (eds) (1994) *Theorizing Masculinities: Researching Men and Masculinities*. New York: Sage.

Bronski, M. (1991) 'A Dream is a Wish Your Heart Makes: Notes on the Materialization of Sexual Fantasy' in Thompson, M. (ed.), *Leatherfolk: Radical Sex, Politics and Practice*. Boston: Alyson Publications.

_____ (1978) 'What Does Soft Core Porn Really Mean to the Gay Male?', *Gay Community News*, Boston, 28/1/78.

Brown, G., Browne, K. and Lim, J. (eds) (2007) *Geographies of Sexualities: Theory, Practices and Politics*. London: Routledge.

Buchbinder, D. (2012) *Studying Men Greek Religion and Masculinities*. London: Routledge.

_____ (1998) *Performance Anxieties: Re-producing Masculinity*. London: Allen & Unwin.

_____ (1994) *Masculinities and Identity*. Melbourne: Melbourne University Press.

_____ and McMillan, P. (1992) *Men, Sex and Other Secrets*. Melbourne: The Text Publishing Company.

Burger, J. (1995) *One Handed Histories: The Eroto-Politics of Gay Male Video Pornography*. New York: Harrington Park Press.

Burgess, J. (2006) 'Hearing Ordinary Voices: Cultural Studies, Vernacular Creativity and Digital Storytelling', *Continuum: Journal of Media & Cultural Studies* vol. 20, no. 2, pp. 201–14.

Burkert, W. (1985) *Greek Religion*. Harvard: Harvard University Press.

Burstyn, V. (1999) *The Rites of Men: Manhood, Politics, and the Culture of Sport*. Toronto: University of Toronto Press.

Butler, J. (1993) *Bodies That Matter*. London: Routledge.

Califia, P. (2000) *Public Sex: The Culture of Radical Sex* (2nd edition). San Francisco: Cleis Press.

Campbell, N. (ed) (2004) *American Youth Cultures*. New York: Routledge.

Cante, R. and Restivo, A. (2004) 'The Cultural-Aesthetic Specificities of All-Male Moving-Image Pornography' in Williams, L. (ed.), *Porn Studies*. Durham: Duke University Press, pp. 142–67.

# Bibliography

_____ (2001) 'The Voice of Pornography' in Tinkcom, M. and Villarejo, A. (eds), *Keyframes*. New York: Routledge, p. 221.

Capino, J. (2005) 'Homologies of Space: Text and Spectatorship in All-Male Adult Theaters', *Cinema Journal* vol. 45, no. 1, pp. 50–65.

_____ (2004) 'Seminal Fantasies: Wakefield Poole, Independent Cinema & The American Avant-Garde' in Holmlund, C. and Wyatt, J. (eds), *Contemporary American Independent Film: From the Margins to the Mainstream*. New York: Routledge.

Caughie, J., Creed, B., Kuhn, A. and Merck, M. (eds) (1992) *The Sexual Subject*. London: Routledge, London.

Champagne, J. (1997) ' "Stop Reading Films!": Film Studies, Close Analysis, and Gay Pornography', *Cinema Journal* vol. 36, no. 4, pp. 76–97.

Chapman, R. and Rutherford, J. (eds) (1988) *Male Order. Unwrapping Masculinity*. London: Lawrence & Wishart.

Clarkson, J. (2006). ' "Everyday Joe" versus "Pissy, Bitchy, Queens": Gay Masculinity on straightacting.com', *Journal of Men's Studies* vol. 14, issue 2, pp. 191–207.

Cockburn, C. (1985) *Machinery of Dominance: Women, Men and Technological Know-How*. London: Pluto Press.

_____ (1983) *Brothers: Male Dominance and Technological Change*. London: Pluto Press.

Cohan, S. (1997) *Masked Men: Masculinity and the Movies in the Fifties*. Bloomington: Indiana University Press.

Cohan, S. and Hark, I. R. (eds) (1993) *Screening the Male: Exploring Masculinities in Hollywood Cinema*. London: Routledge.

Comella, L. and Tarrant, S. (2015) *New Views on Pornography*. New York: Praeger.

Connell, R. (2005) *Masculinities* (2nd edition). Cambridge: Polity.

_____ (2001) *The Men and the Boys*. Berkeley: University of California Press.

_____ (1995) *Masculinities*. Cambridge: Polity

Connell, R. and Messerschmidt, J. (2005) 'Hegemonic Masculinity: Rethinking the Concept', *Gender and Society* vol. 19, no. 6, pp. 829–59.

Cook, R. (2012) 'Lukas Duwenhögger: Homosexual Signs', *Afterall: A Journal of Art, Context, and Enquiry* issue 31, pp. 58–70.

Cover, R. (2015) 'Visual Heteromasculinities Online: Beyond Binaries and Sexual Normativities in Camera Chat Forums', *Men and Masculinities*, pp. 1–17, DOI: 10.1177/1097184X15584909.

Craig, S. (ed.) (1992) *Men, Masculinity and the Media*. London: Sage.

Creekmur, C. and Doty, A. (eds) (1995) *Out In Culture*. London: Cassell.

Dean, T. (2009) *Unlimited Intimacy: Reflections on the Subculture of Barebacking*. Chicago: University of Chicago Press.

De Certeau, M. (1986) *Heterologies: Discourse on the Other*. Minneapolis: University of Minnesota Press.

Demetriou, D. Z. (2001) 'Connell's Concept of Hegemonic Masculinity: A Critique', *Theory and Society* vol. 30, no. 3, pp. 337–61.

D'Emilio, J. (1993) 'Capitalism and Gay Identity' in Abelove, H., Barale, M. and Halperin, D. (eds), *The Lesbian and Gay Studies Reader*. New York: Routledge.

Dery, M. (2007) 'Naked Lunch: Talking Realcore with Sergio Messin', in Jacobs, K., Janssen, M. and Pasquinelli, M. (eds), *C'lick Me: A Netporn Studies Reader*. Amsterdam: Institute of Network Cultures.

Dines, G. (2009) *Pornland: How Porn has Hijacked our Sexuality*. Boston: Beacon Press.

Drucker, P. (2015) *Warped: Gay Normality and Queer Anti-Capitalism*. Leiden: Brill.

Dutton, K. (1995) *The Perfectible Body: The Western Ideal of Physical Development*. London: Cassell.

Dworkin, A. (1991) 'Against the Male Flood: Censorship, Pornography and Equality' in Baird, R. and Rosenbaum, S. (eds), *Pornography, Private Right or Public Menace?* New York: Prometheus.

Dyer, R. (1997) *White*. London: Routledge.

———— (1994) 'Idol Thoughts: Orgasm and Self Reflexivity in Gay Pornography', *Critical Review* vol. 36, no. 1, pp. 49–62.

———— (1993) *The Matter of Images*. London: Routledge.

———— (1990a) *Now You See It: Studies on Lesbian and Gay Film*. London: Routledge.

———— (1990b) *Only Entertainment*. London: Routledge.

———— (1989) 'A Conversation about Pornography' in Shepherd, S. and Wallis, M. (eds), *Coming on Strong. Gay Politics and Culture*. London: Unwin.

———— (1985) Male Gay Porn: Coming to Terms', *Jump Cut* no. 30, pp. 27–9.

———— (1981) *Stars*. London: BFI.

———— (ed.) (1977) *Gays and Film*. London: BFI.

Edmonson, R. (1998). *Boy in the Sand: Casey Donovan, All-American Sex Star*. New York: Alyson.

Edwards, T. (1990) 'Beyond Sex and Gender: Masculinity, Homosexuality and Social Theory' in Hearn, J. and Morgan, D. (eds), *Men, Masculinities and Social Theory*. London: Unwin.

Egan, D. (2013) *Becoming Sexual: A Critical Appraisal of the Sexualization of Girls*. Cambridge: Polity Press.

Eguchi, S. (2010) 'Negotiating Hegemonic Masculinity: The Rhetorical Strategy of "Straight-Acting" among Gay Men', *Journal of Intercultural Communication Research* vol. 38, issue 3, pp. 193–209.

Elias, J. et al. (eds) (1999) *Porn 101: Eroticism, Pornography and the First Amendment*. New York: Prometheus Books.

Erich, J. and Paciotti, L. (1997) *Making It Big: Sex Stars Porn Stars and Me*. Los Angeles: Alyson Publications.

Esch, K. and Mayer, V. (2007) 'How Unprofessional: The Profitable Partnership of Amateur Porn and Celebrity Culture' in Paasonen, K., Nikunen, K. and Sarrenmaa, L. (eds), *Pornification: Sex and Sexuality in Media Culture*. Oxford: Berg.

Escoffier, J. (2009) *Bigger Than Life: The History of Gay Porn Cinema from Beefcake to Hardcore*. Philadelphia: Running Press.

Eyben, E. (1977) *Restless Youth in Ancient Rome*. London: Routledge.

Fanon, F. (1967) *Black Skin, White Masks*. London: Pluto Press.

Fritscher, J. (1991) 'Artist Chuck Arnett: His Life/Our Times' in Thompson, M. (ed.), *Leatherfolk: Radical Sex, Politics and Practice*. Boston: Alyson Publications.

Fung, R. (1993) 'Shortcomings: Questions about Porn as Pedagogy' in Gever, M., Greyson, J. and Parmar, P. (eds), *Queer Looks*. London: Routledge.

_____ (1991) 'Looking for my Penis: The Eroticized Asian in Gay Video Porn' in Bad Object Choices, Fung, R and Mercer, K. (eds), *How Do I Look? Queer Film and Video*. Seattle: Bay Press.

Fung, R. and Mercer, K. (eds) (1991) *How Do I Look? Queer Film and Video*. Seattle: Bay Press.

Gabriel, J. (2013) 'Dreaming of a White … ' in Cottle, S. (ed.), *Ethnic Minorities & The Media: Changing Cultural Boundaries*. Maidenhead: Open University Press.

Garcia, C. (2013) 'Limited Intimacy: Barebacking and the Imaginary', *Textual Practice* vol. 27, no. 6, pp. 1030–51.

Garelick, R. K. (1999) *Rising Star: Dandyism, Gender and Performance in the Fin de Siècle*. Princeton: Princeton University Press.

Gendron, F. (1993) *The Gilded Youth of Thermidor*. Montreal: McGill-Queen's University Press.

Gergen, K. (2001) *Social Construction in Context*. London: Sage.

_____ (1991) *The Saturated Self: Dilemmas of Identity in Contemporary Life*. New York: Basic Books.

Gilbert, J. (2005) *Men in the Middle: Searching for Masculinity in the 1950s*. Chicago: Chicago University Press.

Glazer, N. (2007) *From a Cause to a Style: Modernist Architecture's Encounter with the American City*. Princeton: Princeton University Press.

Graham, P. (2004) *The End of Adolescence*. Oxford: Oxford University Press.

Gutmann, M. (1996) *The Meanings of Macho: Being a Man in Mexico City*. Los Angeles: University of California Press.

Hall, M. (2015) *Metrosexual Masculinities*. London: Palgrave.

Halperin, D. M. (1990) *One Hundred Years of Homosexuality: And Other Essays on Greek Love*. New York: Routledge.

Hamilton, C. (2013) 'Symbolic Amateurs: On the Discourse of Amateurism in Contemporary Media Culture', *Cultural Studies Review* vol. 19, no. 1, pp. 179–92.

Hanke, R. (1990) 'Hegemonic Masculinity in *Thirty Something*', *Critical Studies in Mass Communication* vol. 7, issue 3, pp. 231–48.

Hardy, S. (2008) 'The Pornography of Reality', *Sexualities* vol. 11, no. 1/2, pp. 60–3.

Harris, W. C. (2009) *Queer Externalities: Hazardous Encounters in American Culture*. Albany: SUNY Press.

Hearn, J. (1987) *The Gender of Oppression: Men, Masculinity and the Critique of Marxism*. Brighton: Harvester Wheatsheaf.

Heffernan. K. (2015) 'Seen as a Business: Adult Film's Historical Framework and Foundations' in Comella, L. and Tarrant, S. (eds), *New Views on Pornography: Sexuality, Politics and the Law*. Santa Barbara: Praeger.

Hennen, P. (2008) *Faeries, Bears, and Leathermen: Men in Community Queering the Masculine*. Chicago: University of Chicago Press.

Hill Collins, P. (2006) 'A Telling Difference: Dominance, Strength, and Black Masculinities' in Mutua, A. D. (ed), *Progressive Black Masculinities*. New York: Routledge.

Hitchcock, H. R. and Johnson, P. (1932) *The International Style*. New York: W.W. Norton & Company.

Holmlund, C. (2002) *Impossible Bodies: Femininity and Masculinity at the Movies*. New York: Routledge.

Hopcke, R. (1991) 'S/M and the Psychology of Gay Male Initiation: An Archetypal Perspective' in Thompson, M. (ed.), *Leatherfolk: Radical Sex, Politics and Practice*. Boston: Alyson Publications.

Isherwood, C. (1996) *Wonder Bread and Ecstasy: The Life and Death of Joey Stefano*. Los Angeles: Alyson Publications.

Jackson, E. (1995) *Strategies of Deviance: Studies in Gay Male Representation*. Bloomington: Indiana University Press.

Jacobs, K. (2004) 'Pornography in Small Places and Other Spaces', *Cultural Studies* vol. 18, no. 1, pp. 67–83, DOI: 10.1080/0950238042000181610.

Jeffreys, S. (2015) *Beauty and Misogyny: Harmful Cultural Practices in the West* (2nd edition). London: Routledge.

Johansson, T. (2007) *The Transformation of Sexuality: Gender and Identity in Contemporary Youth Culture*. Aldershot: Ashgate.

Johnson, P. (2008) ' "Rude Boys": The Homosexual Eroticization of Class', *Sociology* vol. 42, February, pp. 65–82.

Johnston, L. and Longhurst, R. (2010) *Space, Place, and Sex: Geographies of Sexualities*. London: Rowman and Littlefield.

Kammeyer, R. (2008) *A Hypersexual Society: Sexual Discourse, Erotica and Pornography in America Today*. London: Palgrave.

Kappeler, S. (1986) *The Pornography of Representation*. London: Polity Press.

Kaufman, M. (1994) 'Men, Feminism, and Men's Contradictory Experiences of Power' in Brod, H. and Kaufman, M. (eds), *Theorizing Masculinities*. Thousand Oaks: Sage.

**222**

Kendrick, W. (1987) *The Secret Museum: Pornography in Modern Culture*. Berkeley: University of California Press.

Kimmel, M. (2005) 'Globalization and its (Mal(e)contents: The Gendered Moral and Political Economy of Terrorism' in Kimmel, M. et al. (eds), *Handbook of Studies on Men & Masculinities*. Thousand Oaks and London: Sage, pp. 414–31.

Kimmel, M. S. (2013) *The Gendered Society* (5th edition). Oxford: Oxford University Press.

_____ (2004) *The Gendered Society* (3rd edition). Oxford: Oxford University Press.

_____ (1996) *Manhood in America: A Cultural History*. New York: Free Press.

_____ (1995) *The Politics of Manhood: Profeminist Men Respond to the Mythopoetic Men's Movement*. Philadelphia: Temple University Press.

_____ (1987) *Changing Men: New Directions in Research on Men and Masculinity*. Thousand Oaks: Sage.

Kipnis, L. (1998) *Bound and Gagged: Pornography and the Politics of Fantasy in America*. New York: Duke University Press.

Kirkham, P. and Thumin, J. (eds) (1993) *You Tarzan: Men, Masculinity and Movies*. London: Lawrence and Wishart.

Kiss, M. and Nielsen, E. J. (2015) 'Sexercising our Opinion on Porn: a Virtual Discussion', *Psychology & Sexuality* vol. 6, no. 1, pp. 118–39.

Komarovsky, M. (2004) *Dilemmas of Masculinity: A Study of College Youth* (2nd edition). New York: Norton.

_____ (1976) *Dilemmas of Masculinity: A Study of College Youth*. New York: Norton.

Kosofsky Sedgwick, E. (1990) *The Epistomology of the Closet*. Berkeley: University of California Press.

Kuhn, A. (1985) *The Power of the Image*. London: Routledge.

Langdridge, D. and Barker, M. (2007) *Safe, Sane and Consensual: Contemporary Perspectives Sadomasochism*. London: Palgrave Macmillan.

Lanzieri, N. and Hildebrandt, T. (2011) 'Using Hegemonic Masculinity to Explain Gay Male Attraction to Muscular and Athletic Men', *Journal of Homosexuality* vol. 58, pp. 275–93.

Lasén, A. and García, A. (2015) ' " … but I haven't got a body to show": Self-Pornification and Male Mixed Feelings in Digitally Mediated Seduction Practices', *Sexualities* vol. 18, no. 5–6, pp. 714–30.

Leadbeater, C. (2010) *We Think: Mass Innovation, Not Mass Production*. New York: Profile Books.

_____ and Miller, P. (2004) *The Pro-am Revolution: How Enthusiasts are Changing Our Society and Economy*. London: Demos.

Lehman, P. (2007) *Running Scared: Masculinity and the Representation of the Male Body* (2nd edition). Detroit: Wayne State University.

_____ (ed.) (2001) *Masculinity: Bodies, Movies, Culture*. New York, Routledge.

_____ (1993) *Running Scared: Masculinity and the Representation of the Male Body*. Philadelphia: Temple University Press.

Levine, M. (1998) *Gay Macho: The Life and Death of the Homosexual Clone*. New York: New York University Press.

Linz, D. and Malamuth, N. (1993) *Pornography*. Thousand Oaks: Sage.

Lister, M., Dovey, J., Giddings, S., Grant, I. and Kelly, K. (2009) *New Media: A Critical Introduction* (2nd edition). London: Routledge.

Long, J. (2012) *Anti-Porn: The Resurgence of Anti-Pornography Feminism*. London: Zed Books.

Lorenz, J. (1999) 'Going Gonzo! The American Flaneur, the Eastern European On/Scene, and the Pleasures of Implausibility' in Elias, J. et al. (eds), *Porn 101: Eroticism, Pornography and the First Amendment*. New York: Prometheus Books.

Luther Hillman, B. (2015) *Dressing for the Culture Wars: Style and the Politics of Self-Presentation in the 1960s and 1970s*. Lincoln: University of Nebraska Press.

Mackenzie, C. (2005) 'Imagining Oneself Otherwise' in Atkins, K. (ed.), *Self and Subjectivity*. Oxford: Blackwell Publishing.

Maddison, S. (2012) 'Is the Rectum *Still* a Grave? Anal Sex, Pornography and Transgression' in Gournelos, T. and Gunkel, D. J. (eds), *Transgression 2.0: Media, Culture and the Politics of a Digital Age*. New York: Continuum Books.

Manley, E., Levitt, H. M. and Mosher, C. (2007) 'Understanding the Bear Movement in Gay Male Culture: Redefining Masculinity', *Journal of Homosexuality* vol. 53, no. 4, pp. 89–112.

Marcus, S. (1964) *The Other Victorians: A Study of Sexuality and Pornography in Mid-Nineteenth-Century England*. New Brunswick: Basic Books.

Martel, F. (2000) *The Pink and the Black: Homosexuals in France Since 1968*. Stanford: Stanford University Press.

Martino, W. (2012) 'Straight-Acting Masculinities: Normalization and Gender Hierarchies in Gay Men's Lives' in Kendall, C. and Martino, W. (eds), *Gendered Outcasts and Sexual Outlaws: Sexual Oppression and Gender Hierarchies in Queer Men's Lives*. New York: Routledge.

Massumi, B. (1987) 'Realer than Real: The Simulacrum According to Deleuze and Guattari', *Copyright* no. 1, pp. 90–7.

McBride, D. A. (2005) *Why I Hate Abercrombie & Fitch: Essays on Race and Sexuality*. New York: NYU Press.

McKee, A. (2014) 'Humanities and Social Scientific Research Methods in Porn Studies', *Porn Studies* vol. 1, issue 1–2, pp. 53–63.

_____ (1999) 'Australian Gay Porn Videos: The National Identity of Despised Cultural Objects', *International Journal of Cultural Studies* vol. 2, no. 2, pp. 178–98.

McKittrick, C. (2010) 'Brother's Milk: The Erotic and the Lethal in Gay Pornography' in Monroe, D. (ed.), *Porn – Philosophy for Everyone: How to Think with Kink*. London: Wiley-Blackwell.

McNair, B. (1996) *Mediated Sex: Pornography and Postmodern Culture*. London: Arnold.

McNamara, M. (2013) 'Cumming to Terms: Bareback Pornography, Homonormativity, and Queer Survival in the Time of HIV/AIDS' in Fahs, B., Dudy, M. and Stage, S. (eds), *The Moral Panics of Sexuality*. London: Palgrave Macmillan.

Mellen, J. (1977) *Big Bad Wolves: Masculinity in the American Film*. New York: Pantheon.

Mercer, J. (2012a) 'Coming of Age: Problematizing Gay Porn and the Eroticised Older Man', *The Journal of Gender Studies* vol. 21, issue 3, pp. 312–26.

_____ (2012b) 'Power Bottom: Performativity in Commercial Gay Pornographic Video' in Hines, C. and Kerr, D. (eds), *Hard to Swallow: Hard-Core Pornography on Screen*. London: Columbia University Press.

_____ (2011) 'Gay for Pay: The Internet and the Economics of Homosexual Desire' in Ross, K. (ed.), *The Handbook of Gender, Sex, and Media*. London: Wiley-Blackwell.

_____ (2006) 'Seeing is Believing: Constructions of Stardom and The Gay Porn Star in U.S. Gay Video Pornography' in, Holmes, S. and Redmond, S. (eds), *Framing Celebrity*. London: Routledge.

_____ (2004) 'Deep in the Brig: The Myth of the Prison in Gay Pornography', *Journal of Homosexuality* vol. 47, issue 3–4, pp. 151–66.

_____ (2003) 'Prototypes: Repetition and the Construction of the Generic in Gay Pornography' in *Paragraph* special issue, Still, J. (ed.), *Men's Bodies*, pp. 280–90.

Mercer, K. (1993) 'Imagining the Black Man's Sex' in Abelove, H., Barale, M. and Halperin, D. (eds), *The Lesbian and Gay Studies Reader*. New York: Routledge.

_____ (1991) 'Skin Head Sex Thing: Racial Difference and the Homoerotic Imaginary' in Bad Object Choices (eds), *How Do I Look? Queer Film and Video*. Seattle: Bay Press.

Merck, M. (1993) *Perversions: Deviant Readings*. New York: Routledge.

Messerschmidt, J. W. (2000) *Nine Lives: Adolescent Masculinities, The Body And Violence*. Boulder: Westview Press.

_____ (1997) *Crime as Structured Action: Gender, Race, Class, and Crime in the Making*. Thousand Oaks: Sage.

_____ (1993) *Masculinities and Crime: Critique and Reconceptualization of Theory*. Lanham: Rowman and Littlefield.

Messner, M. A. (2010) *Out of Play: Critical Essays on Gender and Sport*. Albany: SUNY Press.

_____ (1997) *Politics of Masculinities: Men in Movements*. New York: Rowman and Littlefield.

_____ (1995) *Power at Play: Sports and the Problem of Masculinity*. New York: Beacon Press.

Miller, E. (2013) 'Clean Feet and Dirty Dancing: The Erotic Pas de Deux and Boys in the Sand' in Maes, H. (ed.), *Pornographic Art and the Aesthetics of Pornography*. London: Palgrave Macmillan.

Miller Young, M. (2014) *A Taste for Brown Sugar: Black Women in Pornography*. Durham, NC: Duke University Press.

Mirzoeff, N. (1995) *Bodyscape: Art, Modernity and the Ideal Figure*. London: Routledge.

Moorman, J. (2010). 'Gay for Pay, Gay For(e)play: The Politics of Taxonomy and Authenticity in LGBTQ Online Porn' in Attwood, F. (ed.), *Porn.com*. New York: Peter Lang Publishing.

Morris, P. (2005) 'No Limits: Necessary Danger in Male Porn', available at http://www.managing desire.org/nolimits.html.

Mowlabocus, S., Harbottle, J. and Witzel, C. (2013) 'Porn Laid Bare: Gay Men, Pornography and Bareback Sex', *Sexualities* vol. 16, no. 5–6, pp. 523–47.

Mulholland, M. (2013) *Young People and Pornography: Negotiating Pornification*. London: Palgrave.

Mulvey, L. (1975) 'Visual Pleasure and Narrative Cinema', *Screen* vol. 16, no. 3, pp. 6–18.

Muncie, J. (2004) *Youth and Crime* (2nd edition). London: Sage.

Nardi, P. M. (1997) 'Friends, Lovers, and Families: The Impact of AIDS on Gay and Lesbian Relationships' in Levine, M., Nardi, P. M. and Gagnon, J. H. (eds), *In Changing Times: Gay Men and Lesbians Encounter HIV/AIDS*. Chicago: University of Chicago Press.

Nayar, P. K. (2009) *Seeing Stars: Spectacle, Society and Celebrity Culture*. Thousand Oaks: Sage.

Neale, S. (2000) *Genre and Hollywood*. London: Routledge.

_____ (1983) 'Masculinity as Spectacle: Reflections on Men and Mainstream Cinema', *Screen* vol. 24. no. 6, pp. 2–16.

Newmahr, S. (2011) *Playing on the Edge: Sadomasochism, Risk, and Intimacy*. Bloomington: Indiana University Press.

Nguyen, T. H. (2014) *A View From the Bottom: Asian American Masculinity and Sexual Representation*. Durham: Duke University Press.

_____ (2004) 'The Resurrection of Brandon Lee: The Making of a Gay Asian American Porn Star' in Williams, L. (ed.), *Porn Studies*. Durham, NC: Duke University Press.

Nikunen, K. (2015) 'Intimacy Re-defined: Online Sexual Performances and the Urge of Posing', *Liminalities: A Journal of Performance Studies* vol. 11, no. 1, available at http://liminalities.net/11-1/intimacy.pdf.

Nixon, S. (1996) *Hard Looks: Masculinities, Spectatorship and Contemporary Consumption*. London: UCL Press.

Nye, R. (2005) 'Locating Masculinity: Some Recent Work on Men', *Signs: Journal of Women in Culture and Society* vol. 30, no. 3, pp. 1937–62.

O'Hara, S. (1997) *Autopornography*. New York: Harrington Park Press.

Ortiz, C. (1994) 'Hot and Spicy', *Jump Cut* no. 39, June, pp. 83–90.

Osgerby, B. (2002) 'A Caste, A Culture, A Market: Youth Marketing and Lifestyle in Postwar America' in Strickland, R. (ed.), *Growing Up Postmodern: Neoliberalism and the War on the Young*. Oxford: Rowman and Littlefield.

O'Toole, L. (1998) *Pornocopia: Porn, Sex, Technology and Desire*. London: Serpent's Tail.

Paasonen, S. (2014) 'Things to Do with the Alternative' in Biasin, E., Maina, G. and Zecca, F. (eds), *Porn after Porn: Contemporary Alternative Pornographies*. Rome: Mimesis International.

_____ (2010) 'Labors of Love: Netporn, Web 2.0 and the Meanings of Amateurism' *New Media & Society* vol. 12, no. 8, pp. 1297–312.

_____ (2011) *Carnal Resonance: Affect and Online Pornography*. Cambridge, MA: MIT Press.

Papadopoulos, L. (2010) *Sexualisation of Young People Review*. London: Home Office Publication.

Parrika, J. (2012) *What is Media Archaelogy*. Cambridge: Polity.

_____ and Huhtamo, E. (2011) 'Introduction' in Huhtamo, E. and Parikka, J. (eds), *Media Archaeology: Approaches, Applications, and Implications*. Berkeley: University of California Press.

Patton, C. (1991) 'Safe Sex and the Pornographic Vernacular' in Bad Object Choices (eds), *How Do I Look? Queer Film and Video*. Seattle: Bay Press.

Paul, P. (2005) *Pornified: How Pornography Is Transforming Our Lives, Our Relationships, and our Families*. New York: Owl Books.

Penley, C. and Ross, A. (eds) (1991) *Technoculture*. Minneapolis: University of Minnesota Press.

_____ and Willis, S. (eds) (1993) *Male Trouble*. Minneapolis: University of Minnesota Press.

Phipps, A. (2014) *The Politics of the Body: Gender in a Neoliberal and Neoconservative Age*. Cambridge: Polity.

Pini, M. (2009) 'In the Bedroom: Sex on Video' in Buckingham, D. and Willett, R. (eds), *Video Cultures: Media Technology and Everyday Creativity*. London: Palgrave.

Pleck, J. H. (1983) *The Myth of Masculinity*. Cambridge, MA: MIT Press.

_____ (1980) *The American Male*. Englewood Cliffs: Prentice Hall.

Plummer, K. (2015) *Cosmopolitan Sexualities: Hope and the Humanist Imagination*. London, Polity.

Poole, J. (2014) 'Queer Representations of Gay Males and Masculinities in the Media', *Sexuality and Culture* vol. 18, issue 2, pp. 279–90.

Poole, W. (2000) *Dirty Poole: The Autobiography of a Porn Pioneer*. Los Angeles: Alyson Books.

Powell, A. (2010) *Sex, Power and Consent: Youth Culture and the Unwritten Rules*. Cambridge: Cambridge University Press.

Pronger, B. (2002) '"Ten men{...}hung and well built{...}some smooth, some hairy{...}but all insatiable" or Consuming the Buff Simulacrum' in Miller, B. and Ward, M. (eds), *Crime and Ornament: The Arts and Popular Culture in the Shadow of Adolf Loos*. Toronto: YYZ Books.

_____ (1990) *The Arena of Masculinity: Sports, Homosexuality and the Meaning of Sex*. New York: St Martin's Press.

Radel, N. (2001) 'The Transnational Ga(y)ze: Constructing the East European Object of Desire in Gay Film and Pornography after the Fall of the Wall', *Cinema Journal* vol. 41, no. 1, Fall, pp. 40–62.

Ramakers, M. (2000) *Dirty Pictures: Tom of Finland, Masculinity and Homosexuality*. New York: St Martin's Press.

Rees-Roberts, N. (2008) *French Queer Cinema*. Edinburgh: Edinburgh University Press.

Roche, S. Tucker, R. Thomson and R. Flynn (eds) (2004) *Youth in Society* (2nd edition). London: Sage.

Ross, M. (2005) 'Typing, Doing and Being: Sexuality and the Internet', *Journal of Sex Research* vol. 42, no. 4, pp. 342–52.

Rubin, G. (2011) *Deviations: A Gayle Rubin Reader*. Durham, NC: Duke University Press.

_____ (1991) 'The Catacombs: A Temple of the Butthole' in Thompson, M. (ed.), *Leatherfolk: Radical Sex, Politics and Practice*. Boston: Alyson Publications.

Schaeffer, E. (1999) *"Bold! Daring! Shocking! True!": A History of Exploitation Films, 1919–1959*. Durham: Duke University Press.

Schaschek, S. (2014) *Pornography and Seriality: The Culture of Producing Pleasure*. London, Palgrave.

Scheaffer, R. (2014) 'Smut, Novelty, Indecency: Reworking a History of the Early-Twentieth-Century American Stag Film', *Porn Studies* vol. 1, no. 4, pp. 346–59.

Schlesinger, A. (2008) 'The Crisis of Masculinity' in *The Politics of Hope: And, The Bitter Heritage: American Liberalism in the 1960s*. Princeton: Princeton University Press.

Schroeder, K. (2004) 'Hypermasculinity' in Kimmel, A. and Aronson, A. (eds), *Men and Masculinities: A Social, Cultural, and Historical Encyclopaedia*. Santa Barbara: ABC Clio.

Schwarz, O. (2010) 'Going to Bed with a Camera: On the Visualization of Sexuality and the Production of Knowledge', *International Journal of Cultural Studies* vol. 13, issue, 6, pp. 637–56.

Scuglia, B. (2015) 'The Last Days of Gay Porn', *Psychology & Sexuality* vol. 6, no. 1, pp. 111–17.

_____ (2004) 'Sex Pigs: Why Porn Is Like Sausage, or The Truth Is That Behind the Scenes Porn is Not Very Sexy', *The Journal of Homosexuality* vol. 47, issue 3–4, pp. 185–8.

# Bibliography

Scully, V. (2003) *Modern Architecture and Other Essays*. Princeton: Princeton University Press.

Seidler, V. J. (2006) *Transforming Masculinities: Men, Cultures, Bodies, Power, Sex and Love*. Abingdon: Routledge.

_____ (1997) *Man Enough: Embodying Masculinities*. London: Sage.

_____ (1989) *Rediscovering Masculinity: Reason, Language, and Sexuality*. Abingdon: Routledge.

Seidman, S. (1993) 'Identity and Politics in a "Postmodern" Gay Culture: Some Historical and Conceptual Notes' in Warner, M. (ed.), *Fear of a Queer Planet: Queer Politics and Social Theory*. Minneapolis: University of Minnesota Press.

Siapera, E. (2012) *Understanding New Media*. Thousand Oaks: Sage.

Signorile, M. (1993) *Queer in America*. London: Abacus.

Sigusch, V. (2014) 'Neosexualities and Self-Sex: On Cultural Transformations of Sexuality and Gender in Western Societies' in Schmidt, C., Mack, M. and German, A. (eds), *Post Subjectivity*. Newcastle on Tyne: Cambridge Scholars Publishing.

_____ (2004) 'On Cultural Transformations of Sexuality and Gender in Recent Decades', available at http://www.ncbi.nlm.nih.gov/pmc/articles/PMC2703209/.

_____ (2000) 'Social Transformation of Sexuality in the Past Decades. An Overview', *Fortschritte der Neurologie, Psychiatrie, und ihrer Grenzgebiete* issue 3, pp. 97–106.

_____ (1998) 'The Neosexual Revolution', *Archives of Sexual Behaviour*, issue 4, pp. 331–59.

Simpson, M. (1994) *Male Impersonators: Men Performing Masculinity*. London: Cassell.

Sinfield, A. (2004) *On Sexuality and Power*. New York: Columbia University Press.

_____ (1998) *Gay and After*. London: Serpent's Tail

Smith, C. (2012) 'Reel Intercourse: Doing Sex on Camera' in Kerr, D. and Hines, C. (eds), *Hard To Swallow: Reading Pornography On Screen*. London: Wallflower.

_____ (2010a) 'Pornographication: A Discourse for all Seasons', *International Journal of Media and Cultural Politics* vol. 6, no. 1, pp. 103–08.

_____ (2010b) 'Review of Linda Papadopoulos, Sexualisation of Young Peope Review', *Participations* vol. 7, issue 1, pp. 175–9.

Sontag, S. (1967) 'The Pornographic Imagination', *Partisan Review* vol. 34, Spring, pp. 181–212.

Speck, W. (1993) 'Porno?' in Gever, M., Greyson, J. and Parmar, P. (eds), *Queer Looks*. London: Routledge.

Stadler, J. (2013) 'Dire Straights: The Indeterminacy of Sexual Identity in Gay-for-Pay Pornography', *Jump Cut* no. 55.

Stanley, W. E. (1997) *The Complete Reprint of Physique Pictorial*. Cologne: Taschen Verlag.

Stebbins, R. A. (2006) *Serious Leisure: A Perspective of Our Time*. New Brunswick: Transaction Publishers.

_____ (2004) *Amateurs, Professionals and Serious Leisure*. Montreal: McGill-Queen's University Press.

_____ (1979) *Amateurs: Margin between Work & Leisure*. Thousand Oaks: Sage.

Steigler, B. (1998) *Technics and Time: The Fault of Epimetheus*. Stanford: Stanford University Press.

Stevenson, J. (1997) 'From the Bedroom to the Bijou: A Secret History of Gay Sex Cinema', *Film Quarterly* vol. 51, no., pp. 24–31.

Sullivan, A. (1995) *Virtually Normal*. New York: Alfred A. Knopf, Inc.

Sullivan, N. (2003) *A Critical Introduction to Queer Theory*. Edinburgh: Edinburgh University Press.

Suresha, R. (2002) *Bears on Bears: Interviews and Discussions*. New London: Bear Bones Books.

Taormino, T. (2012) *The Ultimate Guide to Kink*. San Francisco: Cleiss Press.

Tasker, Y. (1993) *Spectacular Bodies: Gender, Genre, and the Action Cinema*. London: Routledge.

Thiers, M. A. (1854) *The History of the French Revolution: Volume 4*. New York: D. Appleton and Company.

Thomas, J. (1999) 'Notes on the New Camp: Gay Video Pornography' in Elias, J. *et al.* (eds), *Porn 101: Eroticism, Pornography and the First Amendment*. New York: Prometheus Books.

Thompson, M. (ed.) (1991) *Leatherfolk: Radical Sex, Politics and Practice*. Boston: Alyson Publications.

Tiidenberg, K. (2015) 'Boundaries and Conflict in a NSFW Community on tumblr: The Meanings and Uses of Selfies', *New Media & Society*, pp. 1–16 DOI: 10.1177/1461444814567984.

_____ (2014) 'Bringing Sexy Back: Reclaiming the Body Aesthetic via Self-shooting', *Cyberpsychology: Journal of Psychosocial Research on Cyberspace* vol. 8. no. 1, article 3, DOI: 10.5817/CP2014-1-3.

Tin, L.-G. (2012) *The Invention of Heterosexual Culture*. Cambridge, MA: MIT Press.

Tinkcom, M. and Villarejo, A. (2001) *Keyframes: Popular Cinema and Cultural Studies*. London: Routledge.

Tortorici, Z. J. (2008) 'Queering Pornography: Desiring Youth, Race, and Fantasy in Gay Porn' in Driver, S. (ed.), *Queer Youth Cultures*. Albany: State University of New York Press

Trujillo, N. (1991) 'Hegemonic Masculinity on the Mound', *Critical Studies in Mass Communication*, vol. 8, pp. 290–308.

# Bibliography

Tsang, D. (1999) 'Beyond Looking for My Penis: Reflections on Asian Gay Male Video Porn' in Elias, J. et al. (eds), *Porn 101: Eroticism, Pornography and the First Amendment*. New York: Prometheus Books.

Tziallas, E. (2015) 'The New "Porn Wars": Representing Gay Male Sexuality in the Middle East', *Psychology & Sexuality* vol. 6, no. 1, pp. 93–110.

Vandello, J. and Bosson, J. (2013) 'Hard Won and Easily Lost: A Review and Synthesis of Theory and Research on Precarious Manhood', *Psychology of Men & Masculinity*, vol. 14, no. 2, 101–13.

Van Doorn, N. (2011) 'Digital Spaces, Material Traces: How Matter Comes to Matter in Online Performances of Gender, Sexuality and Embodiment', *Media, Culture & Society* vol. 33, issue 4, pp. 531–47.

Vonderau, P. (2015) 'The Politics of Content Aggregation', *Television & New Media* vol. 16, no. 8, pp. 717–33.

Ward, J. (2015) *Not Gay: Sex Between Straight White Men*. New York: NYU Press.

Warner, M. (1999) *The Trouble With Normal: Sex, Politics and the Ethics of Queer Life*. New York: Simon & Schuster.

_____ (1993) 'Introduction' in Warner, M. (ed.), *Fear of a Queer Planet: Queer Politics and Social Theory*. Minneapolis: University of Minnesota Press.

Watney, S. (1987) *Policing Desire*. London: Comedia.

Waugh, T. (2004) 'Homosociality in the Stag Film' in Williams, L. (ed.), *Porn Studies*. Durham, NC: Duke University Press.

_____ (2002) *Out/Lines: Underground Gay Graphics from Before Stonewall*. Vancouver: Arsenal Pulp Press.

_____ (1996) *Hard to Imagine: Gay Male Eroticism in Photography and Film from Their Beginnings to Stonewall*. New York: Columbia University Press.

_____ (1993) 'Men's Pornography: Gay vs. Straight' in Gever, M., Greyson, J. and Parmar, P. (eds), *Queer Looks*. London: Routledge.

Weeks, J. (1991) *Against Nature*. London: Rivers Oram Press.

_____ (1986) *Sexuality*. London: Routledge.

_____ (1985) *Sexuality and its Discontents*. London: Routledge.

Weems, M. (2008) *The Fierce Tribe: Masculine Identity and Performance in the Circuit*. Utah: Utah State University Press.

Weitzer, R. (2015) 'Interpreting the Data: Assessing Competing Claims in Pornography Research' in Comella, L. and Tarrant, S. (2015), *New Views on Pornography*. New York: Praeger.

_____ (2011) 'Pornography's Effects: The Need for Solid Evidence', *Violence Against Women* vol. 17, pp. 666–75.

Westcott, C. (2004) 'Alterity and Construction of National Identity in Three Kristen Bjorn Films' in Morrison, T. (ed.), *Eclectic Views on Gay Male Pornography: Pornocopia*. Binghampton: Harrington Park Press.

# Bibliography

Williams, L. (2014) 'Pornography, Porno, Porn: Thoughts on a Weedy Field', *Porn Studies*, vol. 1, issue 1–2, pp. 24–40.

_____ (2008) *Screening Sex*. New York: Duke University Press.

_____ (1989) *Hard Core: Power, Pleasure and the Frenzy of the Visible*. Berkeley: University of California Press.

Woltersdorff, V. (2011) 'Paradoxes of Precarious Sexualities: Sexual Subcultures Under Neo-Liberalism', *Cultural Studies* vol, 25, issue 2, pp. 164–82.

Wright, L. (2001) 'Foreword' in Wright, L. (ed.), *The Bear Book II: Further Readings in the History and Evolution of a Gay Subculture*. London: Routledge.

_____ (ed.) (1997) *The Bear Book: Readings in the History and Evolution of a Gay Male Subculture*. New York: Routledge.

# Index

Notes are represented by the use of 'n' after the page number, e.g. 205n.2